THE RIGHT TO LEARN

The Struggle for Education in South Africa

A Sached Trust/Ravan Press Publication

THE RIGHT TO LEARN

The Struggle for Education in South Africa

Prepared for Sached by Pam Christie

Edited by Helene Perold, Dawn Butler
Designed by Mary Anne Bähr, Ray Carpenter
Illustrations by Elivia Savadier, Anne Sassoon
Additional artwork by Gail Fairlamb
Typesetting by Hirt & Carter

Published by Ravan Press (Pty) Ltd
P O Box 31134 Braamfontein
2017 South Africa and
The Sached Trust
P O Box 11350 Johannesburg 2000 South Africa

First Impression 1985
Second Impression 1986
© The Sached Trust

Printed by Galvin and Sales (Pty) Ltd Cape Town

ISBN 0 86975 286 3

Contents

Introduction

The Right to Learn is intended as a contribution to the current debates about education in South Africa. It does not attempt to be neutral, since we do not believe that it is possible to be neutral about education. Instead, it attempts to look at some crucial issues in education in South Africa, and to put forward ways of understanding them. The book cannot be a blueprint for an education system. What it can do is raise issues for discussion and change.

As this book goes to print, the Minister of Law and Order has announced the banning of COSAS, one of the largest black student movements. Once again this demonstrates clearly how the struggle for education is closely tied to the broader political struggle.

This book is the product of much joint effort and support. Many people contributed their time; discussed the ideas of the book; gave their material; took part in interviews; read and tested out drafts of chapters; and made valuable suggestions for changes. Without the efforts of all of these people, the book would not have been written.

In particular, members of SACHED – staff and students – provided ideas and support; discussed chapters in workshops; gave editorial advice; made suggestions on content and layout; and established contacts with students, teachers, and people interested in education in South Africa.

Members of the Education Departments at Wits University and UCT also provided valuable support.

The writer is particularly indebted to the following people: For editing: Helene Perold, Dawn Butler, Neville Alexander, John Samuel, Gavin Hartford. For workshopping: SACHED staff and students. For material: Adrienne Bird (trade union education), Linda Chisholm (workplace education), Mary Crewe (Veld Schools), Barbara Hutton (resistance), Sue Krige (church schools), Lesley Lawson (alternatives), Jennifer Shindler (statistics), Salim Valley (resistance). For artwork and design: Mary Anne Bähr, Ray Carpenter, Elivia Savadier, Gail Fairlamb. For general assistance: Peter Buckland, Pamela Greet, Duncan Innes, Peter Kallaway, Cynthia Kros, Gilbert Marcus, Ann Moore, Enver Motala, Simon Vilakazi.

August 1985

Abbreviations

AAC	All Africa Convention
AEM	African Education Movement
ANC	African National Congress
ATASA	African Teachers Association of South Africa
AZAPO	Azanian Peoples Organization
AZASM	Azanian Students Movement
AZASO	Azanian Students Organization
BC	Black Consciousness
BCP	Black Community Programmes
BPC	Black Peoples Convention
CATA	Cape African Teachers Association
CATU	Cape African Teachers Union
CED	Cape Education Department
CNE	Christian National Education
COSAS	Congress of South African Students
CTPA	Cape Teachers Professional Association
CYL	Congress Youth League
DEIC	Dutch East India Company
DET	Department of Education and Training
HSRC	Human Sciences Research Council
JC	Junior Certificate
JMB	Joint Matriculation Board
MPLA	Popular Movement for the Liberation of Angola
NEUM	Non-European Unity Movement
NEUSA	National Education Union of South Africa
NP	National Party
NUSAS	National Union of South African Students
PAC	Pan African Congress
PFP	Progressive Federal Party
RSA	Republic of South Africa

SACC	South African Council of Churches
SACP	South African Communist Party
SACTU	South African Congress of Trade Unions
SADF	South African Defence Force
SAIRR	South African Institute of Race Relations
SALB	South African Labour Bulletin
SALDRU	South African Labour and Development Research Unit
SARS	South African Research Services
SASM	South African Students Movement
SASO	South African Students Organization
SATA	South African Teachers Association
SOYA	Students of Young Azania
SPROCAS	Study Project on Christianity in Apartheid Society
SRC	Students Representative Council
SSRC	Soweto Students Representative Council
TAC	Teachers Action Committee
TASA	Teachers Association of South Africa
TATA	Transvaal African Teachers Association
TED	Transvaal Education Department
TLSA	Teachers League of South Africa
TO	Transvaalse Onderwys Vereeniging
UCT	University of Cape Town
UDF	United Democratic Front
UTASA	United Teachers Association of South Africa
WITS	University of the Witwatersrand
WRAB	West Rand Administration Board (now West Rand Development Board)
YP	Youth Preparedness

Chapter 1

What's education about?

As we write this book the education system in South Africa is in crisis. Since 1976 there has been continuing schools unrest. Black students have protested against the education system and also against apartheid in general. Students have marched, boycotted classes, burned schools and government offices, and clashed with the police. They have been expelled, injured, detained, and killed. And they have demanded changes in the education system. Police have fought with birdshot, bullets and armoured cars – and have even used the army to help. But schools unrest continues. Schools and universities are places of struggle; and education is clearly a political issue.

If we look at the education system in South Africa, it's obvious that things aren't equal. There are different education systems for different population registration groups – in fact there are fifteen different education departments. The facilities, like school buildings, classrooms, libraries and laboratories, are not of equal quality. Much more money is spent on schools for white children, so they have better facilities. White children have at least ten years of free, compulsory schooling. Black children certainly don't have that. The drop-out rate in schools for black children is much higher than in schools for white children – so people don't get equal amounts of education. Teachers in the different schools aren't equally qualified. Even at university level there are inequalities. We could go on and on listing these sorts of differences.

But why are there such inequalities in South Africa? Why are the education systems of different quality?

At first, these look like questions about education only. But, in fact, in this chapter we'll be showing that education systems should be seen as part of the wider society. So we also need to ask questions about different ways of understanding society, and therefore about different ways of seeing education. We need to think about questions like: How do schools fit in with the wider society? Can education be used to resolve the problems of society? Can education be used to bring about social change?

The answers that we give to these questions will depend on our views about society. Different people have different opinions about society and about education. To get an idea of these different opinions, we can look at some statements that people have made about education in South Africa.

Different opinions about education

"When I have control over native education, I will reform it so that natives will be taught from childhood that equality with Europeans is not for them."

H. F. Verwoerd, 1953. He was Minister of Native Affairs at the time when Bantu Education was introduced.

"We should not give the Natives any academic education. If we do, who is going to do the manual labour in the community?"

J.N. le Roux, 1945 National Party politician

"There is no place for the Bantu in the European community above the level of certain forms of labour."

H.F. Verwoerd, 1955

"The churches have a concern in education because education and teaching are part of their mission.

It is virtually impossible to reconcile the Christian ideals of self-worth, human development, liberation, service to others, and a willingness for personal sacrifice, with the injustice and exploitation which prevails in South African society.

We need to overcome a long history of discrimination. Education is part of this."

South African Council of Churches, 1980

"We shall reject the whole system of Bantu Education whose aim is to reduce us, mentally and physically, into 'hewers of wood and drawers of water.'"

SSRC, 1976

"Schools boycotts are but the tip of the iceberg – the crux of the matter is the oppressive political machinery itself."

AZAPO, 1981

"There should be an emphasis upon equality of opportunity (for different geographical areas, sexes, social and ethnic groups), with supplementary allocation of resources for disadvantaged groups."

South African Institute of Race Relations, 1979

"Educational policies in South Africa must be dictated by the apartheid philosophy."

F. Hartzenberg, 1980
Minister of Education and Training

"Our aim must be that change takes place without violence, and a prerequisite for peaceful change is an educated and industrious people."

Harry Oppenheimer, 1981
Chairperson of Anglo American Corporation

"South Africa is facing a shortage of skilled workers. We need more technical and vocational education so that we can have more skilled workers. Then we will have greater economic growth in the country."

W. L. Rautenbach, 1981
Consultant for De Lange Commission on Education

"We have to guard against turning our schools into tools of commerce and industry."

Michael Corke, 1981
Headmaster of St Barnabas School, Johannesburg

"I have seen very few countries in the world that have such inadequate educational conditions. I was shocked at what I saw in some of the rural areas and homelands.

Education is of fundamental importance. There is no social, political, or economic problem you can solve without adequate education."

Robert McNamara 1982
Past-president of the World Bank,
on a visit to South Africa

"Our parents have got to understand that we will not be 'educated' and 'trained' to become slaves in apartheid–capitalist society. Together with our parents we must try to work out a new future. A future where there will be no racism or exploitation, no apartheid, no inequality of class or sex."

Committee of 81, 1980

"The education we receive is meant to keep the South African people apart from one another, to breed suspicion, hatred and violence, and to keep us backward.

Education is formulated so as to reproduce this society of racism and exploitation."

COSAS, 1984

Different aims for education

We can see from these statements that people view the education system very differently. They emphasize different aspects of the system. They have quite different aims for the education system.

- Some people see education as a way of *training* people to work in the economy. The statements by Verwoerd in 1953 and Rautenbach in 1981 show this aim. Other people object to this – like the SSRC, the Committee of 81 and educationists like Michael Corke.

- For some people, education is a way of bringing about *social change*. For example, Oppenheimer speaks of preparing people for peaceful change. Certainly, the Committee of 81 is seeing education as part of wider social change. Robert McNamara also sees education as part of social change. (But, of course, all these people have different ideas about social change.)

- For some people, education is a way of getting greater social *equality* and *justice*. Certainly, this is an aim for the SACC and the SAIRR.

- Education is also *political*. For the government, education is part of the overall apartheid philosophy, as we can see from the statements by Verwoerd and Hartzenberg. And the statements by COSAS, AZAPO and the Committee of 81 also see education as being part of a political process.

Obviously, education can be used for different purposes. Different people can have quite different aims, and they can try to achieve quite different results through education.

This is an important point to remember. It warns us that we should be careful when we think about education and social change.

But why? Surely education is important for social change?

Certainly, but that depends on what our aims are, and what sort of education we have in mind.
Do you think that simply giving more Bantu Education would bring social change in South Africa?

I see what you mean.

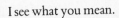

But let's go on to look more carefully at what schools do in society.

15

What do schools do?

Have schools always existed? What would society be like without schools? If there were no schools, would people not be educated?

Actually, schools have *not* always existed. Schools as we know them have quite a short history. In countries like Britain and America compulsory schooling for everyone was only introduced in the last hundred years or so. Before that only rich, upper class people went to school. In pre-colonial African societies there wasn't a schooling system as we know it today. Mostly, people were educated outside of formal schools. But it would be quite wrong to assume that there was no education because there were no schools. All societies find ways of passing on the knowledge that they value to their young people. Different societies have different ways of educating people. Schools are just one way.

But, as you know, our society does have schools. What do these schools do?

- Schools teach people certain kinds of knowledge, like history, geography and science. They pass on the knowledge that a society values.

- Schools teach people a set of values. They teach people how the society expects them to behave.

- Schools prepare people for work. Sometimes they give specific training for jobs – like typing or woodwork.

- Schools grade people – they pass or fail them. Quite often, the jobs people get depend on how many school standards they've passed.

- Schools also give students a chance to meet other people – and to be influenced by each other!

We could go on listing other things that schools do. And not all of them would be about formal learning and teaching!

But remember: we can't look at schools by themselves. We can best understand schools as part of the wider society in which they exist.

Schools and the wider society

If we want to understand the schooling system in a particular society, we can't just look at schools. We also have to look at the society in which they operate.

We've seen that different people have different aims in mind when they talk about education. The statements by Verwoerd, the SAIRR and the SSRC are all quite different. And yet they are all talking about the same schooling system. We've also seen that schools fulfil a number of different purposes. How can we make sense of these different aims and purposes?

If we look at the unequal education system in South Africa, we can see that it is part of the unequal social system. Besides unequal education there are many other inequalities. For example, job opportunities are not equal; salaries are not equal; housing provision is not equal; social services like health and welfare are not equal. So when we look at education, we should remember that schools are only one part of the whole social system.

This means that if we want to understand different views on education, we need to look more deeply into the views that people have about the whole of society. People's views on education fit in with their broader views about society.

But hold on! I understand that people see education in different ways. I also understand that education ties in with other things like jobs and salaries. But I don't know what you mean when you talk of 'different views about society'.

Well, let's go more slowly. People see society in different ways. They have different ideas about how society works, even though they don't always realize it. And they have different ideas about the role of education in society.

I still don't know what you mean. How do they see society? How do they see schools?

17

Let's start with your first question. There are different ways of answering it, but as I see it there are two main views about society:
- Consensus (agreement) views
- Conflict views.

We'll look at these separately.

Consensus views

Consensus thinkers see society like a human body.

The body has many parts (like arms, legs, lungs and brain). These parts work together to keep the body alive and well. They all function in different ways to help the body to work. Each part has a function of its own. Some functions are more important than others, e.g. a body could possibly live without a finger, but not without a head. But all the parts work together – in harmony – to keep the body going.

Consensus thinkers see society as having different parts (or institutions) which co-operate to keep the society going.

The education system, the family, the church, the economy, the law and the government, are all different parts of the social structure. They all have their own functions. But they all work together – in harmony – to keep the society operating more or less as it is.

'Society is like one human body. All the parts work together.'

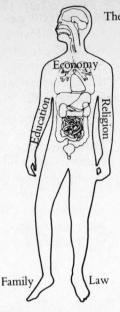

The government

Economy

Education

Religion

'Different institutions in society have different functions but they all work together.'

Family   Law

So if we think about society in this consensus way, then schools are just one part of the social structure. One of the main functions of schools is to prepare people to become members of the wider society.

So, consensus thinkers argue that society has different parts that work together to keep things going.

But how do these people see *change* happening?

Well, keep thinking about a human body. That should help to answer your question.

First, you can see that any drastic or sudden change would be dangerous. So consensus thinkers wouldn't be in favour of that kind of change.

But there are different groups of consensus thinkers. Some of these people are more in favour of change than others. Let's call them conservatives and moderates

Conservatives don't want change *at all* – especially if it is sudden or total or violent. They say that if change does happen it should be slow. Change should not endanger the working of the body.

Conservatives usually prefer the old, established ways of doing things. The existing system suits them as it is. Usually they have benefited from it and they see no reason to change it. They argue that throwing away the old ways leads to problems in society.

Moderates do want *some changes*, but the changes mustn't happen too fast. They don't want the existing society to change too much. Usually they want changes to happen within the existing structure (or body).

Moderates talk about freedom, equality, justice and fairness. But they usually mean that they want everyone to be free and equal within the present system. They don't want to disrupt the working of the present social order.

Conservative

We have developed good ways of doing things in the past. We should try to keep these good ways.

The established school system is the best. We should keep it as it is. If we change it, there could be social problems.

Moderate

We do need to make some changes to make society more equal. But these changes mustn't happen too quickly or be too disruptive.

We should keep the same school system as far as possible. But we should try to give everybody the same chances in the system. People must have equality of opportunity at school. But we must basically keep the present schooling system.

But hold on! I thought conservatives and
moderates were quite different. Aren't they?

Yes, they are different. Conservatives don't want
much change at all. Moderates do want changes,
but the changes mustn't be too disruptive.
  Of course conservatives and moderates are
different in some important ways. But they are
the same in that they both have a consensus view
of society. And they both want to keep the basic
structure of the present society.

I see that!
  But you said that there were two views on
society: consensus and conflict.
  What do the conflict people believe?

Conflict views

Conflict thinkers say that it is wrong to view society like a human
body. They say that society is not unified; everyone does not share
the same interests; and all the social institutions do not operate in harmony.

Instead, they suggest that different groups of people in society have
different interests. People's interests are in conflict. In most societies
there are privileged groups who benefit, and there are groups who do
not benefit equally. There are always power struggles in society – on
a small scale and on a large scale. People do live in the same social
structures, but their interests and values are different.

Some conflict thinkers believe that *racial* differences are the most
important differences in society. For these theorists, racial discrimination is the basic root of social inequality. And they believe that race
conflict is inevitable.

Most conflict thinkers talk about social *classes*. They argue that in
capitalist societies like South Africa the basic division is not race – it is

21

social class. There are people who own wealth (like mines and farms and factories), and there are people who don't own these things but have to sell their labour power in order to live.

According to class theorists, there are two main classes: the capitalist class and the working class. These two classes are in conflict with each other. The capitalist class strives to hold on to the mines, factories, businesses, etc., and to make higher profits. The working class struggles for better wages and working conditions – and also to gain control over the mines, factories, and so on.

Class theorists argue that South Africa is basically a capitalist society. Race may appear to be the main reason for social inequality, but this is only the way things seem. In fact class conflict is the basic conflict in a capitalist society like South Africa.

As we have seen, conflict thinkers are concerned with *fundamental* issues of society. They are often known as 'radicals', from the Latin word meaning 'root', the fundamental part of a plant.

You said that consensus thinkers don't want fundamental change. Do conflict thinkers want change?

Well, remember I said that they don't see society as being stable or in harmony like a body. There are always conflicts. Most conflict thinkers expect fundamental change. And they think that there should be change.

They argue that society will only be really fair and just once there are fundamental changes in the structure of society.

And would these changes affect the schools?

Remember I said that conflict thinkers argue that people have different interests. Conflict thinkers argue that schools themselves are places of conflict.

They argue that schools are part of the unequal society. Schools perpetuate race differences and class differences. In South Africa they keep the different population registration groups separate. They prepare some people to become managers and owners, and other people to become workers. So, in fact, schools help to keep society unequal.

Conflict thinkers say that we can't change society simply by improving education. Changes in education should be seen as part of broader social change.

So, basically what you're saying is that *consensus* thinkers see change as happening gradually, and they want to keep the existing social order with only a few changes.

Conflict thinkers disagree. They say we can't have fundamental changes while we keep the same social structure. Some see race as the basic problem, and some see class as the basic problem. But they all agree that fundamental change is necessary.

Yes, that's basically what I'm saying. But of course, views about society are always more complicated than that! We could spend a whole book just talking about theory!

But it *is* important that you understand this basic difference between consensus thinkers and conflict thinkers. If you're clear about this difference, then you'll find it easier to understand some of the other issues that we'll be discussing later in this book.

23

This discussion illustrates part of the debate about education and society. There are different views about the role of education in society. But most people would agree that education must be looked at as part of the whole society. So the education system in South Africa should be seen as part of the unequal social system as a whole.

But let's return to the debate on education, and summarize some of the points we've made so far. Let's ask the question: Why are there inequalities in education?

What would different people answer?

Conservative

People aren't equal anyway. Not everybody has the ability or the background to be on top. Schools should sort out the leaders from the rest of the people. They should reward people who have potential.

In South Africa blacks and whites have very different traditions. These different traditions should be preserved. Whites have a long history of education. They have experience in running the economy and the government. Their education should continue to prepare them for this role. Blacks have a different set of traditions, which should also be preserved. They should have full economic, political and education opportunities in their own areas.

There should be separate schools for the different groups in South Africa. In this way, the different traditions can be preserved. And if we control society in this way, we can keep order and preserve our way of life.

Moderate

South Africa is a racist society. The inequalities we see around us, for example in education, are the result of apartheid.

We should be moving as peacefully as possible away from racism towards a multiracial society. We should be trying to make these changes gradually and without violence.

One way to get a more just and equal society in South Africa is to give people more education. In fact, education is one of the most important ways to achieve peaceful social change.

We should be giving everyone an equal opportunity in education. That way, educated black people could begin to

24

move into the government and into business. Black people would have more opportunities. They would be less discontented and less likely to want to overthrow the whole system.

We could keep a capitalist system, and allow blacks to take part in it on higher levels. Then we could have a society that is more equal and more just. We could avoid violent change.

And at the same time the economy could benefit from having better trained black workers.

Radical

Certainly, there are racial inequalities in South Africa. But the basic inequalities are actually around social class. The basic conflict in a capitalist society is between people who own wealth (the capitalist class) and people who have to sell their labour power to make a living (the working class). In South Africa, this often appears to be a struggle between races. But it is a class struggle as well.

Education is part of the racist, capitalist system in South Africa. Changes in education alone won't bring social equality and social change. To get equality, we need major social change.

Meanwhile, the present education system helps to prepare people for their class positions. Upper class people have more and better education than working class people. So by expanding the present system, we won't bring change. We don't need more of the same sort of education.

We need to think more carefully about alternatives in education. For example, perhaps we should send kids into factories and farms as part of their schooling. Then we could run adult education programmes so that workers can go to school!

This gives us an idea of three different views on education and inequality in South Africa. Let's now see how the demands of students and parents fit in with all of this.

Demands

We started this chapter by talking about schools unrest. In the school uprisings, people made a number of demands about education. Let's look at some of the things that people were demanding in 1976 and 1980.

Here is an extract from a 1980 Memorandum of Grievances from the Black Schools Boycott, Port Elizabeth, Uitenhage, East Cape and Border Areas. It gives us an example of what one group of people was demanding in 1980.

THE BLACK LEADERS PLEA:-

It is our desire to see an end to the black schools boycott, we bessech those in authority to assist to achieve success in this direction. We are totally opposed to any form of violence, by talking to each other; we believe is the only method that could bring peace and harmony in our beloved South Africa.

We humbly address ourselves to the Honourable the Prime Minister of our country as parents and citizens of South Africa.

R E C O M M E N D A T I O N S:

1. THAT the Honourable the Prime Minister favourably consider the appointment of a Commission of inquiry into the Education system of South Africa. Such Commission to consist of representatives Educationists from all racial groups.

2. THAT the Commission be requested to report to the Prime Minister not later than six to twelve months; to enable the Government to work-out details of a unitary system of education.

3. THAT the blacks totally reject the inferior quality of education. We kindly request the Honourable the Prime Minister to cause for the opening of all educational Institutions to people of all races.

4. THAT the equality of education for ALL- RACES be introduced to allow equal-per-capita expenditure for every pupil or student. Equality in pupil-classroom ratio and construction of more schools and the abolition of double-session system.

5. THAT the Prime Minister be requested to give urgent attention to the present working conditions of teachers with a view of improvement of salaries that would make teaching profession attractive.

6. THAT the Honourable the Prime Minister cause the abolition of Pre-Fabricated schools and provide well constructed permanent schools with well equipped and adequate laboratories, libraries and recreational facilities.

7. WE request the Honourable the Prime Minister to provide, also in the urban areas, sufficient number of teacher training colleges to produce an adequate number of better trained and highly qualified teachers.

8. Provision of free and compulsory education to every child of school-going age up to and including High school Education.

DULY SIGNED ON THIS DATE.............. BY MEMBERS OF BLACK- LEADERS' DELEGATION;

1. Revd. J.M. HAYA,
    CONVENER.
    Rector of the Holy Spirit Church
    of the Province of South Africa.

2. Revd. D.M. SOGA,
    MINISTER-IN-CHARGE,
    Reformed Presbyterian in
    Southern Africa.

3. Mr. J.M. LALI,
    Attorney,
    Member of Special Committee,
    P.E. Schools Boycott.

4. Mr. L.F. SIYO,
    REPRESENTATIVE,
    East Cape and Border Schools
    Boycott. (Mdantsane)

5. Mr. Raman BHANA,
    Member of Indian Council of
    South Africa.

6. Revd. Allan Hendrickse,
    NATIONAL- LEADER,
    Labour Party of South Africa.

Do you think that these demands show a conflict view or a consensus view of education and society?

For comparison, here is another statement of demands from 1980:

RESISTANCE AGAINST RACIST EDUCATION

We are aware as students coming from working class backgrounds that our parents cannot afford to provide shelter, food and

education for us. (I) The policy of the State is to make it financially difficult for us to stay at school. (2) We are then forced to leave school and join the cheap labour force.

We reject APARTHEID AND ITS EDUCATION SYSTEM.

This is the form our grievances take:

(I) A shortage of teachers
(2) No textbooks
(3) Forced uniforms
(4) The Security Branch has free access to school premises
(5) Teachers in Fizeka High have been unfairly dismissed
(6) Corporal punishment is abused in most schools
(7) In the 'Indian' schools students are transported by bus from outlying 'Indian Townships' to make RYLANDS INDIAN HIGH SCHOOL AN APARTHEID PROJECT.
(8) Three teachers have been unfairly dismissed

(9) SRC's are not allowed

We as students identify with students all over the country.

WHITE EDUCATION	R700,00 per child
BLACK EDUCATION	R 59,00 " "
'COLOURED' EDUCATION	R198,00 " "
'INDIAN'EDUCATION	R250,00 " "

This is a strategy to "divide and rule" the masses of South Africa. SOLIDARITY AMONGST ALL STUDENTS AND PARENTS.

WE REJECT APARTHEID AND THE ECONOMIC SYSTEM IT IS MAINTAINING.

EVERY STUDENT IN SOUTH AFRICA SHOULD REALISE THAT THEY ARE THE WORKERS OF TOMORROW AND THEY WILL BE EXPLOITED LIKE THEIR PARENTS.

WE REJECT THE EXPLOITATION OF OUR PARENTS THE WORKERS.

IN SHORT REJECT THE PRESENT POLITICAL SYSTEM.

And these demands? Are they based on consensus views or conflict views?

Conclusion

In this chapter, we've seen that people have very different views on education. We've also seen that these different views on education reflect different views about society and social change.

In the rest of the book we're going to explore some of the issues and debates about education in apartheid South Africa.

Hopefully, this book will provide a forum for discussion. The book will try to open up educational issues for debate, and give a range of opinions on them.

As you'll see, we have our own opinions, but we'll show you that there are many other views as well.

The purpose of the book is not to decide the issues finally. Its purpose is to contribute to an ongoing debate on education in South Africa.

References and further readings

Africa Perspective (1984) 24, Education: Control and resistance

Berger, P. (1970) *Invitation to Sociology*, Penguin, Harmondsworth

Corke, M.A.S. (1979) 'A school system for South Africa' *Social Dynamics* 5(1) 38–42

Corke, M.A.S. (1981) *'Educational enrichment in a changing society'*. NDMF Conference 'The chief executive's challenge', Johannesburg

Corke, M.A.S. (undated) *'Segregated education in South Africa'* Mimeo.

Haralambos, M. (1980) *Sociology: Themes and Perspectives*, University Tutorial Press, Slough

NUSAS (1979) *Education and Development*, Conference papers, University of Cape Town

NUSAS (1982) *Education: Weapon or Tool?*, Conference papers, NUSAS July Festival

SAIRR (1979) *Education for a New Era*, SAIRR, Johannesburg

Chapter 2

A short history

When we look at the education system we have today, it's easy to think that it was always like this. Today we think of school buildings, staffed by teachers and attended by children in uniforms. The whole system looks quite permanent, as if it has always been like this.

But, of course, this wasn't always so. As we've said before, education systems need to be seen as part of the wider society. And just as the wider society has changed with time, so has the education system.

In this chapter we're going to look very briefly at the history of education in South Africa. We'll be able to see how the system started and grew, and what influenced it to change. Our approach will be to look at different historical periods and then to look at education in each period. This should help us to see relationships between education and the wider society. And, hopefully, we'll get some picture of how the education system came to be what it is today.

History helps us to understand the present. It shows us how things came to be what they are. We ourselves are part of history.

History shows us that change is always happening. And we ourselves should expect change. Things tomorrow certainly won't be the same as they are today!

We can divide our history of education into six main sections:

1 Pre-colonial education
2 Education up to 1800
3 British control after 1815
4 The trekker states
5 Social and educational change: 1880 – 1940
6 Industrial growth and apartheid education

Pre-colonial education

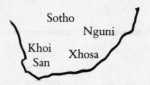

Before white settlers came to South Africa from Europe in 1652, a number of different groups of black people lived on the land. These were the pre-colonial times. Khoi hunters and San herders lived around the Cape. Their economy was based on what they could hunt and gather from the environment. In the Eastern Cape lived Xhosa-speaking people. Other Nguni-speakers lived to the north, in present-day Natal. And Sotho-speakers lived in the interior. These people were subsistence farmers. They kept cattle and other animals, and grew certain crops.

In these pre-colonial African societies there were no formal schools, as we know them today. But this doesn't mean that there was no education taking place. As we said in Chapter One, all societies have ways of teaching people the knowledge that the society values.

In pre-colonial societies education was part of daily life. Children learned about their society and their work from older members of the community. They learned by experience, from doing tasks. And this informal education didn't stop, like schools do, when children reached a certain age. There were initiation ceremonies and rituals, which were part of people's education. People also learned about their history and past traditions through the songs, poems and stories that were passed on orally.

We don't know very much about education in South Africa before the white settlers came. But we certainly know that there was education. And these pre-colonial forms of education continued after the whites settled as well.

Education up to 1800

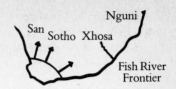

After 1652, Europeans from different countries began to settle at the Cape. The first settlers were part of a trading company called the Dutch East India Trading Company (DEIC). The Company did not intend to set up a permanent colony at the Cape. Instead, it saw the Cape as a halfway station for its trading activities in the East. But in a short time the Cape became a permanent settlement, with different groups of people living there. Let's look briefly at who these different groups of people were, and then see what education they were receiving.

Many of the white settlers established themselves as *farmers and traders,* and settled permanently. They came from Holland, France, Germany and England. Some of them settled around Cape Town and the nearby towns. Some of them farmed for local markets, and also to meet the needs of the DEIC. This group of people formed the local merchant class.

Other farmers, the *trekboers,* moved further inland as cattle farmers. Over time, they set up farms further and further away from Cape Town. In this way they expanded the borders of the settlement. The trekboers took very little notice of the government in Cape Town. In fact, it was hard for the government to keep control over them.

The *Khoi* and the *San* resisted the settlers who were taking their land, but, in time, the settlers established control. Many of the Khoi and San were killed or died of disease; others moved away; and others stayed to become part of the new colony. Some of them were independent, but mostly they worked as servants and labourers for the settlers.

Another group of people living in the Cape were the *slaves*. Settler farmers wanted a cheap labour supply. There were not enough local people to meet their needs. So they imported slaves from other parts of Africa, and the East, to work as unskilled labourers on the farms and in the towns. Soon there were as many slaves as settlers.

Before long, the trekboers met up with the *Xhosa-speaking people* in the Eastern Cape. Both the boers and the Xhosa were pastoralists who needed land for their cattle. Soon the two groups were fighting over land and resources. The frontier wars in the Eastern Cape went

31

on for nearly a hundred years (from 1779 to 1877). At first the Xhosa were fairly successful against the boers. The government could do little to control the situation. But in 1815, the British took over the Cape, and they attempted to gain more control over the frontier area (as we'll see).

This gives us a brief picture of the different people at the Cape, and how they were living.
Let's now look at what their educational provisions were like.

In the early days there were very few schools at the Cape. The DEIC did not pay much attention to education. Mostly, education was in the hands of the church. Two educationists, Behr and Macmillan, describe the education system as follows:

> During the whole period of the Dutch regime at the Cape, formal elementary education meant instruction in the doctrines of the Dutch Reformed Church. The pupils learned prayers, passages from the Bible, and the catechism. These they would recite to the teacher. There would also be singing lessons in preparation for church services. Some of the abler pupils would also acquire the basics of reading, writing, and arithmetic.
>
> (1966:89, adapted)

Even in the towns, not all white children went to school. And schooling was not free – people had to pay for the schooling they received.

In the countryside, the children of the trekboers had even less education. There were no schools for trekboer children. Most of the trekboers were religious, and parents wanted their children to be able to read so that they could read the Bible. Sometimes these parents organized together to pay travelling school teachers who went around the farms, giving instruction. They were not always very suitable teachers.

What about education for black people? In fact, the first school in the Cape was for slaves who were mostly adults. On 17 April 1658, Van Riebeeck, Governor of the Cape, wrote in his diary:

> "Began holding school for the young slaves. To stimulate the slaves to attention while at school, and to induce them to learn the Christian prayers, they were promised each a glass of brandy and two inches of tobacco, when they finish their task."
>
> (Horrell 1970: 3, adapted)

In 1663 a second school was opened. This school was attended by twelve white children, four slaves and one Khoi. It's interesting to see that these first schools were not segregated along the lines of colour. Segregation was introduced quite soon, but at this time lower class whites, slaves and Khoi often attended the same schools.

But generally speaking, not many slaves or Khoi actually attended school. And those who did go to school didn't receive much education. They learned mainly about religion, and some basic reading, writing and arithmetic .

When we look at the schooling that was provided before 1800, we can see that there was very little going on. What schooling there was, usually had religious content and purposes.

But we should remember that the education that was provided – in school and out of school – was enough to meet the needs of that society.

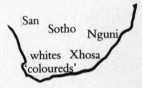

British control after 1815

In 1815 the British took over the Cape from the Dutch, as a result of wars in Europe. And this meant very different treatment for the Cape. The DEIC had been mainly interested in getting agricultural products from the Cape for trading. But the British wanted a more permanent settlement. Britain was building up a large trading empire across the world. Britain took far more interest in controlling the colonies and the people who lived in them than the Dutch had done.

The British set up a system of government in the Cape that was similar to British colonies in other parts of the world. The Cape gradually took over its own government, and in 1872 it became a self-governing British colony.

Economically, the Cape became part of Britain's trading empire. Wool farming developed as an important source of income, and the local merchant class grew more prosperous. Along with increasing trading activity came the growth of towns, the transport system, banking and small businesses.

What about the frontier? After 1815 the British colonial government gave fuller attention to the question of the Eastern frontier. A number of wars of dispossession were fought, the last one in 1877. As a result of these wars the Xhosa people lost their independence and their land, and were forced to work for settler farmers and trekboers.

During this period, missionaries were coming to South Africa in great numbers. They came to spread the Christian gospel. Many of them set up mission stations in the frontier area. They also worked nearer Cape Town, among the Khoi. As part of their missionary activity, they set up schools (as we'll see).

This gives us a very brief outline of conditions at the Cape during this period. As the government grew stronger and extended its control, the education system grew and changed.

Let's now look at the education provisions for the different groups of people at the Cape.

Colonial education

The British authorities paid far more attention to education than the Dutch had done. They wanted to use education as a way of spreading their language and traditions in the colony – and also as a means of social control. They declared English to be the official language, and they attempted to anglicize the church, the government offices and the schools. They set up a number of schools in the British tradition, and they brought over teachers from Britain. In 1839 they set up a proper Department of Education, and also gave financial help to local schools.

During this period, the schooling system gradually became better organized. Primary schooling was eventually made free, but parents had to pay for secondary education. Even so, schooling was very uneven. People were allowed to set up their own schools, so there was a whole network of private schools – some good, and some bad. There were also a few state schools, a large number of state-aided schools and mission schools.

Education developed along the lines of social class. Richer parents could afford to send their children to private schools. Secondary schooling was not free, so it was available only to those who could afford to pay. After 1893 the government gave funds for mission schools to provide education for poorer white communities. But schooling was not compulsory, and many children received no schooling at all.

There were also great inequalities between town and country areas. Over time more local schools were set up in country areas. But many of the trekboer children continued to receive very little education.

In this period we see the development of a more complex system of schooling, as the society became more complex. But it's important to notice how the education system both reflects and shapes divisions in society. In South Africa, divisions based on racial classification are obvious to see. But we can see social class divisions as well.

Let's now look at education for the other groups in the Cape colony.

Khoi and slaves (and 'coloureds')

Khoi and slaves provided an important source of labour, especially on the farms, but also in the towns. British rule brought changes to their position as well. Two laws were passed which were particularly important:

1828   Ordinance 50 gave equal rights to Khoi and other 'free persons of colour'. This meant that the Khoi could move around to look for work as they wished.

1833   All slaves were freed in the British Empire. So the slaves in South Africa were also freed. And Ordinance 50 applied to them too.

These changes meant that white farmers could no longer rely on a supply of unfree labour. They needed different ways to ensure a supply of disciplined labour who would be prepared to work for them. And this is where education again was used. Here is a statement by the historian Horrell, which shows one view of why schooling became important:

> Between 1834 and 1838, some 35 745 slaves were emancipated at the Cape. Some of them migrated from farms to towns and villages or to missionary institutions. Others became vagrants, squatting on government or private land, while numbers went to the outskirts or beyond the frontiers of the colony to start farming on their own. The need for more schools to instil social discipline became acute.   (1970:11)

There is no doubt that schooling was seen as a way of 'instilling social discipline'. Some historians argue that schooling was an important way of bringing 'coloured' people into the dominant society, and preparing them to be wage labourers. According to these historians, schools taught people basic reading, writing and arithmetic. But they also taught discipline, obedience and the value of work.

In fact many 'coloured' people received no education at all. The mission schools – which these people could attend – usually gave elementary education only. Secondary and higher education was for the privileged few. So, education helped to create social class divisions among 'coloured' people as well. But generally it reinforced their lower class position.

Africans

Almost all of the education for Africans was provided by mission schools. As we've said, missionaries set up mission stations in the frontier area, and also in other parts of the country. Part of their work was to establish schools, so that people would be educated enough to take part in church activities. But, as we said in Chapter One, education has many functions. Mission education also aimed to spread the Western way of life among the 'heathen' Africans and to teach them certain work values. In Chapter Three we'll look at missionary activity in more detail. For the moment, let's focus our attention on mission schooling on the Cape Eastern Frontier, and draw attention to some key dates:

1799   The first mission school for Africans was set up at King William's Town.

1824   The famous mission station, Lovedale, was set up in the Tyume Valley. Many other mission stations and mission schools were established at this time.

       Missionaries set up schools mainly for their own religious purposes, but the British governors of the Cape realized that mission schools could be used for their purposes too. They hoped that mission schools could play a part in bringing the frontier under their control.

1841   The government began to give financial aid to mission schools. In this way the government gained some control over the schools.

We can also see from statements made by Cape government officials that they wanted to use mission schools for their own purposes – to bring Africans under their influence:

1848   The government sent a letter to missionaries, asking them:

"What are the best methods to inspire in the Bantu the desire to cultivate their lands by ploughing, and to encourage them to follow industrious habits?"

The letter went on to emphasize:

"Too much pains cannot be taken to impress them with the necessity of wearing clothes and of the use of money, which, industriously gained, honestly obtains whatever they want."

1855   Sir George Grey, Governor of the Cape, said to Parliament:

"If we leave the natives beyond our border ignorant barbarians, they will remain a race of troublesome marauders. We should try to make them a part of ourselves, with a common faith and common interests, useful servants, consumers of our goods, contributers to our revenue. Therefore, I propose that we make unremitting efforts to raise the natives in Christianity and civilization, by establishing among them missions connected with industrial schools.
The native races beyond our boundary, influenced by our missionaries, instructed in our schools, benefiting by our trade, would not make wars on our frontiers."

(Rose and Tunmer 1975:205, adapted)

These statements give us an idea of what the government hoped to achieve through education. But that doesn't mean that the government got what it wanted! In fact, the government often complained that mission education was too religious and not practical enough. But, generally speaking, the government was prepared to leave African education in the hands of the missionaries.

In the next chapter we'll look in more detail at the education which mission schools provided. For our present purposes, we can see three types of mission schools:

●   Mostly, mission schools gave elementary education only.

- Usually, mission schools also taught industrial education.
- A few of the mission schools had high schools and teacher training institutions for a very small number of people.

But, generally speaking, most African people didn't receive any education at all, or didn't attend school regularly.

Once again, we see that different people had different access to education. Again, this reflected and created divisions in society.

Firstly, there were divisions along the lines of colour, with different schools for different groups. But there were also divisions along class lines.

Often, class divisions cut across colour divisions. For example, lower class white and black people were often educated in the same mission schools. Similarly, schools like Lovedale provided higher education for whites and blacks together.

But in fact, most black people were in lower class positions in the society, with very little education.

The Cape governors were generally uneasy about giving higher education to Africans. They saw Africans mainly as unskilled labourers, and they didn't want education to be a path to social equality for Africans.

For example, this is what Langham Dale wrote in a report in 1868:

> "For the educated African there is no opening. He may be qualified to fill the post of a clerk, but either there is no demand for such persons, or prejudice operates against persons of colour being so employed."
>
> (Rose and Tunmer 1975:208, adapted)

In fact, there were a few well-educated Africans who could take up positions as teachers, clerks, interpreters, and so on. In the Cape there was also a non-racial qualified franchise. This meant that people who had certain educational qualifications and certain property were given the vote. By the end of the 1800s there were a number of middle class Africans who qualified to vote. These people enjoyed certain economic and political rights.

But, generally speaking, most Africans did not have much education – and they did not enjoy equal economic and political rights.

The trekker states

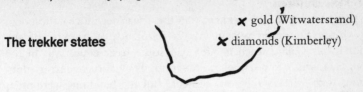

✘ gold (Witwatersrand)

✘ diamonds (Kimberley)

In 1836 the Great Trek started. Groups of trekboer farmers wanted to get away from the British government, and also wanted to look for more farming land. They left the Cape, together with their servants and their cattle, and moved into the interior of South Africa.

Meanwhile, in the land we now call Natal, the Zulu-speaking people were building themselves up into a powerful nation. This had important effects on the Nguni- and Sotho-speaking people in the interior of South Africa. The Zulu waged war on these people, and this warfare spread from group to group in the interior. Many people were killed; others fled; and there were major rearrangements of chiefdoms.

This was a period of plunder and warfare. But it was also a time of nation-building. In this period the Zulu state consolidated itself; Moshoeshoe set up the Sotho kingdom; and Mzilikazi led the Nde-bele into present-day Zimbabwe. This whole process is known in Zulu as the *mfecane* 'crushing' and in Sotho as the *difaqane* 'hammering'.

Because of the disruptions of the mfecane, the voortrekkers were able to move more easily into the interior. But the process wasn't as easy as conservative history books make out. There were a series of wars with the African chiefdoms, and voortrekker communities very often had to negotiate arrangements with local chiefdoms.

The voortrekkers set up states in Natal, the Orange Free State and the Transvaal. Within a few years, Britain annexed Natal as a British colony. The Transvaal and the OFS were independent trekker states. At first these were mainly farming communities, with some trading. As in the Cape, white farmers looked to Africans to work for them – as cattle herders, field workers and general servants. But many of the Africans continued to live independently, sometimes as subsistence farmers and sometimes producing surpluses to trade on the market.

In the 1860s, diamonds were discovered around Kimberley, and in the 1880s, gold was discovered on the Witwatersrand. These mineral discoveries brought great economic changes, and also changes in the social and political arrangements.

39

Education in the Transvaal and OFS

Trekker children

In the early days of the trekker states there was not much educational provision. Education was mainly in the hands of parents and the church. Travelling teachers provided some basic education. In the country towns a few schools were set up. They also gave basic education, with a heavy religious content. But the buildings were often derelict, teachers were poorly qualified and attendance was irregular.

As the Transvaal and OFS grew more established, so more attention was paid to schooling. In 1872 the OFS appointed an Inspector-General of education whose job was to improve the quality of education. More schools were set up, and, in 1895, the first steps were taken towards compulsory education. All children between 14 and 16, who lived within two miles of a school, had to attend for one year. A system of transit schools was set up for country areas. Behr describes the system as follows:

> For a period of six months to one year, a room was hired from a farmer to serve as a school. A teacher was supplied by the state. Children from the surrounding farms were brought there and the farmer undertook to provide board and lodging for the children and the teacher. Obviously, in these schools it was not possible for the teacher to do more than extend the knowledge of the three R's, already partially acquired by the pupil at his or her mother's knee. (1978:19, adapted)

In the Transvaal, education also gradually became more organised. In 1892 an Education Act was passed. It tells us a lot about the way education was viewed. Here is an extract from the Act:

> The Government of De Zuid-Afrikaansche Republiek accepts the principle that it is primarily the duty of parents to provide education for their children. It limits its action to:
>
> 1 the encouragement and support of private schools by giving grants to aid them;
>
> 2 the supervision of schools with a view to ensuring that pupils receive the necessary Protestant Christian education;
>
> 3 the establishment of an institution for higher education principally for the training of teachers and officials. (Behr 1978:13, adapted)

Parents and the church had a strong influence on schooling. The government subsidized schools which met with its requirements. Schooling wasn't free: parents had to pay fees. Inspectors kept some kind of connection between subsidized schools and the government. Most of these schools were in rural towns.

In both the Transvaal and the OFS almost all of the schooling was at a primary level. There was very little provision for secondary schooling. For example, in 1892 92% of scholars in the Transvaal were in primary school; less than 1% were above Std 6. Wealthy parents often sent their children to the Cape for their schooling or overseas to Holland or England. But many children received no schooling at all.

African children

There was even less schooling for African children than for boer children. Mission schools provided what little education there was. Two famous mission schools established at this time were Botshabelo and Kilnerton. But there was no system of funding for mission schools in the Transvaal and OFS. Most Africans did not go to schools at all.

When we assess these educational provisions, it's important to remember how people were living in those societies. Most people in the interior were living as farmers, or else they were traders or labourers. Learning to read and write wasn't always very relevant to their lives. Education outside of schools – in their daily lives – was usually more relevant to them.

In Natal we see similar patterns.

Education in Natal

In Natal the trekker states were soon taken over by Britain. Education was then seen as a government responsibility. A schooling system was slowly established, with state schools, state-aided schools and a system of inspection. A number of teachers came from England, bringing the influence of the English system to the Natal schools. There were also church schools and many private academies providing education of different sorts. Schooling was not free, nor compulsory. As in the trekker states, there was not much schooling in rural areas.

As far as Africans were concerned, there was a general policy of segregation in Natal. The government policy was to place Africans in reserves, or 'tribal locations', and make them carry passes.

More attention was paid to African schooling in Natal than in the trekker states. The general segregation policy also applied to schools. The government set up mission reserves, and granted land to mission societies to be kept in trust for Africans. The missions were allowed to use the labour of the people in the reserves, and they were expected to set up schools. Later, state aid was given to mission schools.

1853   Adams College was opened.

1869   Inanda Seminary was set up for girls.

1882   Mariannhill Mission was established.

In 1884 the control and organization of African schools became the responsibility of the government Council of Education. Separate curricula were drawn up for African schools and a system of inspection was introduced.

As in the Cape, we can see a link between the schooling which people had and the work they were able to do. Many whites believed that schools should teach Africans to do lower-level, manual work. Here is a statement that was made in 1881 to the Natal Native Commission:

"If the natives are to be taught at all, they should be taught industry. I do not myself see much use in teaching the natives to read and write without teaching them to make use of their hands as well.

Industrial instruction should form the most important part of native schooling. There are certain natives who can be educated to get their living without working with their hands; a few of them are clergymen, and there are some schoolmasters. There are also some interpreters in the different magistrates' offices, and so on. And these can gain a good living without working with their hands. But the great bulk of the native people must work with their hands in order to gain an honest living. To teach them to read and write, without teaching them to work, is not doing them any good."

(Rose and Tunmer 1975:213-14, adapted)

And here is another statement to the same Commission:

"In my opinion, schools for natives should give two hours a day to reading and writing, and three hours to manual labour. The importance of manual labour should be brought into prominence at these schools.

As far as possible, I would teach at these schools every occupation that a servant is required to do in the colony. Why is it that I employ the Red Kaffir boy as my groom and gardener? Simply because he demands half the amount that the educated boy does; he does his work as well, if not better, and is more amenable to discipline."

(Rose and Tunmer 1975:215, adapted)

Of course, these are only two opinions given to a government commission. But they do give us some indication of the links which people saw between school and work.

If we look generally at education in the Transvaal, OFS and Natal, we see a number of interesting trends and developments:

1 These states set up education systems which reflected their needs in those days. Certainly, they met the needs of the ruling groups.

2 We can see that patterns of segregation along colour lines were set up early on. Almost always, black people and white people went to different schools.

3 Patterns of class difference were also set up early on. Children of richer parents had more and better education than children of poorer parents.

So, education was part of broader patterns of social inequality – along the lines of both colour and class.

Social and educational change: 1880 – 1940

✗ gold
✗ diamonds

The discovery of minerals in South Africa brought enormous changes. The discovery of gold on the Witwatersrand was especially important. Within a few years the Witwatersrand goldfields became the largest in the world.

The development of mining altered the way of life in South Africa in every possible way. There were economic changes, political changes and social changes. And these changes can still be felt today.

It's worth looking at this period in some detail, because it's in this period that we see the creation of today's society and education system.

As the mines were established, so towns grew up around them. Businesses of all kinds were started. Townspeople needed a whole range of goods, and also food. So trade and farming grew. Roads and railways were built. And a lot of people – black and white – moved to the mines and towns. South Africa was no longer mainly a rural society; it was urban as well.

Mining led to the formation of new social classes. Firstly, there were the *mining capitalists* developed by mining companies, and mining capitalists became extremely wealthy. However, the gold on the Reef was expensive to mine, and mining capitalists made ongoing efforts to keep their profits up. In particular they wanted their labour supply to be as cheap as possible.

Mining was also important in forming the working class in South Africa. The mines needed workers of all sorts. They needed *skilled workers* to do more complicated and responsible jobs. At first, the skilled workers were brought in from overseas – from Europe, America and Australia. These workers usually demanded high wages. And they were prepared to set up unions to fight for their rights.

The mines also needed a large supply of *unskilled workers,* to do the heavier work which didn't need much training or experience. Mining capitalists tried to keep the cost of unskilled labour as low as possible. They looked to unskilled Africans to provide this cheap labour force.

At this time, many Africans were still living subsistence lives in the countryside, or producing surpluses for the market. Most of them still had no need to work for wages. The government devised ways of bringing black subsistence farmers into wage labour. For example, it introduced taxes; to pay taxes, people had to have money; to get money, they had to work for a wage.

The mines used a migrant labour system for these unskilled workers. They argued that migrant workers could be paid less, because they had homes to go back to, and their families were supporting themselves in the country. They argued that they did not need to pay migrant workers a wage that would also help to feed, clothe and house their families.

So, in this period, the working class became divided along lines of colour:

- Most white workers did skilled jobs, at higher rates of pay. They were free to work when and where they liked. And they had bargaining rights: they could form trade unions to negotiate their jobs.

- Almost all black workers did unskilled work, at lower rates of pay. They were controlled by pass laws and the migrant labour system, so they couldn't work when and where they liked. And they had no bargaining rights.

These differences were gradually brought into law, and became the policy of racial segregation.

Obviously, racial discrimination didn't begin in this period of history. We've seen that racialism has a long history in South Africa.

But what is important in this period is that this was the time when the industrial working class was being formed. And while it was being formed, it became divided along lines of colour.

Political changes

This period was also a time of political change. The goldfields were in the Transvaal, which was an independent trekker state. Before long, there was conflict between the Uitlanders – 'foreigners' who had come to the Transvaal because of the gold – and the Kruger government. Britain was also interested in the area because of its wealth.

In 1899 Britain went to war against the boers. After three years of bitter fighting, the boers were beaten. Britain took over the two boer states, the Transvaal and the OFS. In 1910 the four states in South Africa were united into a single British colony, the Union of South Africa.

In 1908 (before Union) representatives from the different states met at the National Convention to draw up a constitution for the new Union government. No black people were represented. In the South Africa Act the Cape kept its qualified 'non-racial' franchise, but this was not extended to the whole country. Instead it was eventually removed altogether, and those black people who previously had the vote, lost it.

After the Anglo-Boer war, even larger numbers of people moved to the towns. This was partly due to hardships and overcrowding in the countryside. People who could no longer make a living in the rural areas came to the towns, and especially Johannesburg, to try their luck. Most of these people – white and black – were unskilled. The question was: Would these white and black workers compete equally as working class people for the same, unskilled jobs?

The answer was 'No'. Instead, the racial division of labour was reinforced. In practice skilled jobs and certain unskilled jobs were reserved for white workers. Most unskilled work was done by black workers – at very low rates of pay.

By the 1920s, this job colour bar was official. A number of laws acted together to put black workers in an inferior position to white workers, and also to remove certain freedoms from them.

1913   The Land Act set up the 'reserves' (later called 'bantustans' and 'homelands'). Africans were zoned to 13% of the total land area of South Africa (though they formed 80% of the population). They were prevented from buying land outside these areas. Property sizes inside the reserves were also restricted.

         As a result of this Act, the majority of Africans could no longer live as subsistence farmers. There was not enough land for everyone. Africans were forced to work for wages on white farms or in the mines or factories.

         The South African Native National Congress (later the ANC) was formed to protest against this Act. (Many of its early members were mission school graduates.)

1920s   The 'Civilized Labour Policy' and the Apprenticeship Act entrenched the job colour bar.

1923   The Natives (Urban Areas) Act was passed. This law stipulated that blacks were allowed in urban areas 'as long as they minister to the needs of whites'.

Pass laws and influx control restricted black rights and black movement to the towns.

Education was an important part of these processes of social change. In this period, there were important changes in education – which set the pattern for today's education system.

Let's now look at some of these changes in education. We'll concentrate on education on the Rand, because this is where most of the changes started.

Education on the Rand

We saw earlier that the schooling system in the Transvaal was not very well organized. Many children didn't go to school at all. And those who did go to school usually had only basic education.

Before the discovery of minerals this wasn't really a problem. But with the development of mining and the growth of trade and industry in the new towns, the old education system was no longer adequate. Many of the new jobs demanded skills – even skills of reading and writing – that the schooling system didn't adequately provide.

This produced great difficulties for the government. It didn't have the money or the teachers or the facilities to provide a large-scale compulsory education system.

Schools were still mainly the responsibility of the church and parents. They were responsible for establishing schools, and appointing and paying the teachers. The government gave grants to schools which met its requirements, and also provided an inspection system. But the government provisions could not adequately cope with the growing demand for schooling.

During this period schooling facilities did expand. For white middle class children there was a system of church schools. These schools were subsidized by the Education Department, and inspected by it. As before, there was also the possibility of going to school in the Cape, or overseas.

But most working class children – black and white – did not have the benefit of proper schooling. There were many private schools which didn't meet the requirements of the Education Department. These are sometimes called 'private adventure schools'. Often, working class parents would hire a hall, or use a private home, and bring together a group of children into a 'school'. The teachers were usually untrained, and the 'education' was very questionable. Attendance at these sorts of schools was irregular – sometimes by teachers as well as by children!

Many people were too poor to send their children to school. Sometimes children only attended for short or interrupted periods. Sometimes poorer parents moved their children from school to school, to avoid paying fees. Many children were out of school.

In this time of social change, there were new demands on the education system. The existing education system could not meet the changing needs of the society. Changes in education were needed.

Important foundations

After the Anglo-Boer War, the British administration took over education in the Transvaal and OFS. This was a period of important development for education. In this period, we see the foundations of the present racially differentiated system of education. We see the introduction of compulsory schooling for whites – but not for blacks.

We've noted that the development of mining, and the Anglo Boer war, brought a period of social upheaval. Many people moved to the towns, and many of these people were poor, unskilled and unemployed. How could these people be brought into the new industrialized capitalist system which was developing? Schooling was seen as one of the answers.

Social reformers were particularly concerned about the children of 'poor white' and working class parents. In many cases parents were too poor to send their children to school. Often children bunked school and formed street gangs, or they took jobs to earn money. Commissions of Inquiry, which were set up to investigate poverty and unemployment, were particularly concerned about the position of children. They hoped that they could solve the social problems by educating the children. The *Johannesburg Times* had this to say in 1898:

"The children of these wretched people need to be rescued from their surroundings and reclaimed for civilization. They must be educated, taught to work, and reared as honest men and women.**"**

Education was seen as a way of bringing about social order, particularly in the time of social upheaval after the war. It was also a way of teaching working class children about work skills and work discipline. Compulsory education came to be seen as an important way of 'rescuing' the children, so as to solve social problems.

After the war the British government concentrated its efforts on developing a system of free, compulsory education for whites. In 1902 a new education ordinance was passed in the Transvaal. The government introduced free primary education 'for children whose parents are of European descent'. It also provided for university and technical education, teacher training – and reformatories!

This was followed up in all the provinces with laws for compulsory schooling for white children between 7 and 14. In the years that followed, the amount of compulsory schooling was increased, so that today white children between 7 and 16 must attend school.

At the same time, black education was not made free nor compulsory. Instead of becoming a state responsibility it remained the responsibility of the church. However, the state was more active than before. Financial aid was given to mission schools throughout the country, and in some cases a special curriculum was drawn up for black schools.

At this time a number of important mission schools were opened.

1906   Grace Dieu School opened near Pietersburg.
1906   Lemana School opened in the Letaba valley.
1922   St Peter's, Rosettenville, was opened.

According to the historian Horrell, in 1905 there were 184 African mission schools, with 310 teachers and nearly 10 000 pupils. (1963:23)

This was an extremely important period in the history of South African education. Free, compulsory education was introduced for white people, but not for black people. This was a highly significant step in the development of the South African education system. And it remains a controversial issue, even today.

There is one more issue to look at before we leave this period. That is, the issue of CNE schools.

Christian National Education schools

Many of the defeated Afrikaners did not like the new system of education. They saw it as a way of forcing the English language and culture on them, and destroying their own language and culture. The new system also undermined the social position of Afrikaner church ministers and teachers, who felt excluded. These people decided to set up their own schools – Christian National Education (CNE) schools.

For a few years, the CNE movement was strong. About two hundred CNE schools were established. But the movement gradually weakened. The schools were not free, nor compulsory – which the state schools were. With time the issues became less significant, especially when more language and cultural recognition was given to Afrikaners.

The CNE movement gradually died out. (Although, as we'll see in Chapter Six, it was revived in the 1940s.) Even so, it shows us a number of important points.

It shows us that opposition groups have been able to influence educational policy. It shows that policy isn't just set out by the government. And it shows that issues like language in schools were sensitive issues, long before Soweto '76!

Education after Union

The Union government, set up in 1910, allowed the different provinces to have control over primary and secondary education (but not higher education). However, African education fell under the control of the Minister of Native Affairs.

1922   New laws were passed concerning the funding of African
1925   education. Government expenditure was 'pegged' – or fixed – at the 1922 level. Any expansion would have to be financed out of taxation paid by Africans themselves.

In effect, this meant that there was a continual shortage of money for African schooling.

In this section, we've looked at some of the important patterns that were set up and continued until after World War II (1939–45).

To sum up these trends:

1 We see a pattern of education differentiated along lines of colour and also along lines of social class.

2 For whites, there was a system of free, compulsory education. This system grew and developed. It included more and more children, at higher levels of education, so that today almost all white children have completed some secondary schooling, and many go on to technical or higher education. At the same time, the system of private schools remains for privileged people.

3 For Africans, education remained in the hands of missionaries. There were continual shortages of money. While a few Africans achieved high levels of education, most received virtually no schooling. So class differences amongst Africans can be seen in schooling as well.

4 This period also shows that education is an area of political struggle. The CNE schools show us that people are able to take action to influence education policy.

And, of course, it shows that education is a political issue.

Reserves

Industrial growth and apartheid education

We saw earlier how the growth of mining brought important changes in South Africa. We saw that patterns of social relations developed along lines of colour and class and that education was part of these social relations.

The 1940s were also a period of important economic growth and change. Between 1939 and 1945 South Africa was fighting in World War II. Because of war shortages local industries developed. In this period manufacturing industries became more and more important.

During this time even greater numbers of black and white people moved to towns to look for work. As with the period of urbanization early in the twentieth century, they were partly attracted by job possibilities, and they partly left because of hardships in the countryside. For black people in particular it was becoming harder and harder to survive in the overcrowded reserves. The towns seemed to offer better chances of survival.

Soon the towns were also overcrowded. There were not enough facilities like houses and schools, for whites as well as for blacks. Many of the black people moved into squatter camps. It was at this time that James Mpanze formed the Sofasonke Party to fight for the housing and other civic rights of Orlando people.

Again, as in the earlier period, there were issues of class struggle. In this period there was a lot of industrial unrest and many strikes, especially among African workers. Many of these strikes succeeded in improving conditions, particularly when wages were low. But strikes were outlawed by the government as a War Measure. Nevertheless in 1946 there was the famous mineworkers strike. When 70 000 black miners downed tools, the police moved in; 12 miners were killed, and over 1 000 were injured.

During this time, the main body of the ANC was still fighting for democratic rights. But the Congress Youth League, impatient with these tactics, was advocating a more confronting position.

Racial divisions in the working class came to the fore once more. Again white workers resisted competition with blacks. They wanted to keep themselves in a privileged position, with better wages, better jobs and better living conditions. In the manufacturing industry there were new skilled and semi-skilled jobs opening up. Many manufacturing capitalists would have liked a settled, skilled urban black workforce. But this was not to be.

In 1948 there was a general election of great significance. The National Party came to power, and introduced its **policy** of apartheid. The NP has remained in power since then. In the 1948 election the NP was supported mainly by the Afrikaner middle class, workers and farmers, united by nationalist beliefs.

As we've seen, there was segregation long before 1948. Patterns of racialism can be traced far back. But the NP took this a step further. They passed a number of laws which enforced segregation more strongly. They also used the 1913 Land Act as a basis for their 'bantustan' or 'homeland' policy. Their policy was to locate Africans in the 'homelands' as far as possible, and to extend the migrant labour system. They didn't want Africans to have rights in urban areas or to settle in towns. As far as possible, they wanted to move Africans to the 'homelands', and call on them as contract migrant workers. These workers would be controlled by pass laws and labour bureaux. Unlike white workers, they would not be free to seek work where and when they liked, or bargain collectively. Their labour was controlled by all sorts of laws.

These apartheid measures were resisted through political organization and strike action. For example, in 1952 the Defiance Campaign was waged against the pass laws and other apartheid discrimination. In 1955 SACTU was formed, a non-racial federation of unions. In 1956, 20 000 women, led by the Federation of South African Women, marched on the Union Buildings in Pretoria to protest against the pass laws. Also at this time the Freedom Charter was drawn up.

The Non-European Unity Movement (NEUM) was another major movement of 'non-Europeans', as they were then called (and called themselves). NEUM campaigned mainly against Bantu Authorities, the 'homelands', Bantu Education, the Group Areas Act and other discriminatory measures.

The government put all its efforts into crushing black resistance. In 1956 the leaders of the Congress Alliance were arrested, and 150 people were charged with high treason. Members of the Unity Movement were also banned. This was followed by the Sharpeville massacre on 21 March 1960. On this day 69 people were killed and 178 were wounded at a peaceful demonstration against the pass laws. The government declared a state of emergency. It arrested 20 000 people, and banned the ANC and the PAC. In the wake of this action, Mandela, Sisulu and other black leaders were imprisoned. Others went underground or left the country.

Once these organizations of black resistance had been crushed for the time being, the government consolidated its position. The capitalist economy continued to grow, organized along racialist lines. Blacks were denied social and political rights in 'white South Africa'. The system of reserves and pass laws and labour bureaux controlled the work they could do, and where and when they could work.

During the 1960s the economy boomed. The country grew richer, and new industries were set up. It was a time of prosperity for capitalism. But during the mid-1970s South Africa entered a recession. Many workers were laid off. The number of unemployed people increased, and many people suffered poverty.

In the 1970s the black labour movement again took shape. New independent trade unions were set up, and black workers once again bargained collectively for better wages and conditions. Organized black workers became a force to be reckoned with.

The government made certain adjustments in the light of this development. In 1979 the Riekert Commission recommended that certain Africans should have permanent urban status, with residence rights and access to jobs. But Africans living in 'bantustans' would be regarded as temporary contract workers. The Wiehahn Commission made important recommendations on labour relations. These included the official recognition of trade union rights for Africans, and the abolition of job reservation.

At the present time, there are other changes that are affecting workers. In industry, new methods of production are being introduced. New machinery has been brought in, so there are changes taking place at work. People are needing different skills. Some black people are getting higher level jobs and moving into middle class positions. Other blacks are becoming semi-skilled workers. But many blacks are unemployed – they are being left out altogether.

You may be wondering where education fits into all of this. Well, the rest of the book answers that question!

What follows here is a very brief outline of education between the 1940s and 1980s, to give you some idea of the picture.

Educational developments:

As we've seen, long before 1948 there was a system of segregated and unequal education in South Africa. White education was free and compulsory, and the system was expanding. Black education was neglected. There had long been shortages of money, which meant that the system suffered in all ways – not enough schools, not enough teachers and not enough children in schools.

In 1936 the government set up a Commission of Inquiry into African education. The Commission pointed to problems with the system, but virtually nothing was done to improve things. As more and more African people came to the towns, so the shortages of schooling became worse and worse.

The National Party viewed education as part of an overall plan for developing South Africa. This plan included the 'homelands' and pass laws, restrictions on blacks in urban areas, and job reservation. Here are some of the most important developments in education under the Nationalist government.

1949   The government appointed the Eiselen Commission to look at African education. The Commission recommended 'resorting to radical measures' for the 'effective reform of the Bantu school system'.

1953   The Bantu Education Act was passed. The Act said that all schools for Africans had to be registered with the government. As a result of the Act, almost all of the mission schools closed down. So did most night schools. This is when the system of apartheid education began.

1954–5   Black teachers and students protested against Bantu Education. The African Education Movement was formed to give alternative education. For a few years, cultural clubs operated as informal schools, but by 1960 they had closed down.

1959   The Extension of University Education Act was passed. This Act set up separate 'tribal colleges' for black university students. Blacks could no longer freely attend white universities. Again, there were strong protests.

1963   The Coloured Person's Education Act was passed. Control over 'coloured' education was placed under the Department of Coloured Affairs. 'Coloured' schools also had to be registered with the government. 'Coloured' education was made compulsory.

1965   The Indian Education Act was passed. Control over Indian education was placed under the Department of Indian Affairs. In 1976, the SAIC took over certain educational functions. Indian education was also made compulsory.

1967   The National Education Act was passed, setting out the principles of CNE for white schools.

1969   The black student organization, SASO, was formed.

Under the apartheid system, patterns of educational inequality were entrenched. Different education systems do not provide equal education for the different population registration groups. And the separate education systems have also entrenched patterns of social class.

In the early years of Bantu Education there was a great increase in the numbers of African students attending school. School enrolments increased dramatically, compared with the years before Bantu Education. But there was a high drop-out rate; the majority of African school-goers did not stay beyond lower primary school (four years). In fact until the 1970s, about 70% of Africans in school were in the first four years – which means that they had very little education. Less than 1% of Africans at school were in matric. The government tried, as far as possible, to set up secondary schools and universities for Africans in the 'homelands'. In fact most Africans went to school in rural areas.

Since the late 1970s, there have been some changes in black education. Numbers have increased – there are more students attending school. There are more students in secondary school than there were in the early years of Bantu Education. More students are getting to matric – though the percentage is still low (1,4% in 1983). The general level of education for Africans is rising, but as we'll see in Chapter Four, there are still patterns of inequality. Many students are at school in the 'homelands', and 30% of African students attend farm schools where the education is very inadequate. Another important feature of education in this period has been the continued resistance by black students to apartheid education (discussed in Chapter Nine).

Here are some of the important dates in this period:

1976   The June 1976 Soweto uprisings began.

1979   The Education and Training Act was passed to replace the Bantu Education Act of 1953. African education was now in the hands of the Department of Education and Training – the DET. But education for Africans remained virtually the same.

1980   The schools boycotts began.

1981   The government set up the De Lange Commission to conduct an in-depth investigation into education and to make recommendations for an education policy for South Africa. The De Lange Report recommended a single department of education for all, education of equal quality for all, and a changed schooling structure.

1983   The Government issued a White Paper, accepting the De Lange guiding principles but refusing to accept the major recommendation of a single education department for all.

1980s   The Government began to place more emphasis on technical education. It encouraged industries to set up training programmes to 'upgrade' black workers. Trade unions also began to play a more active role in providing education for workers.

1984   Continuing schools protest against apartheid education. Start of the Education Charter Campaign.

Conclusion

So far we've looked at the history of education in South Africa, against the background of broader historical events. There are a number of points that stand out:

- We've seen how the system grew and changed over the years, as the society changed. Education hasn't always been the same; it is part of broader processes of social change – which are happening all the time.

- We've seen that segregation and inequality have long been part of the schooling system.

- We've seen that South African schools don't only divide on lines of colour; they also divide on social class lines. Schools play an important part in making up social classes.

- And we've seen that education policy doesn't simply come from the government. It is also influenced by opposition groups (like CNE in the early 1900s).

But we should also be aware that there are different ways of looking at the history of schooling in South Africa. There are different interpretations.

Let's look at the different views of our three theorists: conservative, moderate and radical.

Conservative

If you look at the history of education in South Africa, you can see that blacks and whites have quite different traditions.

Before whites arrived, blacks had no real schools at all. They were living a very simple lifestyle, and they were largely uneducated. Today, there are schools for blacks. Apartheid, in particular, brought improvements in black education. Under apartheid, more blacks have gone to school than ever before. And there are also openings for educated black people in their own communities.

If you look at white education, you can see a completely different history and different traditions. For example, from the earliest days white education has had a religious basis. And this is something which we are still preserving today, as the policy of Christian National Education.

It's important that we recognize that different groups in South Africa have different traditions and different cultures. And setting up different education systems is the best way of making sure that these differences are preserved – to everyone's benefit.

Moderate

If we look at the history of education in South Africa, we can see a long tradition of racial prejudice. And this racial prejudice and racial inequality were worsened by apartheid.

From early on, whites had more education, and better education, than blacks had. Certainly, social class did play a part – wealthy parents could afford to give their children a better education. But of course, most of these wealthy people were white anyway. I think it was mainly a matter of racial prejudice.

And the apartheid government made things worse. I believe that apartheid is really to blame for most of the problems of inequality in education today. The introduction of apartheid laws was a turning point, especially for black education.

Without racial prejudice, the picture would look very different. And we should be doing what we can to move away from racial prejudice, to a more fair, just and equal education system.

Radical

Education was segregated and unequal *before* the introduction of apartheid. So we can't explain the present inequalities simply in terms of racialism and apartheid. Our explanation must stress social class.

Schooling has always been important in helping to form social classes in South Africa. Those few blacks who had secondary and higher education in the mission schools were able to form an elite, middle class. But most blacks were labourers; they were part of the working class. And the same applies to whites – education has also helped to shape class divisions among whites as well.

This process of class formation was taking place before 1953, and it has been continuing in the apartheid period. And it is this process of class formation which explains the fundamental inequalities in South Africa. Certainly, racism is important – but it isn't the fundamental source of inequality.

These different views show us that the history of education is a complex one.

This chapter has presented some of the issues – but it's for you to judge them for yourself.

References and further readings

Africa Perspective (1980) 17

Behr, A.L. and Macmillan, R.G. (1966) *Education in South Africa*, Pretoria

Behr, A.L. (1978) *New Perspectives in South African Education*, Butterworths, Durban

Callinicos, L. (1981) *Gold and Workers: A People's History of South Africa*, vol. 1, Ravan, Johannesburg.

Chisholm, L. (1984) 'Themes in the construction of free compulsory education for the white working class on the Witwatersrand, 1886–1907', Conference papers, Kenton-at-the-stadt Education Conference, Mmabatho

Christie, P. and Collins, C.B. (1982) 'Bantu Education: Apartheid ideology and labour reproduction' *Comparative Education* 18(1)

Collins, C.B. (1980) 'Black schooling in South Africa' *Africa Perspective* 17

Cook, P.A.W. (1949) 'Non-European education' in E. Hellman *Handbook on Race Relations in South Africa*, OUP, Cape Town

De Villiers, R. (1979) 'Remaining essentially Bantu' in NUSAS *Education and Development,* Conference papers, University of Cape Town

Horrell, M. (1963) *African Education: Some Origins and Developments until 1953,* SAIRR, Johannesburg

Horrell, M. (1968) *Bantu Education to 1968,* SAIRR, Johannesburg

Horrell, M. (1970) *The Education of the Coloured Community in South Africa, 1652–1970,* SAIRR, Johannesburg

Kallaway, P. (ed) (1984) *Apartheid and Education,* Ravan, Johannesburg

Molteno, F. (1984) 'The evolution of educational policy' in P. Kallaway (ed)*Apartheid and Education,* Ravan, Johannesburg

Nasson, W. (1984) 'Education and Poverty', Second Carnegie Inquiry into Poverty and Development in Southern Africa, Cape Town

Rose, B. and Tunmer, R. (1975) *Documents in South African Education,* Ad. Donker, Johannesburg

SAIRR (Annual) *Survey of Race Relations in South Africa,* SAIRR, Johannesburg

SARS (1983) *South African Review, vol. 1: Same Foundations, New Facades,* Ravan, Johannesburg

SARS (1984) *South African Review, vol. 2,* Ravan, Johannesburg

Wilson M. and Thompson, L.M. (1969, 1971) *Oxford History of South Africa,* vols. 1 and 2, OUP, Oxford

Chapter 3 The church and education

The church has always been prominent in education in South Africa, and especially in black education. Before 1953 mission schools provided almost all of the education which was available for blacks. During the 1950s under apartheid education, most of these schools had to close down. But that hasn't meant the end of the church's involvement in education. Today church schools – and especially Catholic schools – are admitting black students into their private schools which up till now had admitted white students only. These are the so-called open schools.

The role of the church in South African history is not an easy one to judge. Its role has been complicated and often contradictory. As a result, there are different views about the church's involvement. What follows are examples of three different views:

"There's no doubt that the church has done a lot of good. Missionaries were humane people who spread the Christian faith among the African tribes. And at the same time, they brought education and Western medicine.

Missionaries were the main teachers of blacks in South Africa before Bantu Education forced them to close the schools. Certainly, there were problems with some of these schools. But without these mission schools, blacks would have received no education. The mission schools educated many people. Most of the really prominent black people went to mission schools.

The missionaries deserve praise for what they did."

"Certainly, the missionaries provided education for blacks at a time when there were few government schools. And maybe a lot of prominent people did go to mission schools. But we still need to look critically at what the missionaries did.

I say that the missionaries actually helped in the conquest of the African chiefdoms. They helped to break down African culture, and they imposed Western culture and work patterns. They undermined the way of life of the African people. I think the Bible and the gun went together in the defeat of the African chiefdoms.

You talk about education. Most black people didn't get to school at all. Those who did get to school became an elite, privileged group. So mission education actually divided people.

Overall, I think the missionaries have got a lot to answer for."

"There is a big difference between intentions and actions. The missionaries might have had good intentions. But this doesn't mean that what they did was always good.

Often, they did work hand in hand with the colonial government – which wasn't necessarily to the good of the blacks. And often, they did think in racialist terms, and practise exploitation themselves.

But how far were the missionaries themselves responsible for this? People are very seldom aware of the role they are playing in history. Missionaries were people of their time – as all people are. They reflected and promoted the Western values of those times. Could we expect them to know differently?

And anyway, we are seldom aware of the role we are playing in history. The missionaries were part of the unequal colonial society. That doesn't mean they chose it. Surely we should be trying to understand the past instead of praising or blaming missionaries."

These three views show that there can be a wide range of opinion on missionary education. In this chapter, we're going to trace the story of the church's involvement in education. We'll look at:

- Mission education before 1953
- The response of the churches to Bantu Education
- The 'open schools' movement.

Then, you should be able to make up your own mind about the role of the church in education. You can judge the debates for yourself.

Let's start by looking at mission education before 1953.

Mission education before 1953

Missionaries, merchants and magistrates

At the same time as white merchants, traders and farmers were moving in and settling in South Africa, there was also another very important group of Europeans in the colonies – the missionaries. Missionaries came from Europe with their own purposes in mind. They wanted to spread their Christian faith and way of life. But in South Africa, as elsewhere, missionary activity often went hand in hand with merchants and traders, and the colonial government. This isn't to say that they always had the same aims; but they were often working closely together. As one writer noted in 1877:

> **"**There are close connections between the magistrate, missionary, school master and teacher in furthering the aims of the colonial government: to establish and maintain peace, to diffuse civilization and christianity, and to establish society on the basis of individual property and personal industry.**"**   (Quoted in Trapido 1980:250)

So, the argument is that the magistrate (working for the colonial government), the missionary (working for God) and the merchant (working for profit) were often closely linked.

For a start, let's look at some of the links between merchants and missionaries.

In the 1800s, European merchants and manufacturers were looking for new markets in Africa and the rest of the world. This was the time of merchant capitalism. Merchants and manufacturers often used moral or Christian arguments to justify taking over Africa and other parts of the world. For example, they argued that work on a mine or a plantation was 'good' for people, and that it promoted 'Christian' values, like diligence.

And the link between missionaries and merchants went the other way as well. Missionaries often promoted ideas and practices that fitted in with the ideas and practices of the merchants.

Missionaries came to South Africa to spread the Gospel, and to teach about Christianity. But they also had certain ideas about the way of life that 'civilized' people should lead. Their Christian doctrine was wrapped up in a whole set of Western attitudes and values. And these were often similar to the ideas of merchants, manufacturers and the colonial government. For example missionaries emphasized again and again that Africans had to be 'taught to work'. And work, for them, meant producing goods to sell, or earning wages in exchange for labouring for a fixed number of hours a day. Here is what one missionary said in 1851:

> **"**It is something to have changed the old kraal into a decent village – the old kaross into substantial European clothing – idleness into industry, ignorance into intelligence, selfishness into benevolence, and heathenism into Christianity.**"**   (Quoted in Trapido 1980:249)

And, as the historian Cook says:

> The missionary came to South Africa to preach the Gospel and to dispel the darkness of the heathen. But he taught elements of the same culture to which the trader, the magistrate, and the farmer belong. (1949:348)

So far, we've seen that there were certain links between missionaries and other groups of colonists. Some people argue that the missionaries were 'agents of colonialism', and that the links were strong. Other people argue that the links were not very strong. And others argue that amongst missionaries there were different ideas and practices, so we shouldn't make general statements about them.

We'll pick up on this theme later, when we look at the relationship between the colonial government and the mission schools.

Let's now move on to look at missionary activity, and the schools that were set up.

Mission schools

Missionaries came to South Africa from different European countries – among them Britain, Germany, France, Norway and Sweden – and also from America. And they represented different church groups, or denominations; there were Methodists, Roman Catholics, Congregationists, Lutherans, Anglicans, Presbyterians, and others. They set up mission stations first in the Cape and Natal, and then further inland. In fact, by the end of the nineteenth century, there were more missionaries in South Africa than almost anywhere else in the world!

Different missionary groups had different approaches towards their missionary work among the people. But generally their aims were the same: to establish themselves and their work, and to convert people to Christianity.

Usually, missionaries set up residential mission stations. Here is a description of typical missionary activity elsewhere in Africa – which applies to South Africa as well:

> The initial years were mostly spent in building a church, a school and residential houses for the European priests. The African Christians and their families lived in areas not very far from the mission and regularly came to participate in the various activities. They did the construction work and cleared the surrounding areas for farming. Gradually a complex emerged in which activities like construction, agriculture, evangelical work, literacy training and nursing sick patients were carried on. Besides, the missionaries also visited nearby villages to extend invitations to chiefs to come to the mission. (Hirji 1980:195)

In the course of time mission stations were set up around the country. And where there were mission stations there were usually mission schools. The missionaries saw education as a way of achieving their own aims of converting people to Christianity, and of establishing themselves and their work.

65

There were different sorts of educational activities at mission schools.

- Mostly, the missionaries taught basic reading and writing, along with Christian doctrine. It was easier for literate people to absorb religious ideas by reading the Bible and taking part in hymn-singing. Basic education became an important means for conversion. A short period of basic reading and writing, together with Christian doctrine, was the most common education provided by mission schools.

- At the same time, manual work and practical training were also an important part of mission education. We saw earlier how the missionaries stressed the value of 'hard work' and believed that people should be taught work discipline. Not only did they believe in the value of work, the missionaries also needed work to be done on the mission stations!

   Some people did manual work and farming on the mission stations as part of their education. Others were trained to be carpenters, blacksmiths, masons, joiners, wagon builders, and so on.

- The missionaries also needed to train black people to help them with their work of spreading the Gospel. They had to train catechists and teachers, who could organize services, spread the Gospel among their own people, and teach basic education in the mission schools.

   And so, from early on, the mission schools also provided a higher level of education – and especially teacher training – for a small group of people. These people are often called the mission elite.

From this brief outline, we can see that mission schools produced different sorts of graduates. There were:

1 people with basic literacy;
2 workers, artisans and tradespeople;
3 an elite with higher levels of education.

The education they provided was part of their evangelizing aims, so it was based in Christian values and practices.

Different views on curriculum

Mission educators had different ideas about what black students should learn, especially at secondary schools and teacher training schools.

- Some missionaries thought that blacks should be given exactly the same academic education as whites – which meant, for example, learning Latin and Greek. They believed there should be no discrimination.

- Some missionaries thought that there should be an adapted curriculum for black students. This curriculum should take local conditions into account, and prepare black students for the local society.

- Some missionaries thought that blacks were basically inferior, and shouldn't have too much academic education anyway. Thus, schools should basically prepare people to be trained labourers.

Usually, the prominent mission schools taught a European-style curriculum, but also included industrial training and manual work in the curriculum.

But most mission schools did not emphasize secondary and higher education. They provided mainly basic education, and some provided enough higher education to meet their own needs for catechists and teachers.

Different quality of schools

Mission schools varied greatly in the kind of education and the quality of education they offered. In the course of time, a number of very famous mission schools were established. Here is a list of some of them and the dates when they were established:

Lovedale Institution (1841)
Salem (1855)
St Matthew's (1855)
Healdtown (1857)   Cape
Zonnebloem (1858)
St Cuthbert's (1882)
Mariazell (1899)

Adams College (1853) Inanda (1869) Mariannhill (1882) St Hilda's (1907)	Natal
Kilnerton (1855) Grace Dieu (1906) Lemana (1906) St Peter's (1922)	Transvaal

These schools offered more than basic education. They were usually boarding schools, providing an academic education based on European-type curricula. Most of them were teacher training institutes as well. They emphasized Christian values – and also included practical work and technical training in their curricula. Some of these mission schools were among the best in the country – and Lovedale was one of these.

But as well as these famous schools, there were many many others, often much less well known and much less successful. Most schools had very little money, poor facilities and poorly trained teachers. They usually offered two to three years of basic education – but attendance was irregular, and their educational standards were doubtful.

Here is what the historian Horrell says of these schools:

In 1862, Dr Langham Dale, the Superintendent-General of education in the Cape, went on a tour of inspection. He found that only 5% of the African pupils in these schools had any useful knowledge of reading, writing, or arithmetic. Few of the teachers had passed even Std IV. At outstations unqualified African assistants were in charge of so-called schools, with the nearest missionary some days' journey away. No school books were available in the African languages. There was sufficient school accommodation to admit only a very small fraction of the children of school-going age, and those who did attend came irregularly.

(1963:11-12, adapted)

In 1882 the Inspector-General of the Cape said that Lovedale was 'probably the greatest educational establishment in South Africa'. But he said that half of the other mission schools 'could be closed without loss to educational advancement' (Horrell 1963:54).

So we shouldn't think only of successful schools like Lovedale, Adams College and St Peters when we think of mission schools. We should remember the others as well. And we should also remember that most people didn't go to school at all.

But this brings us to the overall questions: How effective were mission schools? What did they actually achieve? How should we assess them?

To answer these questions, let's start by looking at African responses to mission schools.

African responses to mission schools

In the beginning, missionaries often found it difficult to gain converts and educate them. African leaders sometimes accepted missionaries as intermediaries, traders and healers. But they resisted any attempts to break down their own value systems and authority structures. Here is what the historian Etherington has to say:

> Whole tribes (of Nguni) moved away from stations. Parents withdrew their daughters from mission schools and rotated their sons so that they might earn shirts and wages without risking conversion. Magic and medicines were administered to individuals who seemed to be moving towards church membership. In Zululand and Pondoland converts were isolated on mission stations and ceased to be members of the nation.
>
> (1977:35, adapted)

Often, people who did come to mission stations had their own reasons for doing so. Etherington argues that not many people came for purely religious reasons. Many people came to look for work, or to seek refuge from difficulties in their own communities.

Later on, when the independence of the chiefdoms was being severely threatened, leaders in some African groups allowed a few people, particularly chiefs' sons, to attend school. They hoped that these people could act as intermediaries between the colonial government and the African chiefdoms.

It was only later, with the conquest of the chiefdoms and the growth of the economy in South Africa, that people began to value mission education as a way of advancement in the society.

69

In the earlier period, African people didn't always take mission education seriously. They often had their own aims for sending children to mission schools. If they didn't particularly participate in the white-controlled economy, they didn't necessarily see much value in learning to read and write, or having a mission education. It was only later, in the twentieth century, that people began to demand more education.

New demand for education

By the end of the nineteenth century, the picture in South Africa was changing fast. African chiefdoms were defeated by white conquest, and so authority structures changed. Economic activities also changed. As most of the land was colonized, there was a steady movement of people to towns to look for work. The discovery of minerals and the expansion of economic activities meant that more and more blacks were drawn into wage labour. Most of the small peasants were squeezed off their land.

In these changed conditions people's attitudes to education began to change too. Education was seen more and more as a way into the dominant economic and social system. And so, people began to demand education.

Faced with this situation, missionaries continued to provide schooling and to set up more schools. Some of the schools which were established in this period offered a higher education, and there was also emphasis on teacher training. But most of the schools still provided only two or three years of education. And as people became more urbanized, so the focus of missionary work also broadened. No longer were they simply operating from mission stations. They now also worked in compounds and locations.

And what about mission-educated people? Molteno and other historians argue that these people were part of the breakdown of tribal authority. According to Molteno (1984), there was a division between Christian converts and people who held traditional religious beliefs. Schooled people were more likely to accept the new order. They helped to spread a system of ideas, values and loyalties which fitted in with the colonists' interests, and which helped to undermine tribal resistance.

But at the same time, South African society was divided along lines of colour. Black people – even educated black people – were not treated as equals by the colonists. In the Cape, some black people did have the vote. But in general blacks were in a subordinate position.

Even so, educated blacks were an elite group compared with other blacks who had little or no education, and who could do only lower levels of work.

From this we can see that missionaries and their schools were part of the changes that were happening in South Africa. Mission education played its part in creating new social groups – workers and the elite – in a society divided along lines of colour and class.

But the important question is: To what extent were the missionaries *responsible* for these social changes? Certainly, they were part of the processes of social change. But how important was their part?

As part of our assessment of mission schools, let's look at their relationship with the government.

Relationship with the government

Generally speaking, for most of the nineteenth century mission education operated without much government intervention. As Molteno (1984) says, black schooling was not a high priority for the colonial government. As we saw in Chapter Two, mission schools fell under the authority of the Department of Education. Government funding meant that it was *possible* for the government to exercise some control over the schools. And in some cases they did attempt to influence mission schools. People like Sir George Grey and Langham Dale hoped to use mission education to control the eastern frontier. And the government also encouraged and gave money for industrial education in mission schools. But, generally, the government was prepared to leave black education in the hands of the missionaries.

Gradually, black schooling did receive more government attention. But black schooling was not made compulsory at the time when compulsory schooling was introduced for whites. At the time of union (1910), black education was left in the hands of the separate provinces. Though the government gave funds for black education, money was always very limited. School buildings were owned by missionaries, who also had to spend considerable sums of money from their own funds to run their schools.

71

So, before 1953, the mission schools provided almost all of the schooling which was available for blacks. Along with mission schools, there were a few government schools and a number of community schools. Most of the mission schools were registered with the government, and received government grants. Through registration and funding, the government had a fair amount of influence over mission schools. In return for state aid, the government laid down syllabuses, paid the teachers and appointed managers to oversee the running of the schools.

The vast majority of African people didn't attend school at all. Most of those who did attend had only two or three years of primary schooling. Very few Africans had secondary schooling, and very very few received a matric. Therefore we shouldn't overemphasize the direct impact of mission education – it didn't reach very many people.

Nevertheless, mission education was very important for blacks. Before 1953 it was almost the only education available to them.

And this is where we see a big contradiction. On the one hand, the church was providing, and paying towards, education for blacks. But on the other hand, we could argue that mission schools were 'doing the government's work for it'. They were providing an education which was mainly segregated, and which aimed at spreading Western values, including work values.

Now let's look at three of the common criticisms that are levelled against mission schools.

Some common criticisms

People usually associate segregation and racism with Bantu Education and apartheid. They tend to blame the Bantu Education system for all the problems in today's black education. But many of the patterns of present-day black education were already present in mission education. Let's look at three aspects of mission education which are often criticized:

- Industrial and manual education
- Racism and subordination
- Sexism and women's subordination.

Industrial and manual education

Mission schools usually included industrial education or manual labour as part of the curriculum. This has been a controversial aspect of mission education. This type of education partly reflects the missionaries' belief in the value of hard work; and it was partly because they wanted to train people to take up jobs of different sorts in the economy. The government also encouraged industrial training.

Critics argue that the industrial training offered by missions was not of a high enough standard to prepare people to take up skilled work. Instead of being proper skills training, it was really just training people to have the 'right attitudes' to work. And because there was so little proper training, people were only prepared for lower-level jobs in the economy.

It does seem that industrial education was not very systematically carried out by the missions. The Cape Education Commission of 1891 gave four reasons for this:

- A lack of equipment, facilities and expertise
- Opposition on the part of some missionaries
- The fact that the colonial government had not given the aid it promised
- Opposition on the part of Africans.

And we could probably add a fifth reason:

- Opposition on the part of white settlers who often did not want blacks to receive too much education.

There is no doubt that some mission schools did provide proper training. But it seems that others had token industrial centres, which did not actually teach skills. Here an extract of evidence given to the South African Native Affairs Commission (1903–5):

Question: Have you been to the industrial schools?
Answer: No, I have not been there, but I have studied the result of industrial schools.
Question: Where have you studied it?
Answer: Amongst the natives who have come from those places.
Question: Do you think that all they learn is to knock two bits of wood together with a nail?
Answer: Yes, or to make a box or a table or such little things. But they know nothing about a trade. They do not become skilled workmen.

Here is a complaint made by D.D.T. Jabavu in 1918:

> "In our schools 'manual labour' consists of sweeping yards, repairing roads, cracking stones, and so on, and is done by boys only as so much task work enforced by a time-keeper, and under threats of punishment."
>
> (quoted in Molteno 1984:67)

A government commission report in 1936 admitted that the 'manual work' in black schools was only trivial, and had no educative value. D.D.T. Jabavu claimed that one result of this kind of 'education' was that:

> "the boys grow to hate all manual work as humiliating, 'skulk' from it whenever they can, and ever avoid it at home and in after life."
>
> (quoted in Molteno 1984:67)

In other words, according to Jabavu, this industrial training achieved exactly the opposite results to what it intended.

In addition to inadequate training, there were also problems of race prejudice which blacks faced in looking for jobs which recognized the training they had received. In 1921, H. D. Tyamzashe wrote the following:

> "Of many promising men thus trained, some can be traced to be more or less usefully occupied; but, sad to relate, the majority are not employed in the trades they learned. This is mainly due to the colour bar; there are no openings for native tradesmen."

This gives us an idea of some of the problems associated with industrial education.
What about problems of racism and subordination?

Racism and subordination

It is true to say that mission schools were usually segregated on lines of colour. And even where schools did admit whites and blacks together, segregation was still practised. At Lovedale, for example, students slept and played sports separately. Though they ate in one dining hall, they ate at separate tables. They mixed together in the classroom and during leisure time.

Missionary education usually had little respect for the local African culture. Local culture and history were not included in the school curriculum, and the curriculum was usually based on European schools.

Mission education was rooted in Christian values, and attempted to teach attitudes like patience, humility, piety, discipline and the value of hard work. Critics argue that these values helped to prepare black people to accept a subordinate position in society.

The levels of education which people received also affected their social position. Generally speaking, those blacks who attended school received only two or three years of basic education. This meant that they had limited social and economic opportunities. Critics argue that low levels of schooling, together with missionary values, prepared people for subordinate roles in society and in the workforce.

The general schooling pattern which mission schools promoted was very important. By offering segregated and lower-level education to most of their students, mission education certainly contributed to broader social inequality.

But racism and class differences were part of the society in which the missionaries operated. So the questions are: Were the missionaries responsible for these practices? Could they have done otherwise? And the position of women raises the same questions.

Sexism and women's subordination

The missionaries also brought Western ideas about the place of women in society. Basically, they believed that women should be trained for domesticity – as wives, mothers or servants. Women should not be directly involved in economic production or in politics. Missionary education was open to men and women, but higher levels of education – for catechists and teachers – were aimed mainly at men. Thus, while men were being educated to play a fuller role, at least in the church, the same did not apply to women. The sociologist Cock says:

> The education of black women was largely aimed at socialization into domestic roles, both in their own homes and as servants in other people's homes. (1980:288, adapted)

Sometimes, missionaries were openly sexist. Here is what the Abbot of Mariannhill said in 1889:

> **"**Instruct only the Kaffir boys in reading, writing, and arithmetic, and train them to manual labour. Do not teach the girls any English reading and very little Kaffir. Give them as little education as possible. The system of cramming is too much for the intellect of Kaffir girls. My experience is this: the more that Kaffir girls learn in school, the less they are inclined to work, and the more insolent and dissatisfied they are.**"**
>
> (quoted in Cock 1980:280)

Other missionaries were less prejudiced against women. But, even so, they believed that the main aim in educating women was to prepare them for a domestic life. The Principal of All Saints School at Engcobo saw his task as 'educating Christian women among the natives to be fitting wives for the native clergy and catechists'. And another educator hoped that educated girls would answer 'the divine call to lives of service as helpers at their homes, at mission schools, and at new mission stations'. (Taylor 1928:448)

The missionaries had certain ideas about what girls should learn, and they based these ideas on Western views about the role of women in society. For example, in the mission schools women were not taught agriculture – though this had long been women's work in African society. Industrial education for boys taught a variety of tasks, for example carpentry, wagon-building, stone-masonry, blacksmithing, printing, and so on. But industrial education for girls taught only domestic skills, like cooking, laundrywork, dressmaking and home nursing. As one training institution for girls stated:

> Girls are carefully trained in domestic work – cooking, baking, sewing, ironing and tailoring – in addition to the usual school instruction. The aim is to prepare the girls to make good housewives and mothers, and to lift them and their families to a higher plane of living.　　(Cock 1980:294)

So, from early on, domestic skills were part of the girls' curriculum, and sex discrimination was practised.

For those girls who did attend school, there was a second barrier: they could not easily go on to higher levels of education. In fact, most girls went only to primary school. The total numbers of boys and girls at school were often nearly the same, and sometimes there were more girls than boys. But the girls were mainly in lower classes; it was mainly the boys who went on to secondary and higher education. And this, of course, affected the work women could do and the status they could achieve. For some blacks mission education was a way to advancement in the wider society. But this applied to very few women.

There were limited occupations open to women. Domestic service was the main employment possibility, and industrial mission education certainly prepared women for this role. Those women who did have higher education were still restricted in the work they could do. Nursing and primary school teaching were their best possibilities. And both of these were also 'domestic' kinds of work – just as on a higher level.

Cock (1980) argues that the education offered to women was ambiguous. On the one hand, it gave them the means to earn an independent living (even as domestic servants), and it freed them from tribal subordinate positions. But on the other hand, it encouraged a new set of values, and led them to Western-based roles of women's subordination.

Cock's argument is an important one. It shows us another of the contradictions of mission education. Mission education freed women from one kind of subordination, but prepared them for another.

In general, mission education did not treat women as equal to men, and it prepared women for subordinate roles in society.

But, as with racism and class differences, so sexism was also part of the society in which the missionaries operated. How far are the missionaries themselves responsible?

To sum up these criticisms

These three criticisms show us clearly that many of the patterns of present-day black education were already to be seen in mission education. Generally speaking, mission education was segregated along the lines of colour. It offered limited schooling opportunities to most of its students. It often provided work orientation rather than proper skills training. And it discriminated against women. But at the same time, missions were the only group who gave much attention to educating blacks.

In many ways, mission education was far from ideal. But mission schools were part of a society which discriminated against blacks and against women in education, as well as other aspects of life. And the question we've been asking is: To what extent were the missionaries responsible for this situation?

Perhaps it may help at this stage to look back at the three views at the beginning of the chapter, and see where you stand. Then we can move on with our story of the churches' involvement in education.

The response of the churches to Bantu Education

In 1948 the National Party came to power, and introduced the policy of apartheid. The next year they appointed the Eiselen Commission to make plans for 'the education of the natives as an independent race'. This spelt the end of mission control over African education.

The Eiselen Commission was also critical of mission education. It said that the aims of African schooling were vague and poorly formulated. Instead of valuing African culture, the schools helped to erode it. Nor did the schools realistically prepare Africans for the positions they could hold in society. The Eiselen Commission also criticized the churches' administration of African education. In particular, it criticized rivalry between churches which, it said, led to 'wasteful duplication' and an unsystematic provision of education.

The Commission recommended a radical reorganization of African education. It said that 'Bantu Education' should be brought under the control of the government, and should be used to rebuild and extend 'Bantu culture'. On the basis of cultural differences, people should be separated in education and in other spheres of life. Bantu Education should also help to build up the reserves, so as to 'facilitate and encourage the evolution of a progressive, modern and self-respecting Bantu order of life'. As the Commission put it:

"The schools must give due regard to the fact that out of school hours the young Bantu child develops and lives in a Bantu community, and when he reaches maturity he will be concerned with sharing and developing the life and culture of that community."

(quoted in Rose and Tunmer 1975:251)

On the basis of the Eiselen Commission Report, the Bantu Education Act was drawn up and passed in 1953. And so Bantu Education was born, as a separate education system for Africans, to meet the development plans of apartheid.

We know that many mission schools closed down after the Bantu Education Act. But there's an interesting story about how this happened.

Government control

The Bantu Education Act stipulated that African education should be under government control, and it gave wide powers to the Minister of Native Affairs. All schools had to be registered with the government. Three types of school were allowed:

- Bantu Community schools
- State-aided schools (including mission schools)
- Government schools.

The Bantu Education Act did not state directly that mission schools had to close down. Instead, there were a number of measures which made it extremely difficult for them to remain open and independent.

First, pressure was placed on teacher training institutions (and, as we saw, teacher training was an important activity of mission schools). The government stipulated that teacher training could only take place in Department training centres. Teachers who trained elsewhere would not have their qualifications recognized by the Department. The missions were given three alternatives:

1 to rent or sell the school and hostel to the Department;
2 to rent or sell the school, and retain the hostel with a Department subsidy;
3 to close the teacher training section, and continue as a primary and secondary school.

But the Department would only buy buildings inside the 'Native Reserves'; and this was one way of ensuring that all teacher training would happen in the reserves.

79

You can see that the government was able to get what it wanted by indirectly putting pressure on mission schools. If the missions decided to continue with teacher training themselves, their graduates would not have proper certificates. In fact, they had no option but to hand their teacher training schools over to the government (renting or selling), or to close them down.

What about primary and secondary schools?

As regards primary and secondary schools, missions were again given three alternatives:

1 to remain open as private, unaided schools;
2 to keep control of schools, with a subsidy which was reduced to 75% of teachers' salaries;
3 to rent or sell school buildings to Bantu Community Organizations.

The churches had to decide what to do – and these were difficult decisions to make. Often, it's easy for us to look back and know what they should have done. But, at the time, it was not an easy choice.

Difficult decisions

Other factors complicated the churches' decision. If a mission decided to retain control with a subsidy from the Department (the second option above), the Minister might later 'at his discretion' transfer the school to a Bantu Community Organization. Schools in 'white areas' would also be subject to the Group Areas Act, which meant that they would probably be made to close down at a later date anyway. In 1955 the government announced that subsidies would be phased out completely by 1960. And later it indicated that when the subsidy ended, schools would have to reapply for registration.

And, of course, registration was an important means for establishing government control. Schools could only be registered if they met strict conditions set out by the government. The conditions were:

• they could not charge for tuition;

- the medium of instruction had to be the same as the community school;

- they would be subject to inspection by the Department;

- they had to follow the Department curriculum, except in the case of religious instruction;

- children of other denominations could only attend until an alternative school was available.

These conditions brought schools into line with Bantu Education. In effect, those schools which chose to stay open with a subsidy would later find themselves without subsidies, and would be forced to carry out almost all aspects of Bantu Education anyway.

A mission or church which chose to keep its school as a private, unaided school (the first option above), would find it extremely difficult to continue. Money and staff would be short. And if the school was in a 'white area', it could be closed at any time under the Group Areas Act.

This meant that the most practical alternatives were either to hand the school over to the 'Bantu Community' (the third option above), or to close down altogether.

The churches' views on Bantu Education

Most of the churches (except for the Dutch Reformed Church) objected to the Bantu Education Act and its implications for mission schools. So they did not wish to support the new system. What were their views?

Firstly, most of the Protestant churches objected to Bantu Education because they believed that it was education for subordination and that it denied blacks the right to participate as equals, in areas outside the reserves. The Methodist Church expressed its dismay at a system which 'aimed at conditioning people to a predetermined position of subordination'. The Church of Scotland objected to a policy 'whereby the Bantu are trained for a life in the Reserves'. Most denominations argued that Bantu Education conflicted with Christian principles. The Church of Scotland stated that:

66 We believe that Christian education policy must seek to prepare members of every social group to assume their full share of adult responsibility in the service of the country. 99   (quoted in *SA Outlook,* April 1955)

Secondly, many of the other churches argued against Bantu Education on purely religious grounds, rather than against Bantu Education as a cornerstone of apartheid. The Catholic Church put forward this view most strongly. In a statement to *SA Outlook* (a church newspaper) it said:

> **"**We gravely fear that any Catholic institution entering the community school system cannot retain its Catholic character nor provide the kind of education which accords with our principles. **"**   (November 1954)

Some Protestant churches, notably the Anglicans, also expressed similar views. For example, the principal of Grace Dieu defended his decision to keep his secondary school open by saying:

> **"**This will be the *only* Anglican boarding institution for Africans in South Africa. We feel very strongly that there should be at least ONE school where our faith can still be taught and practised. **"**   (*Grace Dieu Papers*)

Whatever their objections, political or religious, the churches were faced with the problem of what to do with their schools and teacher training institutions. Basically, they could either:
- hand over schools and teacher training institutions to the government;
- run private schools which carried out Bantu Education anyway; or
- close their schools and teacher training institutions altogether.

There was no easy solution. If they handed over their schools to the government, or implemented Bantu Education themselves, they would be in danger of losing the support of many blacks who despised Bantu Education. They might also lose the support of white liberals in South Africa and overseas who funded them.

On the other hand, if schools closed down, many students would be without school, and many teachers would be out of work.

So what did the churches decide to do?

The churches' decisions
Different groups of churches took different decisions:

- Some of the Protestant churches, such as the **Methodists, Presbyterians, and Congregationalists,** decided to rent their buildings to community organizations. As the Methodist Church stated:

> "In order to provide for the immediate educational needs of the African people, the church feels compelled to relinquish control of its schools to the state." *(SA Outlook,* November 1954)

One of the most famous institutions which was handed over to the state at this time was Lovedale.

- The **Anglican Church** took a somewhat stronger stand. In general, it decided to close its schools rather than hand them over, though later it gave some choice to different groups to act as they saw fit. A church spokesperson said:

> "If the Minister of Bantu Education cannot entrust the training of African teachers to Christian missions, we, as a Christian mission, cannot and will not entrust our land or our buildings to him or his Department for educational purposes. We are convinced that the true welfare of the African people is being denied by a political theory."
> *(SA Outlook,* November 1954, adapted)

One of the most famous Anglican secondary schools, St Peters, Rosettenville, decided to close once the present students had completed their course. It was in a 'white area', and would probably be closed anyway. One of its graduates, J.A. Maimane, wrote in *Drum* magazine about the closing of the school:

> "For all the ex-students of this great pillar of learning the announcement that their alma mater would close down in two years was a sad blow. A blow that will bring back many memories of the diligent studying to keep up with the school's high standard; of the easy, happy, disciplined life that prepared them to meet the outside world, proudly and without any fear." *(Drum,* October 1954)

Grace Dieu decided to close its teacher training section, but to continue as an independent, private Anglican boarding school for blacks from Std 6 to Std 10. It asked white members of staff to accept reduced salaries in order to provide funds for the school. In 1957, with the announcement that subsidies would be terminated and that schools would have to be registered, Grace Dieu closed down.

- The **American Board Mission** tried to find legal loopholes by which it could retain control of Adams College. It registered the college as a non-profit making company, which could therefore not be handed over to the government. But the government was able to block them through the registration clause – the school was refused registration after long delays. The buildings were handed over to the state on condition that the name 'Adams College' was never used.

- The **Catholic Church** made a decision which separated it from all the other churches. It decided to keep control of its schools as aided schools. Though some of the bishops felt that they could not support Bantu Education as part of apartheid, the majority felt that it was important to preserve the Catholic faith and to continue Catholic schools.

  Almost immediately, the Catholic Church had problems in financing its schools, as a result of the reduced subsidy. Teachers had their salaries cut by 25%, without consultation, which caused some bitterness. Many lay teachers left, and generally there was a decline in academic standards and morale. The Catholic schools were forced to carry out the provisions of Bantu Education in order to be registered. So the Church found itself becoming a partner with the government in implementing Bantu Education.

  As the Catholic educationist, Flanagan, argues:

The Bantu Education Act placed the bishops in a cruel dilemma. Whatever decision they took was bound to have undesirable consequences. To close the schools would incur government hostility and deprive many blacks of a catholic education. To hand the schools over to the state system would almost certainly mean the total loss of catholic influence in black education, and would deprive blacks of anything remotely resembling an alternative to 'Bantu Education'. They chose the course which they took to be the lesser of two evils.
(1982:88)

But Flanagan also shows the dangers of this position:

However successful the bishops may have been in retaining their schools they paid a price both in moral credibility and in worsened relations with the government.
(1982:88)

The Catholic Church made a religious challenge to the government by keeping control of its schools. But at the same time, this meant a compromise with the government, because they had to run their schools on government lines, in order to stay open.

To sum up, almost all the churches condemned Bantu Education, but in practice tried to make the best of a bad situation.

However they were not particularly supportive of the ANC's boycott – as we'll go on to see.

The churches and the 1955 schools boycott

One of the forms of African opposition to Bantu Education was a schools boycott organized by the ANC in 1955. The ANC planned to withdraw children from Bantu Education schools, and draw up alternative educational and cultural activities. This was a direct challenge to the state. But the campaign failed, partly because it did not mobilize mass support, partly because it was disorganized and partly because of state pressure.

The churches criticized the ANC for two main reasons. Firstly, they disapproved of the boycott tactic as such – both in this case and in the later case of boycotts at Fort Hare. Secondly, they criticized Congress for taking decisions in the heat of the moment which it could not really implement, and for not consulting with many blacks outside the urban areas.

The churches' attitude to the boycott gives an indication of their general stand: they did not support Bantu Education, but they had clear ideas about the 'correct' ways of challenging the government. And some people would say that the position they took was quite a conservative one.

That ends this section on the churches' response to Bantu Education. We can now turn to the final section of this chapter: the 'open schools' movement.

The 'open schools' movement

In recent years, a new theme has emerged in church education – the opening of white private church schools to black students. This is the so-called open schools movement, which started in the late 1970s, and which continues today.

As we'll see, this reflects quite a change in church school policy. To trace this change, let's look at the situation before open schools, and then see what the policy of open schools actually means.

Private church schools

As well as mission schools for blacks, many churches also had white private schools linked to them. Except for Catholic schools, these schools were often small and expensive, and they were usually attended by children of the white elite. These schools were linked to churches 'in matters of doctrine, faith, and worship' only. In most other ways they were independent. They ran their own administration, appointed their own staff, had their own admission policies for pupils, and so on. This split – between matters of religion and matters of education – meant that the churches often had limited influence over the schools.

Many of these white private schools were old, dating back to the end of the nineteenth century. Over the years, it was generally accepted that these schools were for whites only. And when questions were raised, these schools managed to resist any attempts to make them integrated.

- For example, in 1947, when the question of integration was raised, the Standing Committee of Associated Church Schools said that it recognized 'the ultimate equality, in value, of all men before God, irrespective of the colour of their skin'. But it was against having black students admitted to these schools. It referred to the 'damage that would be done by the disturbance and opposition which their admission would undoubtedly provoke'.

- The Bantu Education Act also raised questions about the mission schools and their relationship with apartheid. However, when the Act was passed, there was almost no discussion about the position of exclusive white church schools, which could actually have admitted black pupils from places like St Peters, when they had to close down.

Nevertheless, the Bantu Education Act did open up the debate about the social and political implications of the Gospel. Some of the churches made concerned statements about segregation in church societies, schools and hospitals. But this concern did not necessarily influence the schools. As we've seen, schools were independent from churches in terms of education policy, including the admission of students. Some heads of schools pointed out that integration would be illegal, and used this as a reason for staying segregated. So, in practice, the white church schools refused to confront the question of Bantu Education.

- In 1965 the Anglican Synod (the policy-making body of the Anglican Church) called on Anglican schools not to exclude any children on grounds of colour. But the schools ignored this. In two separate incidents, prominent boys' private schools (St George's and Bishops) each refused to admit a 'coloured' boy. Again, it was clear that there was a large gap between the churches' policy and the schools' policy.

To sum up, we can say that schools generally argued that they could not admit black children because this was against the law. It seems they hid behind the law to avoid giving reasons which were clearly racist.

By stating that integration was against the law, the schools also indicated that they were not prepared to challenge the state.

The churches' attempts to challenge apartheid fell flat because the schools refused to follow their lead. The churches could do no more than make well-meaning statements.

But this situation changed by the end of the 1960s. The elite white private schools 'opened' their doors to black students. In the next section we'll see how this happened.

The open schools

The movement towards integrating the private church schools was led by the Catholic Church. In the 1960s the Catholic Church throughout the world moved towards the 'social gospel'. By the social gospel it meant:

> "The application of the gospel to social attitudes and conduct, and to political and economic systems flowing from them and influencing them."
>
> (*Vatican II*)

In South Africa this meant that Catholics were again called upon to examine their attitudes to apartheid. In the field of education Bantu Education was again condemned. But this time, the Catholic Church took different action. In July 1968 the Catholic Church decided that it could no longer co-operate in implementing Bantu Education, and it handed over a number of Catholic schools to the government. In 1973 a report on Catholic education showed that 70% of the Church's educational resources were being spent on white schools, even though they formed only 30% of the total Catholic schools. This unequal spending led the Catholics to look at the possibility of opening their white schools to black students. (Flanagan 1982:90)

At the same time, the Anglican Archbishop declared that he was in favour of opening schools. The Headmasters' Conference (which represented the heads of Protestant schools) also showed interest. In 1976 the South African Catholic Bishops' conference passed a resolution in favour of opening schools to 'non-white' children.

The word to describe these schools was 'open' rather than 'integrated'. This implied that integration was not compulsory, but simply available. Open schools did not foresee complete integration. Instead, they emphasized the new freedom of parents to choose which Catholic school their children would attend. In practice, the term referred only to white Catholic schools, because the few black Catholic schools were overcrowded, understaffed and inconveniently located for whites.

Once the commitment to open schools had been made, Catholic schools began admitting small numbers of black students. This was done quietly to avoid political trouble. This remained Catholic policy: to keep a low profile and avoid open confrontation with the state.

At the same time, the Headmasters' Conference issued a statement which proposed removing 'all restrictions to the admission of pupils from different races to private schools in South Africa'.

In the open schools policy we see an important new phase in the churches' involvement in education. In this move the churches were actively challenging apartheid education.

But, of course, the open schools movement applied to very few schools – the white, private schools under church influence.

Government attitude

The Catholic and Anglican schools had discussions with the government. In response, the government said that it knew that children had been illegally admitted to open schools. These children could stay, but in future the schools had to consult the authorities about admissions. Each school had to apply to the Provincial Administrator for individual permission for children of other 'races' to be admitted. Most of the Catholic schools ignored this, and continued to admit whoever they wished. Most of the Anglican and Methodist schools chose to comply, and gave their applications to the Administrator. Mostly, applications were approved.

Negotiations continued between the government and church school representatives. In seems that the government itself wanted to avoid public confrontation on the issue. In 1978 it encouraged schools to keep a low profile, and be 'selective' in admitting black pupils. Principals were asked to make sure that applications for 1979 did not exceed the total for 1978. In other words, schools were asked to put into practice their own 'quota system'. The Catholic schools did not comply. But most other schools did comply, and limited their intake. As a result, there were (and are) comparatively few black children in white private schools. In some Catholic schools the percentage of black pupils is as high as 68%. But in most other schools it is no more than 5%.

It's interesting to note that the Catholic schools have been taking a different line from the other church schools, especially in regard to government permission on admissions.

And no doubt the present low numbers in many open schools are one reason why the government is prepared to accept open schools – provided it has some control.

How 'open' are the open schools?

To answer this question, we can look at a number of points:

- Firstly, the open schools are private schools. This means they are fee-paying schools. This immediately limits the pupils to those whose parents can afford to send them there or those who can get bursaries.

- Secondly, the prejudices of white parents have often limited the numbers of black students. Racially prejudiced white parents claim that 'standards' may drop and that white English-speaking 'identity' may be affected. Often white parents will accept only a token number of blacks before threatening to withdraw their children – and their financial support – from the school. So, white prejudice sets another limit on the 'openness' of the open schools, especially the more elite schools.

- Thirdly, certain private school practices count against black students. For example, in some schools there are entrance exams, and the admission of students is often based on their results in these exams. Students from Bantu Education backgrounds may not have a fair chance against students from white (and often private) schools. Some schools screen black applicants to make sure that they will fit in with white cultural and social practices.

- Fourthly, who makes the adjustments: the schools or the black students? Most of the open schools are not, in fact, adapting their curriculum and practices in view of black students. They are simply expecting black students to fit in with the existing practices. And in the exclusive private schools many of these practices are imported from England. There is very little acknowledgement of the unique nature of South African society, its history and its literature.

  The Catholic schools are an exception in this regard. They are making some attempt, as they put it, 'to share the richness of our South African society with one another'. This has included changes in the curriculum, and also attempts to combat racist bias in textbooks.

But if open schools are heavily orientated towards white culture and society, can we really say they are 'open'?

And as well as these considerations, we also need to look at how black parents view open schools. Do black parents (who can afford them) view them as an alternative for their children?

Some black parents' views

"Of course there are cultural differences. The child picks up the culture of the school. His patterns change. I feel I have to talk English to him in the home so that he isn't disadvantaged in comparison with white children in his class.

Once he asked to keep a rabbit for a pet in the house – I can't believe it! Can you imagine an African person keeping a rabbit in the house!

Sure I expected a culture conflict, but I didn't think it would be so bad. I thought I'd be in control. One day he came home singing 'We are marching to Pretoria.' I said 'Come, come, Vuyo, hold that one!'

Still, on balance, I think it's worth it to send him to the convent."

"Where I'm staying in Soweto, we're black and typically black. I won't send my children to these type of schools. I think it creates confusion for the children. They become misfits. In some areas, most children are in white schools. When they play together, they speak English. Other children tease them. They say "By the way, you are white". I don't think it's good for the children."

"Look, what are the choices? The education for African children is inferior. There's no question of that. These white schools offer something a bit better. I want my child to be in a better position than I am. So I send him to a white school."

"These open schools. People think they're going for a better education. They don't think much further. I can't believe they're the answer. I can't believe they're going to make much difference."

Conclusion

That concludes our story of the church's involvement in education in South Africa. As we said at the start of the chapter, the role of the church has been different at different times, and it is not an easy one to judge. Hopefully, this chapter has shown some of the complexities of the story.

References and further readings

Blakemore, K. and Cooksey, B. (1980) *Sociology of Education for Africa*, Allen & Unwin, London, chap. 2 'Colonial education in Africa'

Cock, J. (1980) *Maids and Madams: A Study of the Politics of Exploitation*, Ravan, Johnnesburg

Collins, C.B. (1980) 'Black schooling in South Africa' *Africa Perspective* 17

Cook, P.A.W. (1949) 'Non-European education' in E. Hellmann (ed) *Handbook on Race Relations in South Africa*, OUP, Cape Town

Etherington, N. (1977) 'Social theory and the study of Christian missions in Africa: A South African case study' *Africa* 47 (1)

Flanagan, B. (1982) 'Education: Policy and Practice' in A. Prior (ed) *Catholics in Apartheid Society*, David Philip, Cape Town

Grace Dieu Papers, Church of the Province of South Africa Library, University of the Witwatersrand

Hirji, K.F. (1980) 'Colonial ideological apparatuses in Tanganyika under the Germans' in M.H.Y. Kaniki (ed) *Tanzania under Colonial Rule*, Longman, London

Horrell, M. (1963) *African Education: Some Origins and Development until 1953*, SAIRR, Johannesburg

Majeke, N. (1952) *The Role of the Missionaries in Conquest*, Society of Young Africa, Cape Town

Molteno, F. (1984) 'The evolution of educational policy' in P. Kallaway (ed) *Apartheid and Education*, Ravan, Johannesburg

Randall, P. (1982) *Little England on the Veld: The English Private School System in South Africa*, Ravan, Johannesburg.

Rose, B. and Tunmer, R. (1975) *Documents in South African Education*, Ad. Donker, Johannesburg

South Africa: Official (1905–6) *Reports of the South African Native Affairs Commission 1903–5*, Cape Town

Shepherd, R.H.W. (1971) *Lovedale, South Africa 1824–1955*, Lovedale Press

Taylor, J.D. (ed) (1928) *Christianity and the Natives of South Africa: A Yearbook of SA Missions*, Lovedale Press

Trapido, S. (1980) '"The friends of the natives": Merchants, peasants, and the political and ideological structure of liberalism in the Cape, 1954 – 1910' in S. Marks and A. Atmore (eds) *Economy and Society in Pre-Industrial South Africa*, Longman, London

Wilson, F. and Perrot, D. (1973) *Outlook on a Century: South Africa 1870–1970*, Lovedale Press and SPROCAS

Chapter 4

Reading facts and figures

> **"**I just want to remind the Honourable Members of Parliament that if the native in South Africa is being taught to expect that he will lead his adult life under the policy of equal rights, he is making a big mistake.
>
> The native must not be subject to a school system which draws him away from his own community, and misleads him by showing him the green pastures of European society in which he is not allowed to graze.**"**
>
> (Rose and Tunmer 1975:266)

With these notorious words, Dr Hendrik Verwoerd introduced Bantu Education to Parliament in 1953. This began the era of apartheid education. In 1959 universities were segregated. In 1963 a separate education system was set up for 'coloureds'. Indian education followed in 1964. And an Education Act for whites was passed in 1967. Today education is still divided up along lines of colour. In fact, in 1983, the government rejected the De Lange Committee's recommendation that there should be a single education department for all people.

The problems and inequalities of apartheid education are well known. We all know that there is a shortage of money for black schools. We know that there are too few schools, overcrowded classrooms, underqualified teachers and poor facilities. We also know that black students have expressed their discontent about poor conditions and low standards.

But why do these inequalities exist?

What can be done to end them?

In this chapter, we're going to look in more detail at the apartheid education system, and try to answer the questions above. We're going to do this by looking at figures and graphs and tables. These statistical techniques will show some of the obvious inequalities, like finance, enrolments, teacher qualifications, etc. Using statistics is one way of describing the structural features of the apartheid education system.

But we need to do more than *describe* the system; we also need to be able to *analyse* it. We need to understand where the inequalities are, and also the extent of them. If we know how to read statistics and analyse them we can get a deeper understanding of the system.

It's good to know some facts and figures about the education system. People use statistics in arguments. If we don't know our facts, it's hard to argue back.

Yes! That's certainly happened to me before.

As we'll see, we need to be very careful with statistics. They can be very misleading. It's well known that people can use them dishonestly.

But surely statistics tell us facts? And surely facts are true?

Certainly, statistics tell us facts. But facts don't exist in a vacuum. There is no such thing as a 'fact', pure and simple. Facts are always linked to interpretation or worldview. So we need to study the 'facts' of statistics with great care.

To start with, we should make sure that the facts and figures we see give us enough information about the situation. Often figures and tables only show you part of the picture. The figures should at least help you to compare things. Always be careful of figures that don't give you enough information to compare.

But you'll see what I mean, as we go through the chapter.

In this chapter we'll use statistics to look at the following structural features of apartheid education:

Population
Expenditure on education
School enrolments
Pupil-teacher ratios
Teacher qualifications
University enrolments.

We'll look at each of these structural features in turn.

Population

Before we can look at statistics on education, we need to look at overall population statistics for South Africa. Remember, we can best understand education systems if we view them in the context of the wider society. Population figures show us the size or scale of the problem of educational inequality.

The first table gives the official government population statistics for two years: 1978 and 1980. These figures are divided up into population registration groups according to the official government policy. Note that the 1980 figures do not count people in the 'independent states' of Transkei, Bophuthatswana and Venda. This is also official government policy. And, as we'll see, it makes quite a difference to the statistics.

Dividing up figures is not something which we support – but that's how we're given the figures by the government, who collects them.

95

Table 1 Total population of South Africa: official figures

	1978		1980	
	Number	% of total population	Number	% of total population
African	19 970 000	72,2	15 970 000	67,2
Coloured	2 505 000	9,1	2 500 000	10,5
Indian	778 000	2,8	795 000	3,3
White	4 418 000	16,0	4 500 000	18,9
Total	**27 671 000**	**100,1**	**23 765 000**	**99,9**

(Source: SAIRR Surveys)

There are a number of comments we can make about these overall population statistics:

• First, let's look at the numbers in each population registration group for 1978. Then, let's look at what percentage each group forms of the total population of South Africa.

It's well known that whites are in a minority in South Africa, and blacks are in a majority. The statistics show the *extent* of the white minority: in 1978, whites were 16,0% of the total population.

• Now let's compare the 1978 statistics with the 1980 statistics. Look at the numbers of and percentages for each population registration group for 1980. Notice that the number of Africans *decreases,* while the numbers of the other groups stay more or less the same. Remember: one reason for this is because the 1980 figures don't count people in the 'independent homelands'.

You can see that this makes quite a difference to the percentages. For example:

In 1978, there were 4 418 000 whites

In 1980, there were 4 500 000 whites.

The numbers are almost the same. But the percentages aren't:

In 1978, whites were 16% of the total population

In 1980, whites were nearly 19% of the total population.

So the government's 'homeland' policy does make a difference to the picture!

- But even with the homeland policy, whites are still in a minority in South Africa. They were 18,9% of the population in 1980, and this is still a lot smaller than the percentage for Africans, which was 67,2%.

- Let's think about the political position of the different population registration groups. The voting structures for the Tricameral Parliament make provisions for whites, 'coloureds' and Indians to have separate votes. So far, there are no political arrangements at the national level for Africans in the 'common areas' of South Africa.

- The table shows us the population sizes of the three population registration groups who would have official political rights in South Africa. We can see that these three groups together – whites, 'coloureds' and Indians – are still a minority. Together, in 1980, they made up: 10,5% + 3,3% + 18,9% = 32,7% of the total population. Africans, who have no vote in the President's Council, are 67,2% of the population.

Let's now think about these population figures in connection with education. So let's ask the question:

What can we conclude about education from the statistics?

1 The white system of education applies to a very small percentage of the population – 19% in 1980. So if everyone were to get the same education as whites have, this would mean a very big change.

2 Africans are the vast majority of the people. So if the African education system is the worst off, then the problem of inequality becomes an even greater one.

Do you understand now why I say that the 'facts' of statistics never exist in a vacuum? And what I mean by comparing statistics? In this case, we can see the *extent* of the problem from the statistics. If we didn't know comparative population sizes, we wouldn't have an accurate idea of the apartheid education system.

On the basis of these population statistics, we can now look at aspects of the education system. We'll start with the costs; we'll look at the money that is spent on education for the different population registration groups.

Expenditure on education

In the following table, we can see what the government spends to educate each child every year. This is called *per capita expenditure* (that is, expenditure per person). The table shows us per capita expenditure for the different population registration groups. It also shows how this has changed since 1953.

Table 2 Per capita expenditure on education in South Africa

Year	African	'Coloured'	Indian	White
1953-4	R17	R40	R40	R128
1969-70	17	73	81	282
1975-6	42	140	190	591
1977-8	54	185	276	657
1980-1	139	253	513	913
1982-3	146	498	711	1 211

(Sources: Blignaut, 1981 and SAIRR Surveys)

Let's look at this table more carefully.

- First, read across the figures for 1953-4. The figures are:
  R17   R40   R40   R128
  Notice that there is an enormous difference in the amounts of money that are spent on the different population registration groups.
    Then read across the figures for 1975-6. The figures are:
  R42   R140   R190   R591
  Continue to look across the figures for each year.
    Notice that less money is spent on Africans than on other population registration groups. More money is spent on 'coloureds' and more again on Indians. A lot more money is spent on whites than on any other population group. And if we read across for the other years on the table we can see the same sort of pattern.

- Now, read down the figures in each column, for each group. First, look at what was spent on Africans for each year. The figures are:

  R17
  17
  42
  54
  139
  146

Then read down the columns for 'coloureds', Indians and whites. Notice that the amount increases each year. But it increases for everyone.

What can we conclude about education from the statistics?

1 It's easy to see that different amounts are spent on the education of different population registration groups.

2 A lot more money is spent on whites than on the other groups.

3 Expenditure on education is increasing each year. This applies to all of the population registration groups. Some of this increase is due to economic reasons, like inflation. The question is: Are the increases proportionally the same for each population registration group? The later tables will help to answer this question.

Remember we said that statistics can be misleading. If we looked *only* at the statistics for Africans, we could see the following:

  1975 – R40
  1982 – R146

Then we could say that more money was being spent on African education. That's true.

But the picture looks a little different if we see that more money was being spent on the other population registration groups as well.

You can see this even more clearly from the next tables.

Let's now look at the same figures, but put them in another statistical form. Let's look at per capita expenditure in *ratio* form. Ratio is another way of comparing. If we say that the amount spent on an African child is R1, we can then see how much is spent on other groups in comparison with that R1.

**Table 3 Per capita expenditure
            on education in South Africa in ratio form**

Year	African	'Coloured'	Indian	White
1953-4	R1	R2,35	R2,35	R7,53
1969-70	1	4,29	4,76	16,59
1975-6	1	3,33	4,52	14,07
1977-8	1	3,43	5,11	12,17
1980-1	1	1,82	3,69	6,57
1982-3	1	3,40	4,86	8,27

(Source: as Table 2)

Putting the figures into ratio form is a good way of comparing them.

- If we look across the columns for 1975-6:
     For every R1 spent on an African child,
     R3,33 was spent on a 'coloured' child
     R4,52 was spent on an Indian child and
     R14,07 was spent on a white child.
  So 14,07 times more money was spent on a white child as on an African child.

- If we look down the columns, we can see that the gap remains very large. Since 1976, there has been some change. The gap is narrowing to some extent, but it still remains very large.

- Notice that the ratios drop in 1980-1. If you look back to Table 2 you'll see that a lot more money was spent on Africans in that year, compared with other years. That alters the ratio figures. But notice that the figures for 1982-3 go up again. In 1982-3, the ratio of African to white spending has dropped to 1:8,27 (compared, for example, with the 1976 figure of 1:14,07). But that still means that eight times more money is spent on every white child than on every African child.

- Another general point to remember as you look at these ratios is that the figures from 1975 onwards don't include the 'independent homelands'. The South African government does not directly pay for education in these areas; officially this is the responsibility of the 'homeland governments'. So the most neglected African schools have been excluded from these figures. This would also affect the ratios.

Finally, let's look at the *same* expenditure figures visually, by using a simple bar graph.

Per capita expenditure on education in South Africa in graph form

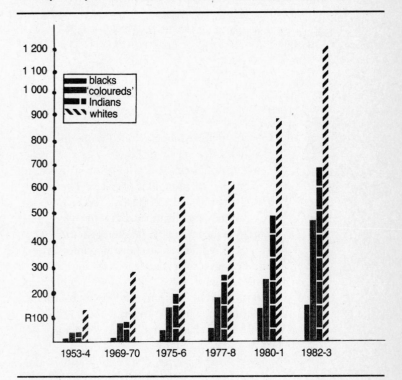

(Source: as Table 2)

Seeing things in graph form really makes the differences stand out! You can get a quick impression of how much more money is spent on whites than on Africans.

So far, we've looked at some of the statistics on expenditure and seen the inequalities that exist. We started off the chapter asking two questions. Here they are again:

Why do these inequalities exist?

What can be done to end them?

I can see that there are huge inequalities in expenditure on the different population registration groups. If I think of the poor facilities in black schools, I can see *financial reasons* for them. The government is spending too little money on black education. If the government spent as much money on educating each black child as it spends on each white child, there would be a great improvement.

Of course, more money would be one answer. But in practice, it isn't that easy.

If we think back to the population statistics, we can see the *extent* of the problem. There are very many more blacks than whites. So it would be extremely expensive to extend the white system to the other population registration groups. It would cost an enormous amount of money to give everyone the same education as whites presently have. In fact, some people argue that it would be economically impossible for the government. There would have to be fundamental changes in the whole system including white education.

And then, of course, there's also the question of whether white education is ideal. (We'll look at that issue in Chapter Six.)

The box below discusses government spending.

Slicing the pie

Each year, the government plans a budget – a fixed amount of money to spend to keep the country running. This money comes from economic activities (like international trading, sale of gold, etc.) and from the taxes which companies and private people pay.

The government allocates money to different sectors, like defence, education, transport, health care, etc. These allocations are *political* decisions; they reflect what the government considers to be important.

One way to look at government expenditure is to use a pie chart. If we think of all government expenditure as a whole pie, we could think of the different sectors (e.g. education, defence) as being slices of different sizes.

In a diagram we can show how the government sliced the pie in 1983–4:

■	Education	6,1%
▨	Primary and secondary industries	8,7%
▰	Defence	14,6%
≋	Finance	17,6%
▩	Constitutional development	18,0%
☐	Other	35,0%

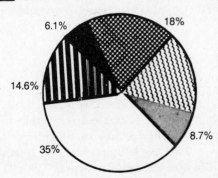

If the government decided to spend more money on education, it would have to take the money from somewhere else. It would have to slice the pie differently.

School enrolments

So far, we've looked at population size and expenditure on education. School enrolments are another important set of statistics on apartheid education.

Again, we can use different statistical ways of looking at school enrolments. Let's start with Table 4, which shows the numbers of people enrolled in school in different years.

Table 4   School enrolments in South Africa, selected years

Year	African	'Coloured'	Indian	White
1970	2 738 564	490 351	161 676	859 352
1972	3 081 162	534 613	172 142	879 755
1974	3 488 043	591 850	180 800	896 819
1976	3 900 454	655 347	188 008	928 640
1978	4 311 616	722 326	205 136	962 561
1980	4 839 806	748 896	217 170	959 243
1982	5 313 016	766 179	223 745	986 276

(Sources: Blignaut, 1981; Horrell, 1968; SAIRR Surveys)

Let's start by reading down the figures in each column (looking at Africans, then 'coloureds', and so on). The table shows that there was a steady increase in school enrolments between 1970 and 1980. More people attended school each year. We should think of this increase in terms of the population increase. We should expect this table to show increases.

As we said before, we need to be able to *compare* statistics. Have a look at the tables that follow.

In the next table we'll take a specific year, 1982, and look at how the pupils were spread out between the different grades. We'll look at the numbers and percentages of Africans and whites in each school grade.

Table 5 School enrolments for Africans and whites, 1982

School grades	Africans		Whites	
	Number	%	Number	%
Sub A	1 008 938	19,0	84 969	8,7
Sub B	768 298	14,4	84 624	8,6
Std 1	690 240	13,0	84 818	8,7
Std 2	574 604	10,8	87 770	9,0
Total lower primary	3 042 080	57,3	342 181	35,0
Std 3	526 363	9,9	89 517	9,2
Std 4	441 205	8,3	88 206	9,0
Std 5	381 441	7,2	83 442	8,6
Special classes	—	—	10 113	1,0
Auxillary classes	—	—	1 244	0,1
Total primary	4 391 089	82,7	614 703	63,0
Std 6	295 326	5,6	85 913	8,8
Std 7	237 660	4,5	81 339	8,3
Std 8	194 583	3,7	74 925	7,7
Std 9	112 383	2,1	63 288	6,5
Std 10	72 501	1,4	55 216	5,7
Unclassified	—	—	30	0,0
Total secondary	912 453	17,3	360 711	37,0
Total:	5 303 542	100,0	975 414	100,0

(Source: SAIRR Survey)

- Let's start by looking at the *numbers* in each class. Look at Sub A (Grade 1) for Africans and for whites. There are many more African children that white children who start school. But we should expect this, because there are a lot more Africans than whites in the total population.

- Now read quickly down both the African column and the white column until you get to Std 10 (Form 5). The numbers for Std 10 are similar, even though the population sizes are very different.

- Now let's look at the percentage columns. These columns treat the total school group for Africans as being 100%, and the total school group for whites as being 100%. The column for Africans

105

then shows what percentage of African school children are in each grade. (And the column for whites shows what percentage of white school children are in each grade.)

So, for example, in 1983 19,0% of Africans who went to school were in Sub A; 14,4% were in Sub B; 13,0% were in Std 1, and so on. By the time we get to Std 10 (Matric), the table shows that only 1,4% of Africans at school were in Std 10.

Notice that the percentages for Africans are dropping. The figures in fact show us the drop-out rate for African children (and white children) year by year. The percentage of African children in each grade gets smaller each year. This shows that African children are not staying at school. They are dropping out.

Compare this situation with the white percentages. The table shows us that the percentage in each grade doesn't change much all the way through primary school, and right into secondary school. The biggest drop-out rate comes from Std 8 onwards (the grade when most white children reach 16, and schooling is no longer compulsory). The table shows us that most white children stay in school and move up to the next class each year. Even though the percentages do drop in Std 8, there is still a high percentage of white children in Matric.

What can we conclude about school attendance from these statistics?

1 There is a high drop-out rate for African children, and a low drop-out rate for white children.

2 For Africans there is a big drop-out after Grade 1. (Notice the big drop from 19,0% in Grade 1 to 14,4% in Grade 2.) This means that many African children have only one year of schooling. Notice the total lower primary percentage. More than half of the African children at school (57,3%) are in the first four years of school. This shows us that many African children don't have more than four years of schooling. We can say that there is a *concentration* at the lower levels of schooling.

3 The drop-out rates for white children show us the effects of free, compulsory schooling for whites. There is a very low drop out rate, even after Std 8.

4 Very few African children get to Std 10; most white children do.

5 The school enrolment figures show very different patterns for blacks and for whites.

6 The table shows us school enrolments; it doesn't tell us about those children who never get to school at all.

Now let's put the percentages from Table 5 into graph form.

Enrolment graphs based on Table 5

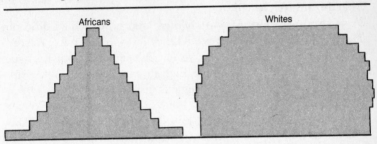

(Source: as Table 5)

These graphs are called *education pyramids*. This is because they are shaped like pyramids: they have a broader base, and then they get narrower towards the top. The more the pyramid changes shape, the more unequal the system is (as we'll see).

- First, look at the pyramid for Africans. It has a very broad base, and a very narrow top. This shows us that most people are at the bottom of the education system. Very few people get to the top.
- Now look at the pyramid for whites. It hardly changes shape at all. This shows that people are evenly distributed through the education system.

In fact, the two pyramids have completely different shapes.

- The black pyramid is similar to the pyramids of poor, less indus-trialized countries – like the countries in the rest of Africa. It shows great educational inequality.

- The white pyramid resembles the pyramids of advanced industrial countries – like Britain and the United States of America. These countries have free, compulsory education. There is less educ-ational inequality.

107

There are two further questions that we can ask in relation to these enrolment patterns:
1 What do children learn in the time they are at school?
2 What is the link between school attendance and social class?

What do children learn?

We've seen that most African children who go to school drop out after about four years. What would they learn in that time? According to the school syllabus, they would be taught in mother tongue. They would learn some simple English and Afrikaans, and arithmetic. They would also learn religious instruction, singing, gardening and crafts.

Most white children have at least ten years of schooling. They would study English and Afrikaans, and some maths. They would also study history, geography, science and biology, as well as other subjects.

There is a strong contrast between the education that most African children receive, and that which most white children receive. This is a contrast of quality of education, as well as quantity. There is an educational imbalance between the different population registration groups.

School attendance and social class

Remember that we said in Chapter Two that education both reflects and shapes social class position. For Africans, those children who get to school are already in a privileged position, above those who don't get to school at all. Social class is also affected by the amount of schooling that people have.

For example, the four years of education which most African school attenders receive would prepare them for unskilled jobs and lower social positions. The few African children who do manage to stay at school have better job opportunities and a chance of a higher social status.

Most white children would have enough education to do clerical jobs, or sales jobs, or apprenticeships – or to do further training. But even although whites are generally more privileged in education than Africans, there are also social class divisions amongst whites. And the level of education which they have is part of these class divisions.

The issue of schooling and jobs is one which we'll look at in more detail in Chapters Seven and Eight. But we all know that job opportunities and social status are linked to the education that people have.

There are four other aspects of school enrolments that we should look at: matric results, the drop-out rate for girls, the illiteracy rate and the enrolment figures for farm schools.

Matric results

We've seen that very few Africans who attend school actually get to matric. In 1982 only 1,4% of Africans who were at school were in matric; 5,7% of white students were in matric. But there's another statistic we need to look at: the matric results which these students achieve.

The number of African students reaching matric has increased greatly in recent years. The graph below shows how the numbers have grown; it also shows matric passes.

Matric results in South Africa, 1976 – 82

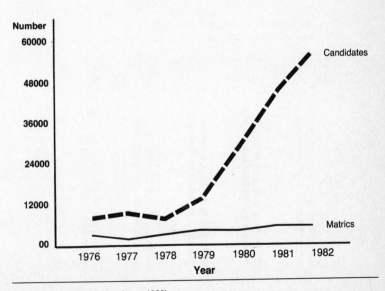

(Source: Shindler 1984; Hartshorne 1983)

109

The top line on the graph shows the increased numbers of matric candidates from 1976 to 1982. You can see how sharply the number has risen especially since 1979. But the bottom line, which shows the number of people who get a university pass (matric exemption), tells a different story. The numbers have risen only slightly.

From this we can see that the matric exemptions for Africans are not keeping pace with the number of candidates. This disparity is at the root of many of the complaints about the African matric exam. There are questions about whether African matric results are a reliable indication of people's ability.

The results for white candidates are very different. For example, in 1981, 94% of white candidates passed Std 10, and 49% of them obtained matric exemption. In the same year, 53% of Africans passed Std 10, and only 13% obtained matric exemption. The contrast is very marked.

Whatever the reasons for these differences, matric results are still used to select people for university entrance. So poor matric results mean that African students have less chance of going to university than white students have.

Drop-out rate for girls

The following bar graph looks at the percentages of boys and girls in high school grades in 1976.

High school attendance in South Africa, 1976

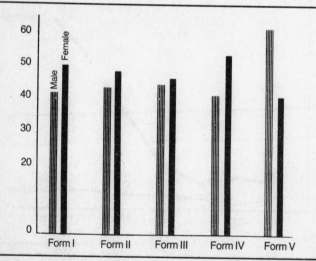

(Source: Cock 1980:270, adapted)

For each form, the graph shows what percentage of the students are boys, and what percentage are girls. For example, in Form I, 45% of the students are boys, and 55% are girls (to make a total cf 100%). So there are more girls in the class than boys. By Form V, this has changed: 65% of the students are boys, and 35% are girls.

What can we conclude from the bar graph?

1 In the lower forms of high school, there were more girls than boys. But by the end of the high school, there were more boys than girls. So more girls dropped out of high school, while more boys stayed on.

2 We need to be alert to gender differences in enrolments at school also.

This bar graph shows only one particular year – 1976. And we need to be careful about drawing general conclusions from one set of statistics.

However, the bar graph does point out something which we should be aware of: that boys and girls may have different amounts of schooling. And, as we've said before, schooling affects job opportunities and social position.

In the next chapter, when we look at the hidden curriculum in schools, we'll consider the issue of sex discrimination in more detail.

Illiteracy rates

So far, we've looked at the number of people who are in school, and what classes they are in. But what about people who can't read and write: those who are illiterate?

The following table shows government figures for adult illiteracy in South Africa. It gives the percentages of adults in each population registration group who are classified as illiterate, as well as the approximate numbers of illiterate people. The 1980 figures exclude the 'independent homelands'.

**Table 6 Illiteracy rates in South Africa
for registered population groups, 1960 – 1980**

| | 1960 | | 1970 | | 1980 | |
	%	Number	%	Number	%	Number
Africans	62,5	4 000 000	51,8	4 500 000	33,0	3 300 000
'Coloured'	38,0	276 300	23,6	260 000	15,5	247 000
Indians	28,7	76 000	16,7	62 000	7,6	39 000
Whites	1,9	40 000	0,9	23 500	0,7	23 000

(Sources: SAIRR surveys; Blignaut, 1981)

Table 6 is worth a careful reading, so let's go systematically through it.

- Firstly, read down the percentage columns for each population registration group for 1960, 1970 and 1980. You can see a general trend from these three columns. The greatest percentages of illiterate people are Africans. The percentages of 'coloureds' are smaller; the percentages of Indians are smaller again; and the percentages of whites are very small indeed. So, we see the same overall pattern of inequality as we've seen in other statistics.

- Secondly, let's compare the percentages across the three decades: 1960, 1970 and 1980. Notice that for each group the percentage of illiterate people is decreasing. That means that a greater percentage of people are becoming literate.

- Now, look quickly at the numbers columns, which show the approximate numbers of people who are illiterate. Leave aside the figures for Africans – we'll discuss them in a moment. Generally, you'll notice that the numbers for 'coloureds', Indians and whites are reducing; generally, there are fewer people who are illiterate.

- But now let's look more carefully across the African figures. There are some surprising things to notice. Let's start with the percentages:

  In 1960, 62,5% of Africans were illiterate
  In 1970, 51,8% of Africans were illiterate, and
  In 1980, 33,0% of Africans were illiterate.

  So the percentages are dropping.

112

But now let's look at the corresponding numbers columns for 1960 and 1970.

In 1960, approximately 4 million Africans were illiterate.
In 1970, approximately 4½ million Africans were illiterate.

In other words, the numbers *rose* between 1960 and 1970. More people were illiterate. How can this be?

The answer is quite straightforward. Over the years, the population size has increased – the numbers of people in each population group have grown. And this affects the percentage figures. So while it's true that the *percentages* of African illiterates dropped between 1960 and 1970, the actual *numbers* increased.

Can you see how misleading statistics can be?
But read on for another example.

Now let's look at the 1980 figures for Africans. Notice that there is a much lower figure in the percentage column of illiterate Africans for 1980, than for the other years:

In 1960, 62,5%
In 1970, 51,8%
In 1980, 33,0%

That looks like a very big improvement. But notice also the *numbers* column. The 1980 figure is also lower:

1960 – 4,0 million
1970 – 4,5 million
1980 – 3,3 million.

Here, we have a problem of interpretation. Remember: the 1980 figures don't include the 'independent homelands' – where there are a lot of illiterate people. So we can't actually tell from this table whether or not the illiteracy rate has actually dropped between 1970 and 1980. We would need more information.

That's a real example of just how important it is to read tables carefully – and also how important it is to be able to make proper comparisons.

Now let's look briefly at the enrolment figures for farm schools.

Enrolment figures for farm schools

The following is an extract from a report in *The Star,* dated 5 November 1984. It gives enrolment figures for farm schools, information on teachers, class sizes and the level of schooling provided.

● There are **486 975 black pupils in farm schools, comprising 30 percent of the total enrolment. The average South African farm school has 90 pupils.**

● Of 5 219 such schools, 2 330 are one-teacher schools that normally do not go further than Standard 2. About a quarter of farm school pupils are in the latter category. On average, the remaining schools have three teachers.

● There are no figures for dropouts.

● In general, the opportunities for schooling are far more limited for black children on white farms, than in any other sector of the educational system in South Africa, either rural or urban.

From these figures there is no doubt that farm schools offer very limited educational opportunities – and they cater for 30% of black school children.

Pupil-teacher ratios

It's well known that black schools are overcrowded. There are shortages of classrooms and teachers. Facilities like libraries and laboratories are inadequate – or not there at all. And these problems are particularly bad in rural areas. Obviously, the shortage of funding explains some of these problems.

One way to show overcrowding is to look at the numbers of students as compared with the numbers of teachers. This is called the pupil-teacher ratio. This ratio gives us an idea of the average number of children in one class. The following table shows the pupil-teacher ratios for the different groups between 1971 and 1982. (The figures for 1980 exclude Transkei, Bophuthatswana and Venda. The figures for 1982 exclude the Ciskei as well.)

Table 7   Pupil-teacher ratios in South Africa, selected years

Year	African	'Coloured'	Indian	White
1971	1:58	1:31	1:27	1:20
1976	1:52	1:30	1:27	1:20
1977	1:50	1:29	1:27	1:20
1978	1:49	1:29	1:27	1:20
1980	1:47	1:29	1:25	1:19
1982	1:39	1:27	1:24	1:18
1983	1:43	1:27	1:24	1:18

(Source: SAIRR Surveys)

Let's start by looking at the figures from 1971 to 1978.

- In 1971 there was one teacher for every 58 children in African schools. There was one teacher for every 20 children in white schools.

  In 1978 there was one teacher for every 49 children in African schools. There was still one teacher for every 20 children in white schools.

  If we read down and across the columns, we can see general trends. The class sizes in African schools are much larger than the class sizes for the other groups. Class sizes for Indians and 'coloureds' are more or less the same. Class sizes for whites are smaller. Over the years, the pupil-teacher ratio for 'coloureds', Indians and whites has remained more or less the same. The pupil-teacher ratio for African schools has reduced, but it is still much higher than the others.

- The figures for 1980 and 1982 alter slightly. Notice that the pupil-teacher ratios for white, 'coloured' and Indian schools have dropped slightly. The pupil-teacher ratio for African schools has also dropped. But notice once again that these figures don't include the homelands. So we can't make an accurate comparison of class sizes. The information which is available seems to indicate that pupil-teacher ratios in many of the homelands are still very high. They are generally higher than the 1982 figure of 1:39 and the 1983 figure of 1:43 in Table 7. This is shown by the examples in Table 8:

Table 8 Pupil-teacher ratios in homelands, 1981

Bophuthatswana	1:45,7
Kwazulu	1:49,7
Lebowa	1:49,2

(Source: SAIRR Surveys)

The tables give us an idea of *average* class sizes. But remember: to make an average of 49, some classes would be a lot bigger, and others would be smaller. We all know of cases where class sizes are around 100! Once again, we can see how important it is to read statistics carefully.

But let's go on to draw some conclusions from these figures.

What can we conclude from the tables on pupil-teacher ratios?

1 The pupil-teacher ratios reflect the same general patterns of inequality between groups, as the other statistics do.

2 The tables show a trend towards improvement, but it also shows that the gap is still very wide.

3 Thinking of population size, we would need a *lot* more teachers in black schools if we wanted to get equality with white schools.

The next question to ask is how well qualified the teachers are.

Teacher qualifications

Teachers in the four population registration groups are not equally well qualified. The following table shows teacher qualifications for 1979. The figures exclude Transkei and Bophuthatswana.

Table 9 Teacher qualifications in South Africa, 1979

Highest qualification	African	'Coloured'	Indian	White
University degree	2,3%	4,2%	19,4%	32,0%
Std 10	15,5%	26,3%	65,3%	68,0%
Below Std 10	82,2%	69,5%	15,3%	–

(Source: SAIRR Surveys)

This table doesn't need much explaining. But it's worth pointing out that the table shows that in 1979 there were *no* white teachers without a matric-level qualification. *Most* African teachers (82,2%) and over two-thirds of 'coloured' teachers (69,5%) had no matric. Not many African and 'coloured' teachers had university degrees.

And, in fact, the situation is worse than the table actually shows. Many black teachers have only passed Std 6 or Std 8. So their qualifications are a lot lower than those of white teachers.

The position has improved slightly since 1979, but it is still serious. Here is what the De Lange Report of 1981 said about teacher qualifications:

> The position with regard to Black teachers gives most cause for concern. To reduce the teacher-pupil ratio from the present 1:48 to 1:30, the number of teachers will have to increase from 95 501 in 1980 to 239 943 in the year 2000. These figures also include the needs of the independent Black states.
>
> In view of the above, the present rate at which teachers are being trained for primary and secondary schools is totally inadequate. The quality of the teachers in the Black educational system in particular is also a problem.

And this comment comes from a government-appointed commission. The position is obviously very serious.

Finally, let's look quickly at university enrolments.

University enrolments

The following tables show university enrolments for the different
population registration groups between 1969 and 1983.

Table 10 University enrolments in South Africa, 1969 – 1983

	1969	1974	1976	1983
Black students in 'white' universities	4 886	9 196	12 565	28 129
African students in African universities	1 581	3 541	5 204	12 550
'Coloured' students in 'coloured' universities	774	1 440	2 508	4 487
Indian students in Indian universities	1 621	2 342	3 124	5 388
Total black students in all universities	**8862**	**16 519**	**23 401**	**50 554**
Total white students	**68 550**	**95 589**	**105 879**	**126 609**

(Sources; Blignaut: 1981 and SAIRR Surveys)

Table 11 Increase in university enrolments in South Africa, 1967–1976

	Number	Annual rate %
Black students in 'white' universities	7 679	22,4
African students in African universities	3 623	32,7
'Coloured' students in 'coloured' universities	1 734	32,0
Indian students in Indian universities	1 503	13,3
Total black students in all universities	**14 539**	**23,4**
Total white students	**37 329**	**7,9**

(Source: Blignaut: 1981)

Table 11 shows the increase in numbers of students in the nine years between 1967 and 1976; and it also shows the increase as a percentage.

What can we conclude about university enrolments?

By now, we've had a lot of practice in reading tables, so we'll go very quickly through Tables 10 and 11. There are other points from the tables that you can pick out for yourselves.

1 Reading across Table 10, we can see that there has been a great increase in the number of black students at all universities.

2 But the starting point was very small. In 1969 the numbers of black students were very low as compared with white students. So although there has been a big increase, the numbers are still small – especially compared with whites, who are a smaller population group.

3 Table 11 shows increases in numbers, as well as percentages. Although white enrolments increased by only 7,9%, the actual number is large – 37 329 students.

 Black enrolments increased by a much larger percentage – 23,4%. But the actual numbers – 14 539 students – are much lower than increase in enrolment for white students.

4 So black enrolments are still lagging behind white enrolments.

Again, we see the same patterns of inequality along lines of colour.

 But don't let's forget the inequalities of social class as well. University education is very important when we consider social class. Different patterns of university enrolments would also be part of social class formation.

Conclusion

We've now analysed some of the structural features of apartheid education, and we've seen that there are great inequalities.

Let's return to our questions which we posed at the beginning of the chapter.

Why do these inequalities exist?

What can be done to end them?

Different people answer these questions differently. To conclude this chapter, lets look at some of the common arguments about apartheid education.

Conservative

Under the apartheid education system, there are better schooling provisions for blacks than there were before. Before apartheid very few blacks went to school. Under apartheid there has been an enormous increase in school attendance. There are far more schools and far more teachers than there were before.

Educational inequalities date back to the pre-apartheid period. The DET is doing all it can to reduce these existing inequalities.

When apartheid was introduced, the government's policy was to educate as many people as possible, within separate education systems. The Bantu Education system concentrated on providing primary schools, because so many people hadn't been to school at all. That's why there are more people in primary schools than in secondary schools. When we have given people primary education, then we can spend more time and money on secondary education.

We have to be practical. We have to start somewhere. Even if we want equality, we can't overcome the backlog overnight. We have, in fact, achieved a lot. Things are much better than they were before.

Moderate

When we look at apartheid education, the first thing we see is racial discrimination. That, basically, explains everything.

Certainly, there were inequalities before apartheid. But mission education before 1953 was far better than apartheid

education. Apartheid education has extended and formalized racial inequality.

We need to find ways of increasing expenditure on black education. We need to build more schools and train more teachers. Then, hopefully, people will be able to stay at school longer. We also need more black university graduates to meet the economic needs of the country.

We need to think about ways of upgrading the education system. Of course this will cost money – but the expense will be worthwhile. The whole country will benefit.

Radical

Verwoerd himself said that Bantu Education should prepare blacks for certain forms of labour. And that's exactly what's happening in apartheid schools. Blacks are being prepared for lower-level jobs in the economy.

If blacks have four years of schooling, then they can basically understand the language of their white employers. Meanwhile, schools have taught them suitable attitudes and values: for example, they have been taught to be punctual and obedient and polite.

And, of course, those blacks who have no schooling at all can only get the lowest-paid jobs in the economy.

Bantu Education is designed to prepare most blacks for the working class, and a few of them for the middle class. Bantu Education is designed to keep most blacks in an inferior class position.

If we improve the system in its present form, blacks may indeed benefit by getting a better education. That's good. But we won't necessarily be changing the class position of blacks. We won't necessarily be changing the basic inequalities of our society.

Well, that's the debate.

What do you think, as reader? It's up to you to make up your own mind on the basis of the facts and figures you have at hand.

References and further readings

Blignaut, S. (1981) *Statistics on Education in South Africa, 1968–79,* SAIRR, Johannesburg

Christie, P. and Collins, C.B. (1982) 'Bantu Education: Apartheid ideology or labour reproduction?' *Comparative Education* vol. 18 no. 1

Cock, J. (1980) *Maids and Madams: A study in the Politics of Exploitation* Ravan Press, Johannesburg

Hartshorne, K.B. (1983) 'Black secondary school leavers: Trends in Senior Certificate/Matriculation 1960–82', *Indicator SA* vol. 1 no. 3

Horrell, M. (1968) *Bantu Education to 1968,* SAIRR, Johannesburg

HSRC (1981) *Investigation into Education vol. 1: Provision of Education in the RSA* (De Lange Report), HSRC, Pretoria

SAIRR (Annual) *Survey of Race Relations in South Africa,* SAIRR, Johannesburg

Shindler, J. (1984) 'African matric results: 1955–83' SAIRR Topical Briefing, Johannesburg

Chapter 5

The hidden curriculum

What do we learn at school?

If we were asked this question, we would probably think of the subjects that schools teach. We would probably think of English, and history and accountancy, and so on. We might also think of sport and singing. All of these subjects are part of what is called *formal curriculum* of schools. But if we think more about it, there are many other things that we also learn at school.

We learn about authority figures like headmasters, teachers and prefects. We learn how these people expect to be treated.

We learn about rules, and what happens if we break them.

We learn about work discipline too. We learn that we have to sit down and work when we would far rather be doing other things!

We learn that people aren't equal in society. Those who do better at school are usually able to get better jobs.

In most schools we learn that we should work by ourselves, for our own rewards. In fact, sharing work is often called cheating!

We also learn a lot from our friends!

So, at the same time as we learn English and geography, we also learn all sorts of other things. These other things (which aren't written down in any syllabus document) are called the *hidden curriculum*. They are the less obvious aspects of what we learn at school. And some people argue that the hidden curriculum is actually more important than the formal curriculum!

In the rest of this chapter, we're going to look at examples of the hidden curriculum of apartheid education. We're going to try to 'uncover' some of the hidden effects of schooling, and see how these work. We'll be looking at a number of areas:

The divided schooling system
Government control
The authority structures of schools
Organization in schools
School and work
Syllabuses and exams and certificates
Teaching methods.

These are some of the most important areas where the hidden curriculum operates. And they are aspects of schooling which we very often take for granted.

As we look at each of these seven areas, we'll think about two important questions on the hidden curriculum:

1 What does this particular aspect of schooling teach children?

2 What can we, as readers, learn about South African society from this?

Here is a very well-known statement on the hidden curriculum by Basil Bernstein, a British theorist:

> We should look at the way schools select subjects for the curriculum, the way they teach these subjects, and the way they examine them.
>
> These things tell us about the distribution of power in society. They also tell us about social control. (1975:85, adapted)

Bernstein and other theorists argue that if we look carefully at the way schools are organized and what they do, we can learn a lot about the wider society. The hidden curriculum teaches children about the society they live in: its values, its rules and its power structures. So it's a very important part of schooling. Not everyone agrees with Bernstein. But read on, and see what you think.

The divided schooling system

As we know, there are separate education departments for the different population registration groups. In fact, if we count the homeland departments, there are 15 departments of education in South Africa!

But schools are not only separated according to population registration groups. There are other divisions as well. For example:

- There is *mother-tongue* instruction for all population registration groups; so Sotho-speakers are separated from Zulu-speakers – and English-speakers are separated from Afrikaans-speakers.

- There is a big difference between *city schools* and *rural schools* e.g. children in farm schools have very different experiences from children in township schools.

125

- Some schools are *richer* than other schools; richer parents are able to pay for better facilities and more equipment.

- Sometimes there are separate schools for boys and girls, so *gender* is another way that schools may be divided.

- There is also a system of *private schools* (mainly for middle class English speakers). High fees (sometimes thousands of rands) make these schools a privilege for rich children only.

- There are also different *religious schools* which parents may choose to send their children to, e.g. Catholic schools, Jewish schools, etc.

If we look at the education system overall, we can see that there are a lot of divisions – and we haven't even mentioned them all. Hidden curriculum theorists argue that these schooling divisions prepare children for social divisions outside of school. Because there isn't time to examine all of the divisions, we'll concentrate on only one of them: the division according to population registration groups. Let's ask our two hidden curriculum questions about these divisions:

1 **What do these divisions in schooling teach children?**
2 **What can we, as readers, learn about South African society from this?**

Here are some answers:

- One of the aims of the apartheid education system has always been to build up an awareness of 'racial' difference. The following statement from the Eiselen Report of 1951 shows this point well:

> "We must remember that we are dealing with a Bantu child, i.e. a child trained and conditioned in Bantu culture, endowed with a knowledge of a Bantu language, and imbued with values, interests and behaviour patterns learned at the knee of a Bantu mother. These facts must dictate to a very large extent the content and methods of his early education.
>
> The schools must also give due regard to the fact that out of school hours the young Bantu child develops and lives in a Bantu community, and when he reaches maturity he will be concerned with sharing and developing the life and culture of that community."
>
> (quoted in Rose and Tunmer 1975:251, adapted)

- Schooling in apartheid South Africa was never designed to bring population registration groups together. It was designed to keep them separate. Separate schools were part of an overall plan for the social, economic and political development of apartheid. Schools were part of creating and maintaining an awareness of separateness and difference.

  This still applies. In 1983, the government rejected the recommendation made by the De Lange Committee that there should be a single education department for all groups. It reaffirmed its policy that each population registration group should have its own schools and its own education departments.

- Another important point is that the separate education departments don't necessarily provide equal education (as we saw from the 'facts and figures' in Chapter Four).

  The British writer Olive Banks (1955) made the following point about the separate schooling system that existed in Britain:

  The language of equality could never fit the actual practice. One kind of school (grammer schools) recruited for elite occupations. The other kind (secondary modern schools) were designed for manual workers.

The same thing could be said about the separate schools in South Africa. No matter how much goverment supporters talk about equality, no one could argue that the present system gives all children an equal chance. The statistics in the previous chapter show this. And the children know it. Here is what one 'coloured' Johannesburg headmaster said in 1983:

"Of course my kids know they're disadvantaged as compared with white kids. You only have to have assembly outside in the winter to know that. You only have to sit in overcrowded classrooms with broken windows to know that. You don't need agitators to tell you that you aren't equal to white kids."

So, according to this example, the hidden curriculum of separate schooling for different population registration groups teaches children to expect separation and inequality along the lines of colour.

What do *you* think of this argument?

127

Government control

Although there are separate education departments, the government keeps tight control over the education system. We can give a number of examples of this:

- Let's ask: Who chose the system of separate education? The answer to this question should tell us something about the hidden messages of power in the education system.

  Black people have been opposed to separate education departments since these were introduced. Even the Eiselen Commission of 1951 noted that blacks did not want separate education. And blacks have made their opposition clear on many occasions since 1953. Yet, in spite of this opposition, separation was introduced and still continues.

  This certainly tells us who has the power to decide about education systems, and who hasn't.

- The issue of white staffing in black education also illustrates hidden issues of power and control. Here are some examples:

Another area in which something could be done is that of proper grading and promotions. All the most senior positions in the Department of Bantu Education are manned by Whites. All the five floors in its Scheiding Street are occupied by Whites. Are there really no Blacks who could fill at least some of these jobs?

The Voice 29.5.75

White universities

THE four black universities in SA are dominated by white staff, with white lecturers outnumbering their black counterparts by 551 to 240.

Last year, the first 14 lecturers appointed to the new Vista University were all white.

At Fort Hare 131 of the 188 staff are white; at Turfloop, 140 out of 228; at University of Zululand, 111 out of 187; and at Medunsa 155 out of 174.

These figures were given in Parliament this year by the Department of Education and Training.

City Press 27.3.83

- In fact, strict government control applies to white schools as well. They also have a hidden curriculum of government control. They cannot appoint their own teachers – teachers are appointed by the authorities. They cannot teach what they like – the government lays down strict syllabuses. And there are hundreds of departmental regulations governing all aspects of white schooling. (We'll talk more about government control of white education in Chapter Six.)

Remember Basil Bernstein's statement on the hidden curriculum: that schooling systems show us the distribution of power in society, and ways of social control.

You can judge whether Bernstein's statement applies to the above examples of government control.

Let's briefly consider the position of the homelands, bearing in mind the issues of control.

Homeland education

Since the 1960s, the government has been developing its 'homeland' policy. It has fragmented the African population registration group into ten ethnic groups. These ethnic groups are the basis for ten ethnic nationalisms and homelands. The government has been trying to restrict the movement of Africans into 'white' South Africa. And it has been 'relocating' people into homelands.

Until recently, government policy was to build secondary schools in homelands. This way, it hoped to move people out of towns, and also to build up the homelands to become 'independent states'. The government has also been trying to encourage industries to move into the homelands.

Homelands have a measure of political and economic independence. But in fact, the homelands are ultimately dependent on South Africa, especially in terms of trade and finance. They also rely on South Africa to employ their workers.

In detailed terms, the situation varies greatly from homeland to homeland. Some are 'independent', others are not. Some homeland people are rural, some are commuter-labourers living in bantustan townships near 'white' towns – like Umlazi near Durban, and Garankuwa near Pretoria. There are also different social classes within homelands. So we shouldn't think of the homelands as being all the same.

In theory homelands have control over their own education systems. But in practice they are closely tied in with the South African education system.

In fact, there are more African students at school in the homelands than there are in 'white' South Africa, as the following table shows:

**Table 1   African school enrolments
in 'white' South Africa and homelands, 1982**

	'White' areas	'Independent' and non-independent homelands	Total
Primary	1 374 964	3 016 125	4 391 089
Secondary	245 850	666 603	912 453
Total:	1 620 814	3 682 728	5 303 542

(Source: SAIRR 1983:435)

Thus the homelands – independent and non-independent – are responsible for providing schooling for larger numbers of Africans than 'white' South Africa is. And this raises financial questions. For example, do the homelands have the money to provide education for an increasing number of people? They rely on money from South Africa for education. The homelands are responsible for their own budgets and spending on education. But the South African government gives 'professional and technical help', and also budgetary grants. Table 2 below shows South Africa's estimated expenditure on education in 1983–4:

**Table 2   Total estimated expenditure
on education for all population groups, 1983–4**

African education in 'white' areas	R561 318 000
Education in non-independent homelands	289 891 134
Education in 'independent' homelands	317 509 000
Indian education	235 052 000
'Coloured' education	450 736 000
White education	2 062 624 000
Total	R3 907 130 134

(Source: SAIRR 1983:419)

Writing about homeland education, De Clercq states:

The past few years have seen a rapid expansion of secondary schooling for Africans which unfortunately wasn't accompanied by a corresponding increase in school budgets nor in the supply of qualified teachers. This resulted in serious overcrowding of classrooms and a general drop in the quality of schooling and in academic performance. In 1977 the number of African Std 10 candidates was 1 876 for the 'white' areas, with 71% of them passing the Senior Certificate exam. There were 9 216 for the homelands, with a 68% passrate. By 1981, the candidates for the 'white' areas had increased to 14 447, with a low 56% passrate. In the homelands there were 44 964 candidates, with only 47% of them passing the exam.   (1984:6, adapted)

Homelands have limited resources and facilities as compared with the South African government. But they also have some political freedom. And they can decide to turn their backs on Bantu Education, and adopt other education policies.

- In KwaZulu the Buthelezi Commission stated that Kwa-Zulu should be seen as part and parcel of South Africa. Its educational problems are also part and parcel of the unequal South African system. The Commission therefore called for the reorganization of *all* educational provisions in the whole of South Africa. That would allow all students to compete equally for jobs.

- In Bophuthatswana the Popagano Report saw the educational problems as being those of an independent state, not part of South Africa. It says that Bophuthatswana's problems are the problems of a Third World country, like any other African state. They are problems of underdevelopment and must be solved through adopting policies of economic modernization.

Although these two Commissions give quite different reasons for educational problems, and different solutions, there are also similarities. Both KwaZulu and Bophuthatswana rely on South Africa to employ the graduates from their education systems. So both of them – and the other homelands too – need to ensure that their education systems are acceptable to South African employers. In fact, the Popagano Report says that Bophuthatswana's education system needs

"to gain acceptance of its standard in Southern Africa, and elsewhere so that young people coming out of such a system will not be hampered in their future education or in their future careers. **"**

(De Clercq 1984:15)

Thus Bophuthatswana's external exams, syllabuses and certificates fall under the DET. The same applies to other homelands. The Transkei is a member of the JMB. Education in the homelands is very closely influenced by South African education structures – and the South African government.

Having looked briefly at homelands, let's now look at what goes on inside schools.

The authority structures of schools

If you go into any school – white or black – you'll soon know who is in charge. There is a ladder of seniority, with the principal at the top, then deputy principals and vice principals, then senior teachers, then ordinary staff. You can even tell this hierarchy from the position and size of their offices, and where they sit in the staffroom! Somewhere at the bottom of the hierarchy are the students. But even amongst students there is a hierarchy as well – prefects, senior students, etc.

This isn't to say that people lower down in the hierarchy have no power. Students certainly have the power to disrupt classes or to boycott school. And teachers can disobey orders or teach things that aren't on the syllabus. But then, the school principal (or the Department) has the power to punish them for their behaviour! We all know that students can be punished in all sorts of ways – including corporal punishment – and they can also be expelled. Teachers can be dismissed with very little warning.

Usually schools have a fixed set of rules, and also a range of punishments for breaking these rules.

Let's ask our two hidden curriculum questions:

1 What do the authority structures of schools teach children?

2 What can we, as readers, learn about South African society from this?

● Children certainly learn how authority works – in schools and also in the wider society. They learn that they are expected to conform to rules – and they learn what happens if they don't conform.

- Some schools are more authoritarian than others. In fact, certain writers have argued that working class schools are often more authoritarian than middle class schools – and that this prepares children for different positions as adults in society. On this argument working class children would be more used to having strict rules forced on them; middle class children would be used to having more freedom. (We'll look at this argument again in the section on work.)

Here are some opinions about different amounts of authoritarianism in different South African schools.

"In my opinion, African schools, around Johannesburg anyway, are more rigidly authoritarian than white schools. Some African schools are known for their strict headmasters, who enforce rules by corporal punishment and even expulsion. Children in these schools are strictly disciplined – even regimented. The discipline is much stricter than in English-speaking white schools, at least."

White educationist in Johannesburg

"I feel really sorry for children in Afrikaans schools. They are really educationally underprivileged, to my way of thinking. Their schools are so rigid – students are not allowed to think for themselves, or to question things. These students are being prepared to be 'good Afrikaners' – that's for sure."

'Coloured' headmaster in Cape Town

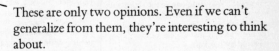

These are only two opinions. Even if we can't generalize from them, they're interesting to think about.

- Another example of authority structures in the hidden curriculum of schools is the presence of the army (the SADF). In white schools, we can see the influence of the army in Cadet Training and in the Youth Preparedness Programme (which we'll discuss in Chapter Six). In black schools, there are teachers in army uniform, and there are also 'youth camps' organized by the SADF.

133

What are the hidden messages of the army's presence in schools? Here is what the teachers' union, NEUSA, writes in its newsletter:

Military presence grows

The SADF infiltration into S.A. education grows daily

'MILITARISATION' IS a broad catch-phrase used to refer to many aspects of South African society. In regard to education, it refers to the increasing influence of the SADF over the racially divided educational system in this country: the extended cadet and Youth Preparedness (Y.P.) programmes in white schools, and the uniformed teacher and 'youth camps' in black schools.

White Schools

Education plays a large role in the process through which people come to accept the values of the current social order. South African history is largely taught from a white perspective and, for example, students of geography are taught that the racial differentiation of residential areas is natural.

With the authoritarian hierarchical structure of most white schools, the increasing militarisation serves to ensure the acceptance by pupils of the intensifying war and the SADF's role in it. This attitude is revealed in the army vs. terrorist themes of many essays received by teachers.

Direct SADF involvement in education is seen in the cadet system and Y.P. programmes, and in the veld and leadership schools.

Cadets

With official SADF-assisted cadet training from 1976, and participation in this being compulsory at most white schools, it is thought that 210,000 cadets are involved at present. The extension of cadets to include white girls is expected. Many schools already have marching and other cadet activities for girls.

The purpose of cadet training was blatantly expressed by Col. Viljoen, director of school cadets in 1979: acknowledging the 'total onslaught' against South Africa, the colonel stated that the youth should be involved in the total national strategy and that cadet training prepared the youth for military training.

It is compulsory for cadets to wear uniforms provided by the SADF on marching day. The SADF also provides weaponry and co-ordinates cadet programmes and officer training. Camps for selected pupils, who are later given rank, include activities such as rifle shooting, guard duty, ambush practice and grenade training. Leadership and discipline are highly stressed.

Black Education

As part of the SADF's campaign to win the 'hearts and minds' of the black population, the SADF has established itself in black education. In 1975 the Theron Commission recommended compulsory military service and cadet training for coloured pupils. Although resistance is high, some schools do participate in cadet programmes.

Militarised holiday 'adventure camps' for coloured and Indian children have existed for six years, essentially indoctrinating the relatively privileged. Participants are encouraged to develop 'leadership, patriotism and military discipline.' Recently, the SADF was involved in youth camps for children from Langa, Nyanga and Guguletu. The West Cape Administration Board and local community councils were also involved.

Parents of children who went on the camps complained of the lack of information about the camps: the participation of the SADF was not known prior to the departure of the children in SADF trucks.

- We can also look at prefects and SRCs as part of school authority structures. Some schools have elected student bodies to represent student interests – the SRCs. Sometimes schools have SRCs instead of prefects. Sometimes there are prefects as well as SRCs. SRCs played a very important role in the 1980 Cape school boycotts.

  Democratically elected SRCs were also one of the demands made by students in 1984. The government responded to this demand by offering to set up SRCs – along certain lines. The students rejected this offer, saying that government-organized SRCs would not be representative of student democracy. This issue also shows that there can be different kinds of SRCs!

  Some people argue that SRCs are an important means for teaching students about participation and democracy. Students gain experience from working on SRCs. They also have the opportunity of learning about a different, less authoritarian form of organization. Other people argue that SRCs themselves should be looked at critically. They aren't necessarily democratic, and they can be quite conservative.

Here are some comments on prefects and SRCs:

"The prefects in our school really take things too far. They just do the principal's dirty work – they are like his servants. If we don't come with proper school jerseys, they confiscate our jerseys. Sometimes, we never see them again. I can't admire such people."   Alexandra student, 1983

"There's a big difference between prefects and SRCs. SRCs are elected by students. Prefects are chosen by the staff. So, I mean, SRCs are responsible to us, man. We can have some control over them. And they can organize and get things going, man."
                                                          Cape Town student, 1983

But, for other people, it's not as simple as that.

"Listen, some SRCs are so conservative, you wouldn't believe it. They just organize beauty contests and cake sales. You can't simply assume that SRCs will be any good. It really depends on the students at the time. If the students are socially concerned and interested, SRCs can be powerful. Otherwise, they don't do much."
                                                          Cape Town teacher, 1983

135

It's quite difficult to say for sure what children actually learn from things like authority structures.

We can't assume that children learn what they are taught – or that they remember it!

But we can say that it is likely that they pick up some impressions or attitudes. And this is how the hidden curriculum functions.

Obviously, all societies have laws and ways of dealing with people who break the laws. Some of these laws and punishments are just – some are unjust. What we are looking at here is the way in which education systems prepare people to obey rules and laws.

While we're thinking about authority in schools, let's give some thought to the position of teachers.

The position of teachers

Teachers – in both black and white schools – are in a difficult double position.

- On the one hand, they are the employees of the government. They are responsible for carrying out the government's education policy. We could see them as agents of apartheid education.
- On the other hand, teachers are also workers and members of the society. They have to struggle for better pay and working conditions. Many of them are against the apartheid system, and want social change.

These two positions may often mean a difficult contradiction for the teacher.

As 'servants of the state', teachers have to be registered with the government; otherwise they may not be eligible for employment. The government sets out codes of behaviour and also binds teachers to the principles of Christian National Education (which we'll be looking at in Chapter Six). And teachers have very little choice.

Teachers in government schools also have very little freedom of speech. If they oppose the government they may be blacklisted and not given a job. In black schools especially teachers

136

may lose their jobs if they have 'wrong attitudes'. Teachers also face hardships with administration. There are problems like wrong classifications, wrong salaries or no salaries paid at all, and so on.

But this doesn't mean that teachers are necessarily 'part of the system'. Teacher organizations in South Africa – especially black teacher organizations – have often been prominent in political struggles. For example, in 1953 teacher organizations opposed the introduction of Bantu Education. And they have been active in other struggles too.

What follows are statements made by seven black teachers in South African schools. We can't make generalizations from these statements – there are only seven of them. But they do illustrate the contradictions of the teacher's position:

"Some students say we are just the means for the government to promote apartheid. And of course I understand why they say that.

But as I see it, we should just go on with education. It's better to take half a loaf than nothing at all. If we don't get certificates, we don't get jobs. Then we stay poorly paid in bad jobs. The more we stay uneducated, the more we help the government.

"The students don't always appreciate the difficulties we face. Our promotions are blocked, especially if we take a political stand. The Department underpays us and moves us around. We also struggle with this education system – not just the students.**"**

"I am a strong supporter of progressive teacher organizations. I think they make a lot of difference to the position of the teacher. As isolated individuals, teachers may well be weak. But when they are organized into groups and leagues and unions, the picture is different. History has shown that teacher organizations have been able to struggle effectively for better working conditions – and for the needs of their communities.**"**

"Listen, I think there's an important job to be done in the schools. We teachers need to be really well educated ourselves, then we can be giving our children a *good* education. Not just this syllabus and exam stuff. I mean an education that *really* shows what's going on.**"**

❝I support SRCs. I advise my students to listen to them and take part. 'But the day the SRC can hire and fire teachers, that day I leave teaching.**❞**

❝Students say 'We must do away with the system'. I say to them 'What exactly do you mean? What do you *want*?' But they don't really know.

I think a lot of students are just in school to grow. They are waiting until age sixteen, to get a reference book, and go to work.

A lot of students are just trouble-makers. And a lot of the unrest is just the work of these trouble-makers.**❞**

❝Students sometimes say that we aren't part of the struggle. But how can that be? This apartheid system is bad for me too. Just because I have a house and car, and I teach in a school, and I have a university degree – that doesn't mean I'm outside the struggle.**❞**

These statements are simply illustrations of some teachers' views. But they do highlight the contradictory position – and the contradictory views – of teachers in black schools.

After that comment on teachers, let's continue with our discussion on the hidden curriculum, and look at organization in schools.

Organization in school

Most schools are highly organized places. Schools bring together children of certain age groups into the same place, and organize them. The children wear uniforms which identify them with their particular school.

Schools divide children up in a number of ways. All children are organized into classes. Classes are age-graded, from Sub A through to matric. Sometimes children are divided up according to 'ability' – called 'streaming'. And there may be separate classes, or even separate schools, for boys and girls.

Schoolwork is also highly organized. The day is divided into periods, each separated by a bell ringing. There are set times for schools to begin and end, and people are expected to be punctual. Work schedules are controlled by syllabuses, and inspectors check that the work is covered. For each subject, at each level, syllabuses set out exactly what is to be done and in what order.

At the end of the year, children are assessed and graded. Those who pass go into the next standard (and go up in status). Then the whole process repeats itself.

All of this shows us that schools have set patterns which they follow regularly.

1 What does school organization teach children?

2 What can we, as readers, learn about South African society from this?

- Children's lives at school are highly controlled. After spending a number of years at school, children are likely to expect this sort of control. And to some extent this prepares them for social control outside of schools.

- According to Basil Bernstein, school practices teach children the values and beliefs of the wider society. Some practices – like assemblies and uniforms – bring people together. Other practices – like having separate classes or separate activities for boys and girls – divide people up. They teach people to accept different treatment, both inside school and in the wider world outside school.

Here are several comments on a practice which brings people together – school uniforms.

> "The Regional Director for Education in Johannesburg sent circulars to all schools in Soweto assuring parents that uniforms were no longer compulsory, and that no child should be punished for not having one."
>
> Rand Daily Mail, 16.6.81

> "Our students have a long tradition behind them. This uniform was introduced when the school was founded about a hundred years ago. It's an important part of the tradition of the school. And it's important that students feel that they are part of that tradition. We certainly wouldn't change our uniform without very good reason."
>
> Head of private school, 1983

139

Interviewer: I see all your students are wearing a uniform.

Principal: Certainly. I insist on that. Wearing a uniform gives the children a sense of belonging to the school. It's important for the children to know that this is *their* school – and also for people in the street to know who they are. They can be proud of it.

Interviewer: But aren't uniforms an unnecessary expense for parents?

Principal: Not at all! Why shouldn't parents spend the money on their children? They'd only spend it on liquor or gambling otherwise.

Interview with Soweto principal, 1982

"They like us to wear a uniform here. Most students do. I make sure I don't. I see uniforms as a way of controlling us – of making us all the same. I won't go along with that."

Student at a black teacher training college, 1983

Here is an example of another school practice, one which divides people:

"School sport is a really good example of inequality between boys and girls. At co-educational white schools, a lot of emphasis goes on boys' sport like rugby and cricket. Girls are expected to go along to boys' matches and be spectators. It's a whole ritual.

But it hardly ever works the other way around. Imagine boys spending every Saturday afternoon watching girls playing netball!

Boys are active and privileged. Girls are spectators – and treated as second-best." White Johannesburg school teacher, 1983

Of course, all of these points are controversial. You, as reader, may choose to disagree with them. But you should think carefully about them as examples of the hidden curriculum. Often, these sort of practices may be important in shaping students' attitudes and values.

School and work

A number of writers have pointed out that the way schools are organized is very similar to the way work is organized – and this is another aspect of the hidden curriculum. For example, two American writers, Bowles and Gintis, have done an important and controversial study on school and work in a book called *Schooling in Capitalist America*. Bowles and Gintis argue that schools specifically prepare people for the world of work. Schools are organized so that they 'correspond' with the organization of work. That way, people learn to cope with the discipline and demands of the school first, and the workforce later.

The following table shows the similarities between school and work, according to Bowles and Gintis:

Schools	Workplace e.g. factories
There is a **hierarchy** of power. Headmasters delegate power to teachers, who control students. Senior students have more status than junior students.	There is a **hierarchy** of power. Owners delegate power to managers and supervisors, who control workers. There is a hierarchy among workers – skilled workers have more status than semi-skilled or unskilled workers.
Knowledge is **divided up** into separate subjects. It is fragmented. Students don't have a complete picture of what they are learning.	Jobs are **divided up** into specific tasks. Work is fragmented. There is job specialization. Workers usually perform only one repetitive task. They have little understanding of the production process as a whole.
Students are expected to show **correct attitudes and behaviour.** They are expected to accept authority and their place in the hierarchy. They are expected to be polite and punctual. They are made to wait until the end of the year before they get their rewards – that is, being promoted into the next standard.	Workers are also expected to show the **correct attitudes and behaviour.** They are also expected to accept authority and their place in the hierarchy. They are expected to be polite and punctual, and to wait – until payday – for their rewards.

And we could add another point of comparison to the Bowles and Gintis list:

Students organize themselves into **student organizations** like COSAS, AZASO, AZASM, and so on, to give them solidarity and to fight for their rights.	Workers organize themselves into **unions** to give them solidarity and to fight for their rights.

Bowles and Gintis also argue that school children learn more than work discipline and behaviour. They also develop a self-image and a way of presenting themselves that fits in with the level of work that they will go on to do. Some people are taught to give orders; others are taught to obey orders.

Bowles and Gintis say that schools are different for different social classes. According to them, American schools reflect the social backgrounds of their students. And this also relates to the kind of work discipline the students will go on to experience.

Bowles and Gintis write that:

In America, blacks and other minorities go to schools that are strict and repressive, with coercive (forceful) authority structures. These schools mirror the sorts of job situations that students will move into.

Schools for middle class children are generally less strict. Children have more freedom of action, and can participate more. The authority structures are less coercive. These children are being prepared for higher level jobs, where they need to show more initiative, and be able to work by themselves. (1976:132, adapted)

People have criticized the Bowles and Gintis 'correspondence' theory. Certainly there are similarities between school and work. But can we say that schools are organized in a certain way *because* this is the way capitalist work is organized?

Nevertheless, their argument is worth thinking about. It gives us another way of looking at what schools do.

Let's look at another important issue: sexism and the position of girls in schools.

Sexism and the hidden curriculum

In recent years a number of writers have been concerned with the schooling of girls and how this prepares them for later life. These writers have shown how the hidden curriculum of schools treats boys and girls differently. The hidden curriculum builds up an awareness of gender (or sex) differences so that students expect different treatment for boys and for girls. And it also discriminates against girls. Boys and girls don't have equal experiences at school, and they don't have equal chances in life after school either.

Studies of work, for example, show that women are less likely than men to rise to higher positions. And they usually get lower pay than men do. Often the jobs they do are similar to their role in the home. As wives and mothers they do cooking, cleaning, clothing and child care. At work they often get jobs in food and textile factories, and they do cleaning and domestic service. In the professions they are teachers, nurses and social workers. These are the 'caring professions', with lower status than professions like doctors and lawyers.

What follows are a few examples from research on the hidden curriculum of gender differences. What do children learn from this hidden curriculum? Do you think that schools prepare girls for 'women's work'?

School textbooks
Studies done of textbooks show that boys and men are mentioned more often than girls and women are. Most typically, men are active – they are doing things and achieving things. Women are shown as passive, weak and dependent on men. As one writer says, 'they are hardly ever shown in roles of leadership, adventure, heroism, scholarship, or career expertise'. (Biraimah 1982:164) Textbooks give stereotyped pictures of the different roles of men and women in society. They don't offer the same role models to girl students and to boy students. And usually the role model they give to girls is a very limited one.

School subjects
We all know that boys are timetabled to do subjects like woodwork while girls do domestic science. Often the school timetable is organized so that it is hard for girls to do science and

143

maths. History and typing are often seen as 'better subjects for girls'.

Classroom activities

In classrooms, teachers usually ask boys to do the 'heavy work', like moving desks. Girls are asked to do more 'domestic' jobs. How often do teachers ask boys to get them their tea at break?

Studies of classrooms show that teachers ask boys questions more often than they ask girls. Often they don't expect girls to succeed or be able to do more difficult work. They expect boys to be energetic, independent and lively. They expect girls to be obedient, tidy and conscientious.

School organization

A lot of the daily routines of schools are based on gender differences. Teachers often seat girls and boys separately and have different registers for girls and boys. There are different uniforms, playgrounds and sports facilities. All these differences are part of the hidden curriculum of schools. They teach people to expect that boys and girls should be treated as different.

Teachers

Most primary school teachers are women. Most head teachers are men. Why?
Many women go into teaching, and stay there. Very few get to the top. Why?
And what hidden messages do girls pick up from this?

These are just a few examples. But they should make us more aware of sexism in the hidden curriculum.

Now let's look at our next section in the hidden curriculum: syllabuses, exams and certificates.

Syllabuses, exams and certificates

Syllabuses and exams also tell us a lot about the hidden curriculum of schools. Here is a statement made by the Department of Education and Training in 1981:

"The same standards apply in Black schools as in the schools of other education departments with regard to syllabuses and examinations. The same core syllabuses are used and the Joint Matriculation Board requires the same standards from black pupils for university entrance as from any other pupil in South Africa.**"**

This statement by the DET claims that content, the exam system, standards (and therefore certificates) are equal for all population registration groups. But, for hidden curriculum theorists, these are the very areas that we need to look at more carefully. Remember that Basil Bernstein argued that these are the very areas which show us about power and social control.

We all know that the education departments lay down syllabuses for school subjects. But who decides what should be taught in schools? And how do these people make their decisions? For some people, these questions don't present problems. But actually, the issue isn't that simple. If we think about all the different knowledge that people have in our society, we can see that there are all sorts of things that schools don't teach:

What about law?
What about computing?
What about traditional medicine?
What about development studies?
What about astrology?
What about African history?
What about politics?
What about psychology?

If we think about it, it's obvious that schools teach only a small part of the collective knowledge of our society. The formal school curriculum is a *selection* of the knowledge we have in our society. At different times and in different societies schools teach different things. In other words, societies have to select what their schools should teach from a whole range of knowledge. So the questions of what they select and how they select it become important!

Michael F. D. Young, in his book called *Knowledge and Control,* writes:

> The curriculum is a result of choices that are made. These choices reflect the *values* and *beliefs* of *dominant groups* in the society at a particular time.
>
> (1971:24, adapted)

145

According to Young, there is a strong link between school knowledge and power. Those people who have power are able to decide what knowledge schools should teach. The school curriculum itself reflects what these people think is important. In this way it indirectly reflects the power arrangements of the society.

Not everybody agrees with Young. Nevertheless, he does raise some important questions about how school knowledge is chosen. He gives us insights which are useful.

There are certainly a number of questions which we could ask about the South African curriculum:

- It is compulsory for black children to learn through the medium of English or Afrikaans at school. Why isn't it compulsory for white children to learn through the medium of an African language?

- Why do we spend so much time at school learning about European history? Why don't we learn about Third World history or African history?

- Why do black children learn gardening, when white children don't?

- Why do girls and boys learn different subjects, e.g. girls learn sewing and boys learn woodwork? Shouldn't both genders learn to mend their clothes and fix their furniture?

These questions – and the answers we give – certainly tell us something about power arrangements in the South African society.

Now let's take some specific examples of syllabuses and exams in South Africa. As we look at the examples, we can raise the same questions that we've been asking about the hidden curriculum:

1 What does this aspect of schooling teach children?

2 What can we, as readers, learn about South African society from this?

Syllabuses

As an example, we can compare the Std 2 geography syllabus for the Cape Education Department (CED) and the Std 2 environment studies syllabus of the DET. The two education departments set out different syllabus aims, and they also set aside different amounts of time for the study of geography.

Two of the aims listed in the CED syllabus for geography are:

"To lead the pupil to a closer acquaintance with
- his own country and its people
- other lands and peoples of the world, and
- the natural phenomena of the earth in so far as he is able to understand them.

To develop in the pupil a concept of common humanity by
- leading him to take an interest in national problems of his own country
- encouraging a sympathetic attitude towards other races and their problems, and
- creating a clearer understanding of the interdependence of the peoples of the world."

So white children are expected to have:

- a knowledge of the earth and its people;
- an understanding of the population groups in South Africa; and
- an understanding of international relations and problems.

The DET gives a different set of aims in its environment studies syllabus:

"The person should realize that he is a member of a particular community and that he is bound by various ties to particular groups of people in that community, as they are represented, for example, by his home, his school, church, residential area, and his tribe. These groups serve him directly and indirectly and he in turn owes them loyalty and co-operation. At a later stage, larger loyalties can be developed."

So black children are expected:

- to know about their own community;
- to be loyal and co-operative members of this community; and
- to learn about 'larger' things later on.

147

It's obvious that the two sets of syllabus aims are quite different, and this tells us something about the way the hidden curriculum works.

A second example of how the hidden curriculum of syllabuses can work comes from this comment on farm schools:

"Farm schools are extremely poor. They are the worst off in the whole system. The facilities are really bad. Children usually have to walk miles to school. Sometimes, during busy seasons, they don't go to school at all; they work on the farms instead.

The government supplies money for exercise books. Sometimes there is only one book for each child for the whole year. That dictates how much writing the child will do during the year – one exercise book full.

In this case, the amount that children write has nothing to do with the teacher or the syllabus. It simply depends on how much paper they have.

Talk about the hidden controls in schools."

Researcher on farm schools, 1983

What about the DET's claim that everyone has the same syllabus?

This in itself may produce hidden consequences. Here are some comments made by Soweto teachers.

"It's all very well to talk about African schools having the same syllabus as white schools. But no account is taken of the tremendous difficulties with the language switch from vernacular to English.

In deep Soweto – Meadowlands and Phiri – some children in Standard Three can hardly speak a word of English. And it's supposed to become the medium of instruction! There they are, in biology, learning about 'carnivores', when they don't even know the words for 'cup' and 'saucer'.

It's just not as simple as saying 'they all have the same syllabus'. These children are educationally disadvantaged."

Primary school teacher in Soweto, 1983

"The reading books are all about white middle class children in England. This bears no relation to the culture of black children in Soweto – never mind the rural areas. It has nothing to do with the world they experience outside of school. These kinds of books do nothing to instil a love of reading in black children."

Soweto English teacher, 1983

"The syllabuses are very full. They have so much in them we can never finish them. If we keep to the syllabus, we have no time at all to teach anything else. The Department makes sure of that!

Packing the syllabus is one way of controlling what we can teach in schools." Soweto high school teacher, 1983

According to Young, these sorts of syllabus examples reflect issues of power and control. Whether or not we agree with Young, this point is worth thinking about.

Tests and exams

Tests are a familiar part of the education process. They are one way of seeing how much people know – and grading them. But they are also an important part of the hidden curriculum.

Here is one opinion on a hidden purpose of testing. It's an opinion that's quite often expressed in other countries as well.

"Instead of writing half-year exams, we now have to write monthly tests in all our subjects. This keeps us working all the time. We have no free time. With half-year exams, you had more time. You could cram at the end, before the exam. Now it's just always schoolwork – one test after the next.

I think the DET is using monthly tests to keep students out of politics. They are trying to silence us by making us busy." Soweto student, 1982

Inspectors and advisors

One of the functions of inspectors and advisors is to help teachers. They see that the work is being properly taught. But they can also be doing other things.

"After the 1980 boycotts, the Department set up a system of subject advisors. They were supposed to be there to help teachers – to improve the quality of education, and all that.

Man, they're always visiting us and checking up on what we're doing! Every second week they're there. They make sure that we stick to the syllabus. They listen to our lessons. They look at the tests we set.

They're there to *control* us man, not to help us. With all this inspection, there's no time left for real education – only for drilling students." Cape Town teacher, 1983

149

Obviously, not all testing and inspecting is about this sort of control. But the comments made by the student and the teacher do give us certain insights.

Certificates

Remember that the DET statement claimed that exam standards are equal for all population registration groups. The following *Drum* article gives us one perspective on whether or not qualifications are equal.

CHAOS IN BLACK EDUCATION

"**S**IES. The whole thing stinks. Our parents have to work themselves to death for our education. We strain throughout the year so as not to disappoint them while other people get their examinations through the back door. We might as well give up," a Soweto student told DRUM.

He was commenting on the utter chaos in black education.

There have been a spate of Press reports about the leaking of examination papers in JC and matric throughout the country, as well as reports of students buying certificates. This affected coloured, Indian and Bantu education departments.

DRUM made countrywide investigations. The different education departments assured us that tight security measures were taken to ensure that no exam papers could be leaked. But the fact was that many students were having full dress-rehearsals of the exams they had to sit for.

DRUM spoke to some of the principals after hearing that students at their schools had been caught with leaked exam papers.

All but one admitted that students had been found with exam papers.

Drum, January 1982

We often hear complaints by black people that their certificates are worth less than the certificates that whites get.

The *Drum* article gives us one perspective on this. We obviously can't see it as the whole picture, but it does tell us something of importance.

And here, for interest, is some material on compulsory education. You can draw your own conclusions on the hidden curriculum of compulsory education.

Compulsory education

First, here is a statement by the government, taken from a DET publicaton:

<u>Compulsory Education</u>

In 1981 free and compulsory education was introduced in 202 schools in 38 areas. This affects all pupils who turned 6 before or on 31 December of the previous year. Compulsory education will be extended horizontally to higher classes from year to year and also to other areas with the full consent and co-operation of parents.

The right to learn

This is what NEUSA (the teachers' union) has to say:

Compulsory Education

Along with the age laws went the introduction of compulsory schooling in about 201 schools in 38 townships mainly in the Transvaal. The system applied only to sub A students in 1981, but 45 000 students were affected. Pupils in Sub A were given free books and stationary at the cost of R4 per child. (Not very much considering how much books cost these days!) However parents still had to pay school fees.

Compulsory education does not mean that the state has to provide education for all children, it means that parents who can afford to send their children to school must sign an undertaking to keep their children in these schools for a set period of time. This means that its up to the parents to make sure that children don't boycott or miss school. If they do then they have broken a contract and can be justifiably expelled.

This is just another way to force students to attend school without making it free and without changing the content of the schooling that students have been protesting against.

Here is an article from *City Press*, 27.3.83:

IT'S A FLOP

Two years after the Government introduced the scheme with much fanfare, a mere six percent of those pupils eligible are taking part.

And despite the compulsory nature of their education, there was a massive 23 percent drop-out rate last year.

These figures were released in Parliament this week when the Department of Education and Training (DET) filed its annual report.

It revealed that only 75 000 out of a total of more than one million Sub A and Sub B pupils were involved in compulsory education.

And the figures show that of the 45 000 pupils who started compulsory education in Sub A in 1981, only 34 500 were attending Sub B classes in 1982 — a drop-out figure of more than 16 000.

Top educationalists say the failure of the scheme — which is only implemented in areas where school committees opt for it — is caused by parents' "distrust of the system".

Educationalist and university lecturer Mr Thamsanqa Kambule said the feeling of distrust was the result of parents' experiences with the education authorities during the '76 riots.

"After the upheavals, the Government, instead of giving genuine education reforms, dragged its feet," said Mr Kambule.

"So when compulsory education was introduced in 1981, parents were suspicious."

His views were echoed by Professor Es'kia Mphahlele of the Council of Black Education and Research, who added: "Compulsory education is impossible with the over-crowding in our schools, and in any event there is no-one to ensure the children attend classes."

The DET's deputy chief public relations officer, Mr Edgar Posselt, admitted the department was not enforcing the scheme.

He said the drop-out rate was a matter for grave concern.

"The DET is working on school readiness and remedial education programmes to arrest the problem."

He said the department had also started an advisory panel to deal with the problems of Sub A and Sub B "compulsory" pupils.

153

Let's turn to our final aspect of the hidden curriculum – teaching methods.

Teaching methods

Remember how Bernstein argued that teaching methods themselves also give us examples of the hidden curriculum. Other educators, like Ivan Illich and Paulo Freire, have also argued that teaching methods are very important.

In most schools the teacher usually stands up front, while the students sit passively at their desks. The students' role is to listen to and to memorize what the teacher says. The students are not active – they simply 'receive' the knowledge which the teachers 'deposit' in their minds.

Paulo Freire and others have called this system the 'banking system of education'. Teachers 'deposit' or 'transfer' knowledge into the 'empty' minds of their students. Knowledge is treated like an object – a commodity that can be exchanged – instead of something which people create. Most students are not given the opportunity to think for themselves or to discover things for themselves. They don't develop a critical awareness of the world. And all of this shapes their view of the world and what they can – or can't – do to change things.

Freire also calls this kind of education 'education for domestication'. He argues that other forms of education are possible, and that if we want social change we need to develop new forms of education. These would be based on collective learning – or dialogue – on the part of teachers and students. They would both be active participants in the learning situation.

The example of Freire is important for two reasons:
1 it shows us that teaching methods are also part of the hidden curriculum, shaping the way people view the world;
2 it also shows us that alternatives to the present system *are* possible.

Conclusion

In this chapter we've looked at many examples of the hidden curriculum in apartheid education. What can we conclude from this? At least two points seem important.

● As we've said before, schools need to be seen in the context of the wider society in which they operate. The examples of the hidden curriculum show this clearly.

   Schools teach more than the content knowledge that is set out in the formal curriculum. They also teach a whole range of attitudes, values and assumptions which prepare people for the wider society.

   Apartheid schools are no exception to this. They are part of the unequal, racist, capitalist society in South Africa. The hidden curriculum of schools teaches about the structures and social relations of the society.

● But at the same time we should remember that children don't always learn exactly what schools try to teach. It isn't a watertight situation. Children don't always accept the messages of the hidden curriculum – as we'll see when we look at resistance in education.

References and further readings

Banks, O. (1955) *Parity and Prestige in English Secondary Education,* Routledge Kegan Paul, London

Barrett, M. (1980) *Women's Oppression Today,* Verso, London

Bernstein, B. (1975) *Class, Codes, and Control: vol. 3,* Routledge Kegan Paul, London

Biraimah, K.C. (1982) 'Different knowledge for different folks' in P.G. Altbach et al. *Comparative Education,* Macmillan, New York

Bowles, S. and Gintis, H. (1976) *Schooling in Capitalist America,* Routledge Kegan Paul, London

Cock, J. (1980) *Maids and Madams: A Study in the Politics of Exploitation,* Ravan, Johannesburg

De Clercq, F. (1984) 'Education and training in the homelands: A separate development?' Second Carnegie Inquiry into Poverty and Development in Southern Africa, Cape Town

Donaldson, A. (1983) 'Present structures and constraints: The provision of educators in Transkei' in D. Freer and P. Randall *Educating the Educators,* Conference proceedings, University of the Witwatersrand

Harvey, R. (1980) 'The farm school system and Bantu Education' *Reality* May

Jaff, R. (1981) 'Education for Popagano' *Perspectives in Education* 5(1)

Levy, B. (1976) 'Farm schools in South Africa: An empirical study' SALDRU Farm Labour Conference, Cape Town

Nasson, B. (1984) 'Bitter Harvest: Farm schooling for black South Africans' Second Carnegie Inquiry into Poverty and Development in Southern Africa, Cape Town

NEUSA (undated) *De Lange . . . Marching to the Same Order,* NEUSA, Johannesburg

NEWSA (newsletter of NEUSA)

Plaut, T. (1976) 'Farm schools for African and Coloured children in South Africa' SALDRU Farm Labour Conference, Cape Town

Rose, B. and Tunmer, R. (1975) *Documents in South African Education,* Ad. Donker, Johannesburg

SAIRR (Annual) *Survey of Race Relations in South Africa,* SAIRR, Johannesburg

Young, M.F.D. (1971) *Knowledge and Control,* Collier Macmillan, London

Chapter 6 White education: The worldview of CNE

'One education system for all!'

This is a common demand from people who want educational change in South Africa. It is one of the demands of student organizations. It was also one of the recommendations made by the De Lange Commission in 1981.

But what system do people have in mind when they demand a single education system? Sometimes people think of the education system for white people. They imagine that everyone should have the same system as whites have. But is the education system for whites really a good one? This is a question which we need to think about carefully.

Obviously, there are many advantages in the white education system, compared with the education for other population registration groups. Whites have compulsory education: by law they attend school from age 7 to age 16. Their schooling is largely free, though a law passed in 1982 states that they may have to pay certain fees. We have seen that white teachers are generally better qualified; class sizes are smaller; and facilities are generally better than those for the other groups. In these ways, the system for whites certainly has advantages.

But there's more to education than this. We need to remember that the white education system is also part of apartheid education. And it is based on a specific worldview – the worldview of Christian National Education (CNE). In this chapter we'll look at the way this CNE belief system shapes white education. We can then judge better whether the white system would be a good one for everybody.

Worldviews and education

All education systems are shaped by certain worldviews and values. Education is not neutral. In Chapter One we saw that different people have different aims for education. People have different worldviews, and these worldviews influence the sort of education that they want. In this chapter we're going to look at the worldview which influences the education system for whites in South Africa. This is the worldview of Christian-Nationalism.

I understand that there are different worldviews, and that people have different ideas about education. But then how do some worldviews come to have more influence than others? Why does a particular worldview – like Christian-Nationalism – come to influence the education system in South Africa?

Well, in this chapter you'll see how it is that people who have power are able to influence the ideas of other people. But let's carry on, and this should become clearer.

In this chapter we're going to look at the principles and beliefs behind the education system for white students. We'll also look at how these beliefs are expressed in the white schooling system. We'll look at:

● The CNE movement, its history and its basic beliefs;

● The 1967 National Education Policy Act (which is the basis of white education) and the CNE policies it sets out;

● Specific programmes in white schools which are designed to promote Christian Nationalist beliefs, especially the Youth Preparedness programme and Veld Schools;

● The government's response to the De Lange Report, where the government repeats that CNE remains its policy and that CNE must be the basis of education in South Africa.

As we've said before, we're concentrating on the *ideology* of white education. We've chosen to look at the belief system, rather than to look at facts and figures, or the way the system operates in practice. Obviously, ideology is only part of the story – it doesn't tell us everything. But, as you'll see, it's a very important part.

Let's start by looking at CNE.

Christian National Education

In Chapter Two we mentioned the CNE schools that were set up after the Anglo–Boer War. Groups of Afrikaners were opposed to the schooling system which the British introduced, and they opened their own alternative schools based on Christian-National principles.

But the ideas of CNE go back even further than this to the early days of British settlement at the Cape. After the British occupied the Cape in 1806, they introduced a state schooling system. A number of boers disagreed with state schooling. They believed that the church should have a strong influence over schools. They wanted to preserve their particular Calvinist religion, and also the identity of the Dutch-Afrikaner people. And they wanted their schools to reflect these views. Later the education systems in the Transvaal and OFS gave a prominent position to the church in education.

After the Anglo–Boer War, the British introduced different schooling provisions. They hoped to use the schools to break down boer nationalism and to promote the language and values of the British. Education was brought under state control and the church's influence was reduced. The Dutch language was given less prominence in schools.

In response to this, the Commission for CNE was formed in 1902 by boer teachers, military leaders and church people. About 200 private CNE schools were set up, with financial help from Holland. A SPROCAS Report describes these schools as follows:

> At these schools, Dutch was the medium of instruction for most subjects at the primary level, although in the CNE high schools in towns English continued to be the main medium of instruction. In all CNE schools there was a strong emphasis on Christian teaching according to the Calvinist doctrine. The majority of Dutch-Afrikaner children were sent to these schools. (1971:72)

The CNE schools did not last for very long. They struggled to raise the money they needed. It was hard for them to compete against the free, compulsory schooling offered by the state. Soon the state schooling system moved to compromise a little with the CNE movement. More recognition was given to Dutch, and prayers and religious instruction were included in the school curriculum. As the language and cultural position of the Afrikaners grew stronger, so CNE schools gradually became part of the state system. By 1907 there were very few private CNE schools left.

But this did not mean the end of the CNE movement. The historian Hexham writes: 'The few CNE schools that remained became a symbol of hope and a focal point for the movement.' (1980:393)

Small informal groups of people kept the ideals of CNE alive. They managed to turn the Potchefstroom Theological Seminary into the Potchefstroom University College for Christian Higher Education. This was based on CNE principles, and helped to keep CNE alive.

During the 1930s and 1940s Afrikaner nationalism grew, and CNE was part of this. At an Afrikaner Volkskongres in 1939 an Institute for CNE was founded. In 1948 this Institute published a well-known pamphlet setting out CNE policy. The introduction to the pamphlet stated:

> We want no mixing of languages, no mixing of cultures, no mixing of religions, and no mixing of races. The struggle for the Christian and National school still lies before us. (SPROCAS 1971:74)

It's important to realize that CNE is not a neutral theory of education. The CNE movement expressed the worldview of Dutch-Afrikaner people. It expressed their views about the role of the church – their particular Calvinist church – in education. It expressed their views about a nationalist education for Dutch-Afrikaner children.

But more than this, it was part of the Afrikaner nationalist struggle. In 1902 CNE schools were set up to resist British culture and language and to preserve the culture and language of the boers. And the 1948 CNE pamphlet was born out of the Afrikaner nationalist movement of the 1930s and 1940s.

So CNE is both part of a particular worldview and part of a nationalist struggle. Certainly, we could never describe CNE as a neutral and non-political educational policy.

But the next question is: To what extent does the CNE worldview influence white education today? To answer that, let's look at the Education Act that makes provision for white education.

The National Education Policy Act (1967)

Under apartheid, different laws have been passed to provide separate education for the different population registration groups. So there is the Bantu Education Act of 1953, the Coloured Persons Education Act of 1963 and the Indian Education Act of 1965. In 1967 the so-called National Education Policy Act was passed, which laid down the guiding principles for white education.

The 1967 Act was welcomed by apartheid politicians as a mile-stone in the history of South African education. And it remains the basis of white education today. But, as the liberal educationist E.G. Malherbe points out, the title of the 'National Education Policy Act' tells us a lot. Malherbe writes:

> The education referred to is specifically limited to white persons. It would seem, therefore, that the Act would have been far more accurately named, had it been called simply *The White Persons' Education Act*.
>
> (1977:142, adapted)

The 1967 Act makes sure that white education is equal in the four provinces, and it also sets up a framework of ten principles for white education. Here is a summary of the ten principles:

161

National Education Policy Act, 1967

(a) Education in schools, maintained and managed by the state or by a provincial education department shall have a Christian character, but the religious conviction of the parents and pupils shall be respected in regard to religious instruction and ceremonies.

(b) Education shall have a broad national character.

(c) The mother tongue, if it is English or Afrikaans, shall be the medium of instruction.

(d) Requirements as to compulsory education, and the limits relating to school age shall be uniform in all provinces.

(e) Education (including books and stationery) shall be free, except in respect of pupils studying part-time, and apprentices.

(f) Education shall be provided in accordance with the ability and aptitude of and interest shown by the pupil, and the needs of the country and that appropriate guidance shall, with due regard thereto, be furnished to pupils.

(h) The parent community shall be given a say through parent-teachers' associations, school committees, boards of control or school boards or in any other manner.

(i) Consideration shall be given to suggestions and recommendations of the officially recognized teacher's associations when planning for purposes of education.

(j) Conditions of service and salary scales of teachers shall be uniform.

(Behr 1978:42, adapted)

The first six principles are key statements for understanding the basic assumptions of white education – in particular, principles (a) and (b). These two principles are familiar statements about the 'Christian' and 'National' basis of education. They provide the cornerstone of the Christian-National worldview, and they show clearly that white education is based on CNE principles.

The Act is quite open about its Christian-National worldview – there's no doubt about that. And although parents and teachers are supposed to have a say – according to principles (h) and (i) – they have no choice about CNE.

Obviously, the terms 'Christian' and 'National' are very broad in their meanings. They can mean different things to different people. So in 1971 the Minister of Education gave official definitions. These definitions are worth a closer look.

Christian Education in schools shall have a Christian character founded on the Bible and imprinted **(a)** through religious instruction as a compulsory non-examination subject, and **(b)** through the spirit and manner in which all teaching and education, as well as administration and organization, are conducted.

The religious convictions of the parents and pupils shall be respected in regard to religious instruction and religious ceremonies.

(Malherbe 1977:147)

There are a number of points to make about this definition:

- The definition talks about 'Christian character' – as if we all know what this means. But the question is: What do we mean by 'Christian'? Many people who call themselves Christians *reject* the CNE policies of the government. The government has a particular interpretation of 'Christian'.

- The definition shows that 'Christian' education doesn't only mean teaching about religion. It also means 'imprinting' these views in a less obvious way. Note especially point (b). It shows quite clearly that 'Christian' principles will be the basis of the hidden curriculum of white schools. As it says, the teaching, education, administration and organization of white schools will be 'Christian' in 'spirit and manner'.

The values that filter through the whole school are hard to dodge. If people don't want to learn religious instruction, they can avoid it. But there's no choice when it comes to the 'spirit and manner' of schooling. These things are much harder to avoid – and sometimes it's even hard to see them operating.

'National' is a longer definition with more parts. But read it carefully and see what you can pick up.

National Education in schools shall have a broad national character which shall be imprinted **(a)** through the conscious expansion of every pupil's knowledge of the fatherland, embracing language and cultural heritage, history and traditions, national symbols, the diversity of the population, social and economic conditions, geographical diversity and national achievements; and **(b)** by developing this knowledge in each pupil into understanding and appreciation by presenting it in a meaningful way where appropriate, in the teaching of the two official languages, national history of the fatherland, civics and geography in school teaching and further through the participation of pupils in national festivals, and their regular honouring of the national symbols, so as to
(i) inculcate a spirit of patriotism, founded on loyalty and responsibility towards the fatherland, its soil and its natural resources;
(ii) enable every pupil to gain a balanced perspective; and
(iii) achieve a sense of unity and a spirit of co-operation.

(Malherbe 1977:147-8)

Again, there are a number of points to make:

- White education is specifically aimed at building up a sense of nationalism. This is a stated aim of the system. School subjects, especially languages, history, geography and civics, are intended to 'inculcate' (or convince people about) patriotism. Nationalism is also 'imprinted' through 'honouring national symbols' and participating in ceremonies.

- But the definition of 'nation' is very limited and specific. It refers only to white South Africans, and not to blacks. But, even more narrowly than this, it is based on a specific form of nationalism – Afrikaner nationalism. Yet when the statement talks of 'language', 'cultural heritage' and 'national symbols', there is no indication that these very things are the outcome of a particular nationalist struggle – *Afrikaner* nationalism.

  In the 1920s Afrikaners fought for their language to be recognized. They fought to have the present South African flag instead of Britain's flag, the Union Jack. And they have fought for the recognition of their culture. So these things are not fixed and given. They are not neutral and value-free. They are part and parcel of the struggle for Afrikaner nationalism.

  The 1967 Act and the official definition of nationalism ignore all of this. They ensure that the Afrikaner form of nationalism applies to all white children – including English-speaking children.

- As Malherbe points out, it is interesting that the official definition of nationalism talks about 'unity', when, in fact, the 1967 Act *divides* white children according to language and culture. (Remember: mother-tongue instruction means that English-speaking and Afrikaans-speaking children go to different schools.)

We can see that the 1967 Act is clearly based on a particular worldview – that of CNE

But, more than that, CNE should be seen in political terms. Nationalism is a political policy, and has been the policy of the ruling Afrikaner political party. And Afrikaner nationalism is a policy which has been contested by many South Africans.

So white education has a specifically *political* basis. It expresses the ideas and worldview of a specific power group. There is no way that this education is based on neutral, value-free principles.

But let's go on to look at our next point: some of the school activities based on CNE.

CNE programmes in white schools

So far we've seen that the 1967 Act is based on a specific Christian-National worldview. CNE principles assume that whites should be separated from blacks (as a 'nation') and that Afrikaans-speaking children should be separated from English-speaking children (by mother-tongue schooling). The government aims to 'imprint' CNE principles on all white children, not only through the formal curriculum of schools but also through the hidden curriculum.

But how does this affect what goes on in schools? The CNE worldview is certainly expressed in the hidden curriculum of white schools. The official statements and definitions give some clear pointers about where to look. Flag-raising, festivals 'honouring' (white) heroes, religious assemblies, and so on, are all designed to 'imprint' Christian-National views.

But CNE is also very obviously expressed in special programmes in white schools which openly teach morals and values. There are two special programmes in Transvaal schools where we see this most clearly: the Youth Preparedness Programme and Veld Schools.

Remember, in this chapter we have chosen to look at belief systems and ideology. We're looking at the government's educational policies and its statements of intention.

What actually goes on in schools may be a little different. We can't assume that policies are always put into practice as they are intended. But policies and statements certainly tell us a lot.

Another point to understand is that many white parents aren't actually aware of the CNE ideology. They may not realize what their children are being taught. It's often especially hard to pick up the hidden curriculum in schools.

But let's look at the Youth Preparedness programme in more detail, and see its links with CNE.

165

The Youth Preparedness Programme

In 1972 a new compulsory subject was introduced into white schools in the Transvaal. This was the Youth Preparedness Programme (YP). The educationist A. L. Behr writes that 'this programme flows in part from the requirements of principles (a) and (b)' of the 1967 Act – the CNE principles. (1978:44) In other words, it is a programme designed specifically to teach CNE values.

At that time, in the early 1970s, the government began to say that South Africa was experiencing a 'total onslaught'. They claimed that various groups, who were inspired by communism, were plotting to undermine South Africa. They said that there was evidence for this in sports boycotts, talk of sanctions and the growing world sympathy for Frelimo, MPLA and the ANC, and other organizations in the South African liberation movement.

This talk of threat and 'total onslaught' was echoed by high-placed officials in the Transvaal Education Department. They claimed that children needed to be physically and morally prepared for the hard times that lay ahead. In 1972 Dr A. L. Kotzee, Director of Education in the Transvaal, launched the Youth Preparedness Programme (YP). In a speech to school principals he said that the South African value system and South African youth were under attack, and he suggested a course of action. His speech tells us a lot about his own values and also the values of the goverment. So it's worth looking more closely at what he had to say. Here is a summary of his speech:

Kotzee's speech on Youth Preparedness

The speech starts by talking about a breakdown in Western civiliza-tion. It claims that there is 'moral and physical decay' in the world and that this 'corruption' is particularly affecting the youth. It goes on:

> **"**Today there are such calculated forms of treason that it is often difficult to identify it. But there is something going on in the world today which I would like to identify and to give a name, and that is the treason against youth of some intellectuals, writers, thinkers and philosophers. Some of them speak and write in such a way as to make, for instance, sex immo-rality and drug abuse seem to be natural and normal, while self-discipline is made out not only to be old-fashioned but to be downright queer. Too many people are prepared to surrender too many principles and stan-dards.**"**

The standards being abandoned are moral ones, religious ones and social ones. They include the state, the church, the home, the school – every 'existing form of civilization'.

> "Political, financial and military pressure from without, and undermining of everything dear to us from within – that is our real unpleasant and dangerous situation at present. We have to be physically and mentally fit and on the alert to weather the storm."

The speech goes on to talk about physical dangers:

> "You have already seen the sirens which are to sound the warning when the bombs start falling. Would you know what to do with your pupils if this should happen during school-time? Would you know how to extinguish fires, how to save people from under the ruins and how to nurse them?"

But Kotzee feels that there is another important issue to consider:

> "We are only 3¾ million whites, and for the time being we still have to render many services to other population groups in our country. If we wish to ensure our future we shall have to realize that each one of us is a key person holding a key post, no matter what it is. This holds for every pupil entrusted to our care. We cannot afford to lose a single one on the way."

Terrible consequences would follow if the youth are not prepared:

> "If we fail, we can say goodbye to Western civilization as we see it today, and to all the values that have been characteristic of our civilization through the ages."

The speech ends saying that the school is strategically important, and principals and teachers have a important mission:

> "In the name of our youth I appeal to you to launch and execute the Youth Preparedness Programme with enthusiasm."

(TED Educational News Flashes, no. 30, 1972:2-4)

167

You can see that this speech clearly expresses certain values. Let's look at some examples:

- It assumes that changes in the modern world are leading to a breakdown of Western civilization;
- It talks about 'decay' and 'corruption' – these are value-laden words;
- It assumes that white children need to be prepared for emergencies at school – but what about black children?
- It assumes that white people should be in a superior position in society, and that white children should be 'prepared' for this.

The values and worldview of YP are quite obvious. And it's also obvious that YP is closely tied to CNE.

In 1972 YP was introduced as part of Guidance. A syllabus was drawn up, with differences based on age and gender. Some of the compulsory components of YP are:

Emergency planning
Fire fighting
Drilling and marching
Drilling, shooting and orchestra
Shooting and self defence
Vocational guidance
Moral preparedness.

The Education Department has supplied detailed manuals to each school in which the programme is outlined lesson by lesson.

Military components

If we look at the list of compulsory components for YP, we can see that the first five components emphasize military kinds of activities. They seem to be designed to 'prepare' people for the 'total onslaught'. Children are taught to march and drill and shoot and defend themselves. And they are also mentally 'prepared' for 'emergency situations'.

The YP programme links in closely with the South African Defence Force of its military aspects. For example, in one of the manuals called *Marching and Drilling,* schools are referred (with page references) to the following SADF manuals:

> *Drill, All Arms,* 1971 SADF
> *Drill Manual,* 1955 SA Army
> *Ceremonial Manual for the SADF,* 1971
> *Compliments and Saluting,* 1971 SADF.

The SADF is also used for the components on Map Reading and Field Tactics.

You'll notice the YP puts stress on military practices and values. Using the army is a clear indication of this. You can also see that there's an emphasis on ceremonies and rituals which 'prepare' children physically and at the same time, 'imprint' military attitudes and values.

For some people, this militarism isn't worrying. But there are other people who are strongly against militarist practices and values. For them, the militarism of YP is a real problem.

The YP Programme also actively encourages different treatment for boys and girls. For example, both boys and girls are expected to do drill and marching, but only Std 9 and 10 boys are required to do musketry (gun drilling). And here is a statement by the TED:

> Girls' schools will probably have to appeal to boys' schools for help with marching and shooting practice and perhaps also with other components, possibly also in exchange for help in respect of components with which the boys' school has difficulty.
>
> (*TED Educational News Flashes,* no. 30, 1972:7)

One of the important hidden messages of YP is gender difference – the assumption that boys and girls have different interests and different abilities. In fact, in terms of the hidden curriculum, YP actually encourages people to be aware of gender differences. Generally the assumption is that girls are less able to cope with certain activities than boys are. And this assumption can certainly be questioned!

Moral preparedness

As Kotzee's speech on YP showed us, one of the important aims of YP is to teach certain moral standards, within the context of CNE. In the YP Programme there is a component called 'Moral Preparedness' which includes the following content:

- Citizenship, which deals with 'the official emblems of the RSA', 'our national holidays', 'the strategic position of South Africa to the rest of the world', 'the Bantu', etc.
- Human relationships
- Things worthwhile in life – work, human virtues, authority and liberty, etc.

(TED Manual, 1972)

No doubt you'll recognize some of the activities mentioned under 'citizenship'. They are the activities for 'imprinting' nationalism suggested in the CNE policy and definition.

You can see that the syllabus teaches about values and beliefs. It is a programme for **moral** education. And here again some people object to this, especially because a particular set of morals is being taught.

Teachers of YP

The government realised that the YP Programme would not succeed unless teachers were committed to its ideals. The following statement is made about the section on 'Use of the Road and Vehicle Care' but it could equally well apply to the whole programme:

Only competent, responsible teachers who are inspired with enthusiasm and earnestness, who are prepared to make a study of the above-mentioned problem and who will consequently be able to inspire pupils· and arouse their interest, should be used. Should this work, however, be entrusted to persons who are not interested or not aware of the extreme gravity of the matter, it is doomed to failure from the outset.

(TED Manual, 1972)

Not all white teachers support the YP Programme, but it has been very difficult for them to express their resistance. Unco-operative teachers have been discriminated against, and some teachers have even been blacklisted for attempting to organize against the Programme.

You now have some idea of how the YP
Programme is designed. In its aims, its content
and the way it is organized it is clearly worked
out to teach a set of values. And it is based on a
CNE worldview.

What about the other special programme –
Veld Schools?

Veld Schools

Veld Schools are another part of the white education system in the
Transvaal which are specifically set aside for physical and moral
teaching. As the name tells us, they are schools in the veld. Their
stated purpose is to bring urban children into a rural environment.

Dr J. Pasques, who has been an important thinker on Veld
Schools, has this to say:

> Urbanization is one of the most important revolutions of our time. Many
> factors arise from this which have a detrimental influence on the child's
> ability to become mentally and morally prepared for life. Various social
> studies have revealed that these detrimental factors can be eliminated to a
> large extent by allowing the child to make intimate contact with nature. It
> is, therefore, essential to provide accommodation for youth groups in re-
> mote places in nature still unspoiled. He *sees* the stars twinkle, he *smells*
> the scent of a bloom, he *feels* the wild fruit and he *hears* the wind whistling
> through the mountain peaks. By focusing his attention on the wonders of
> nature – the beauty of the spider's web, the symmetry of the flower, the
> wonder of the cosmos – the child's attention is centred on the wonders of
> creation.　　　　　　　　(*TED Educational News Flashes,* no. 61, 1981:28)

You'd think from Pasques's speech that girls
didn't go to veld schools, wouldn't you? But
that's not true! They do!

On one level, there is nothing wrong with
taking city children into the country.

But if we read more carefully about Veld
schools and look for the hidden curriculum, we
see another set of aims. And these aims should be
quite familiar by now.

Other aims of Veld Schools

In a recent study Buwalda set out the aims and objectives of a typical Veld School as follows:

1 To lead the pupil on the road to maturity and adulthood.
   N.B. The aim of this course is not simply to impart knowledge but to reinforce the norms, values and morals (customs) of our society.
2 To encourage the pupil to be a better South African.
3 To encourage pupils to become better Christians.
4 To provide an adventure.
5 To show that a threat to South African's existence and stability does exist, and what we can do about it.
6 To provide pupils with an opportunity to get to know and appreciate nature.
7 To prepare our young for emergencies which may take place.
8 To assess leadership qualities.
9 To impart knowledge.   (1979:1-4)

If you look at this list of nine aims, you can see that only one (aim no. 6) deals with nature.

The rest of the aims are promoting a particular worldview. For example, pupils should be taught to be 'Christians', and 'better South Africans'. They should be 'prepared' for emergencies. And, very importantly, they should accept the norms and values of the society (aim no. 1).

There is no doubt that the broad aim of Veld Schools is to teach a particular worldview.

The aim of Veld Schools is to impress on children the dangers which are facing them, their society and the 'South African way of life'. Children are taken away from their familiar urban environment and placed in an unfamiliar rural environment. They are given lectures on topics like discipline, respect and understanding, patriotism, race relations, communism and the Creation. They also do strenuous physical activities such as obstacle courses, compass work, overnight hikes, bush survival and shelter construction, and first aid.

Children are grouped into teams. Competition is encouraged, and throughout their stay children are rated for their 'leadership potential'. Reports are sent back to their schools and 'outstanding pupils' may then be encouraged to attend 'Leadership Camps'.

As with YP, there are physical activities and also lectures which directly teach about values. And then there is a whole hidden curriculum of values – which you should be able to pick out for yourselves.

Pupils attend Veld Schools twice in their school careers: once in Std 5 and once in Std 8. The aim is ultimately that all children at TED schools will spend about ten days at Veld School. Veld Schools are not optional: children have to attend when their turn comes.

There have been criticisms of Veld Schools, which the TED has denied. Here is an extract from the 1982 *Survey of Race Relations:*

Veld schools

The Transvaal Education Department (TED) came under attack this year for its veld schools.

A report was compiled at the end of 1981 by a group from the Johannesburg College of Education, who had visited the Schoemansdal veld school. According to the report, group discussions were held on such topics as: 'Must we rebuild schools burnt down by blacks?' and 'Insurgency: how would you gain the support of the non-white for your government?'

Mr Joel Mervis (PFP) said in the provincial council that although the teaching of party politics was forbidden in TED schools, 'the NP political theory is central to veld school teaching'.

Mr Peter Nixon, PFP provincial spokesperson on education, criticised the schools saying they were aimed at mobilising the youth for the 'total onslaught'. Mr Nixon said that 'the coupling of half-truths with sweeping emotional statements during lectures and talks at the Transvaal Education Department's veld schools, led to confusion and fear in the minds of children'.

In response to the criticisms, a TED spokesperson said that the teachers running veld schools did not want to indoctrinate children with National Party propaganda. He also said that the lectures were just one part of the programmes and that the TED was more interested in stimulating group discussion.   (1982:493)

Perhaps what this really shows is that you can't fully judge an education programme without looking at its broader ideological basis. You learn a lot by looking at the worldview that it's based on.

But let's pause at this point to see what our three thinkers – conservative, moderate and radical – would say about YP and Veld Schools.

Conservative

Children need to be taught morals and values. In the modern world moral standards are dropping. The youth of today have let go of the values and moral standards of the past. Long hair, rock music and bad manners are all indications of this. We need to guard against this decadence. We need to make every effort to preserve civilized standards.

And, of course, South Africa is in a particularly vulnerable position. The communist countries would love to see the end of our government and our way of life. So we need to be on guard and watchful all the time.

The Christian and National values outlined by the government are important, stable values. They are a good basis for building up a strong and upright youth. We should support these values. We should also support programmes in schools which are designed to teach these values and to make our youth morally upright.

Moderate

I agree that it's important to teach children about morals and values. It's very important for people to have moral standards.

The main thing is that people mustn't have particular morals and values forced on them. They must be able to make up their own minds about moral issues.

It's important that moral education helps people to make choices. YP and Veld Schools should show more than one point of view. As long as people are shown all sides of the picture, there's no problem. Then people can make up their own minds.

Moral education programmes should be balanced and unbiased. I would have no objection to YP and Veld Schools, as long as they tried to be balanced and to give different viewpoints.

Radical

Of course people should have moral standards. Certainly, morality is very important.

But we need to recognize that programmes which teach morals and values don't operate in isolation. We need to be aware of the specific social and political context that they operate in.

You can't look at YP and Veld Schools just by themselves. They are part of the apartheid education system, and they're designed to promote specific morals and values. They have a political purpose – to spread the particular worldview of the people in power. We can't view them simply as if they are neutral, open, education programmes. They just aren't.

Surely you don't believe that YP and Veld Schools could ever be neutral and unbiased? They're too political for that.

Moderate: You radical thinkers can't just turn morals into issues of power. You're too one-sided in your approach.

Radical: Perhaps. But maybe you're being too simplistic when you overlook issues of power.

These debates certainly get complicated! You said earlier that CNE is still at the basis of white schooling. Is that so?

Yes, it certainly is. In fact, the government stated this very clearly when it responded to the De Lange Report in 1981 and 1983. We can look at that now.

The government's response to De Lange

As you know, the government appointed the De Lange Commission to investigate educational provisions in South Africa. In its report the De Lange Commission made a number of recommendations. In 1983 the government issued a White Paper (an official statement) in response to the De Lange Report. It accepted some of the De Lange recommendations and rejected others. And it took the opportunity to restate CNE principles.

The following extract from the White Paper shows that the government remains firmly committed to CNE principles.

> ... the Government reaffirms that it stands by the principles of the Christian character and the broad national character of education as formulated in section 2 (1) (a) and (b) of the National Education Policy Act, 1967 (Act 39 of 1967), in regard to White education and as applied in practice or laid down in legislation in regard to the other population groups. Any changes or renewal in the provision of education will have to take these principles into account, with due regard to the right of self-determination which is recognised by Government policy for each population group.

175

Well, that concludes our discussion on the worldview of white education. Remember what we said earlier on: there may be a difference between the ideas we read about, and what actually goes on in practice in the schools. But there's no doubt that the CNE worldview influences the education system for whites.

So now we can return to the question we asked at the beginning of the chapter.

Do you think the white education system would be a good one for everybody?

References and further readings

Behr, A.L. (1978) *New Perspectives in South African Education*, Butterworths, Durban

Buwalda, R. (1979) Veld School Report (unpublished)

Education News Flashes (Series) Transvaal Education Department

Hexham, I. (1980) 'Afrikaner nationalism, 1902-14' in P. Warwick *The South African War: The Anglo-Boer War 1899–1902*, Longman, London

Kotzee, A.L. (1972) 'Why a programme of Youth Preparedness in our schools?' TED, Pretoria

Malherbe, E.G. (1977) *Education in South Africa, vol. 2*, Juta, Cape Town

Pasques, J. (1978) 'Die Filosofie van veldskole', TED Mimeo.

Pasques, J. (1981) 'The philosophy of Veld Schools' *Educational News Flashes* 6(1)

Randall, P. (1982) *Little England on the Veld: The English Private School System in South Africa*, Ravan, Johannesburg

Republic of South Africa (1983) White Paper on the Provision of Education in the Republic of South Africa, Pretoria

Rose, B. and Tunmer, R. (1975) *Documents in South African Education*, Ad. Donker, Johannesburg

SAIRR (1982) *Survey of Race Relations in South Africa*, SAIRR, Johannesburg

SPROCAS (1971) *Education beyond Apartheid*, Report of the SPROCAS Education Commission, Johannesburg

TED (1972) *Manuals for the Implementation of Youth Preparedness*, Pretoria

Chapter 7

Education work and certificates

YOU'D BETTER DO WELL AT SCHOOL OR YOU'LL NEVER GET A GOOD JOB!

We all know that there's a link between the schooling we've had and the work we do. But why do we work anyway? And are qualifications really necessary for jobs?

This chapter will be divided into two parts, to answer these two questions. In the first part, we'll look at the nature of work in our society and the link between education and work. In the second part, we'll look at the issue of certificates and qualifications.

Part One: Why do we work?

Harry Braverman, a famous theorist, has this to say about work:

> All forms of life sustain themselves on their natural environment. Plants absorb moisture, minerals and sunlight; animals feed on plantlife or prey on other animals. But to seize upon the material of nature ready-made is not work; work is an activity which alters these materials from their natural state to improve their usefulness. The bird, the beaver, the spider, the bee and the termite, in building nests, dams, webs, and hives, all may be said to work. Thus the human species shares with others the activity of acting upon nature that changes its forms to make them more suitable to its needs. (1974:45)

177

In other words, people work in order to survive. We do things that change the world around us, so that we can meet our needs for survival. Firstly, we have to produce food and clothes and shelter so that we can keep ourselves alive. But then we also have to make sure that we can continue to do this in the future. Farmers need to sow and harvest, and sow again. Factory owners need to make sure that machines can be fixed if they break down; they need to make sure that goods can be made and sold tomorrow, as well as today.

So, we work for two main reasons:

- to meet our immediate needs for survival
- to meet our needs for renewal.

Work is a central human activity. The way we work – the way we produce and renew our conditions – affects almost everything we do. It affects where we live and how we spend our days. It affects how we see ourselves, and it affects our relationships with other people. It also affects the material conditions under which we live.

The changing nature of work

At different times diferent societies have survived and renewed themselves by doing different sorts of work. For example, South Africa was once a land economy. People lived off the land. They produced what they needed – food, clothes and shelter – from the land. People worked together, and children learned the ways of the society from their parents and the people around them. Today South Africa is a capitalist country, based on wealth from industries and mines. The society provides schools for children to learn. The work we do and our way of life have changed enormously. In fact the basic system of production has changed so much that we can call it a revolution – the Industrial Revolution.

The Industrial Revolution

The Industrial Revolution began in Britain and Europe in the 1700s. Early capitalists made their money through trade – buying and selling goods around the world. As the amount of trade increased, so trading posts were set up in different parts of the world, and colonies were established; for example, Holland and Britain both colonized South Africa. As trade and profits increased, so capitalists looked for new ways to increase the production and sale of goods. And this process, as we'll see, was the basis of the Industrial Revolution.

Before the Industrial Revolution

Before the Industrial Revolution, most people in Britain and Europe worked at home or in small groups. People lived in small towns or in the countryside. Certainly, there was a division of tasks between people. Some people worked at farming; other people produced goods like clothing and material; other people provided services like health care. We can call this the *social division of labour*.

Skilled workers were organized into groups called craft guilds. For example, there was a blacksmiths' guild, a textile workers' guild, and so on. These guilds were organized in a hierarchy, with master craftsmen at the top, then journeymen, then apprentices. Through apprenticeships, guilds trained people for work. But at the same time they were able to close out 'unqualified' people from doing certain kinds of work.

People produced goods by hand or with very simple machines. They had a degree of control over how they produced the goods, and when they produced. Most people didn't have formal education for work. They learned their skills on-the-job, either in the craft guilds or in their small production units.

Changes due to the Industrial Revolution

With the growth of the Industrial Revolution the organization of work changed. As we've said, capitalists looked for new ways of increasing the production of goods. New, large, expensive machines were introduced into the production process. Small craftspeople could not compete. Factories were set up, which brought people together to work in groups, producing goods for the profit of capitalists. In return they were paid a wage. Industrial towns grew up around the factories as people moved from the countryside to look for work. Peoples' way of life changed dramatically as their work changed.

With the changing nature of production, people needed different skills. Instead of knowing how to produce things by hand, people had to learn how to operate the machines that produced these things. As time passed many workers lost their old skills and became machine-minders.

People also lost control over their work. In the factories, workers could not decide what would be produced, or how it

179

would be produced, or how long they would take. Owners and managers made these decisions.

This is not to say that workers were passive in these processes of change. Workers joined together in trade unions. They resisted unpopular measures, and they won for themselves better conditions, hours of work and rates of pay. They also won political rights. The right to education also formed part of their struggle. Alongside industrialization, schools for the children of workers were gradually set up. On the one hand, these schools protected children by removing them from the pool of wage labour. But on the other hand, they also taught attitudes and values which fitted in with the changing processes of capitalist work.

A new industrial revolution?

Work continues to change all the time. Today new technologies – computers and microchips - are bringing enormous changes in work. More and more jobs are being done by machines, and in some production processes, there are hardly any human workers left! Some people argue that we are at the start of a new industrial revolution – the computer revolution.

In Chapter Two we saw how economic activities in South Africa changed as time passed. But there is a basic principle which has remained the same since whites settled. And this is the principle of capitalism.

Capitalism

Countries like South Africa, America and Britain are organized along capitalist principles. Basically this means that individual people or groups of people own the mines, factories and farms. (We can call these the 'means of production'.) In capitalist countries the means of production are not owned by the state or by the people as a whole. They are owned by individuals or private groups.

As a result, a relatively small number of people own the wealth of the country. These people are the capitalist class. Most of the people earn their living by working for a wage. They work in the production process. They sell their labour power (their ability to work) to capitalists for money. These people are the working class.

The capitalist system is also called the free enterprise system or market system. Supporters of capitalism argue that individuals should be free to set up businesses (or 'enterprises'). They should then compete with each other on the 'open market'. Competition among capitalists will ensure that they provide quality goods and services at reasonable prices (so the argument goes). The laws of supply and demand will regulate production. Workers, then, will compete for jobs on the job market. According to capitalism, workers are free to sell their labour power on the open market and to look for jobs with better wages and conditions.

Opponents of capitalism disagree with this 'free enterprise' view. They argue that the system is basically unequal. They say that a few people get very rich by exploiting the labour of other people. Most people don't share the wealth of the country. They remain relatively poor. Opponents of capitalism argue that the 'free market' isn't as free and open and equal as capitalists say it is. And in South Africa there is no such thing as a free job market; whites and blacks don't compete equally for the same jobs. Nor do men and women.

Perhaps you've been wondering where education fits in with all of this. So let's make some general comments about education and capitalism.

Education under capitalism

Along with the growth of capitalism has come the growth of schooling. Before industrialization not many people went to school. It is only since industrialization that mass schooling has developed.

As we've seen in other chapters of this book, there is a link between schooling and social class. For example, in Chapter Two we saw how children of richer parents had better schooling opportunities than children of poorer parents. In Chapter Four we saw how the apartheid education system prepares many African children for lower class positions. We've seen that education is influenced by people's social class position, and it also helps to shape social classes.

Obviously, schools don't create the social classes of capitalism. Social classes are basically groups of people who own, or do not own, the means of production. Classes exist in relation to each other and in relation to the means of production. Whether you belong to one class or another is not basically decided by education. It is decided by whether or not you own the means of production and the kind of work you do.

However, there is no doubt that education does have a role in class formation. Education under capitalism creates and perpetuates inequalities. It is not coincidental that working class people usually have less education, and poorer quality education. Certainly, we can say that education prepares people for the jobs they do. They learn skills, attitudes and values which are relevant to their work situations. They learn their place in the social arrangements of capitalism. And all of this is part of social class.

Education is also part of the power struggles in society. Schools and universities may themselves be places where struggles take place. And education itself is constantly changing through these sorts of struggles.

But we'll talk more about education as we move through this chapter. We can now spend some time looking at the main features of work in capitalist societies, and how education fits in with this.

Work in capitalist societies

As we've said, work is a central human activity. People spend a large part of their lives working, in one way or another. And some of the basic divisions in capitalist societies come from the kind of work that people do.

In Chapter Five, we read about the Bowles and Gintis theory of the correspondence between school and work. Remember that they – and other theorists – argue that there are very close links between what goes on in schools and the world of work. Hidden curriculum theorists argue that schools prepare people for the work they do. The arguments on the hidden curriculum are relevant to this chapter also.

If we think about the way work is organized in capitalist societies like South Africa, we can see a number of features. We'll look at four features in some detail:

- Work is divided into different categories, with different status and education levels
- There is a division of labour
- There is a split between mental work and manual work
- The labour market is divided up or segmented.

We'll look at each of these in turn.

Different categories of work

In all societies there is a *social division of labour*. The work is divided up between people. For example, some people are farmers; others are builders; others are teachers. That way people are able to combine their work so that different needs in the society are met.

Some of this work needs special education or training. Sometimes people learn to do different jobs at school, college or university. And sometimes they learn on the job.

It's easy to think of all sorts of different work that people do in society. And, when we think about it, it's obvious that all jobs don't have the same social status – or the same rates of pay! In capitalist societies people are not equally rewarded for the work they do. In fact there are big differences in status and pay.

For example, *professional* workers like doctors and lawyers are highly esteemed in our society and highly paid. Many *service* workers, for example rubbish collectors, are not highly esteemed, nor highly paid. Housework is often not paid at all. Yet both lawyers and rubbish collectors perform necessary work for the society. In fact some people argue that the work of rubbish collectors is even more socially useful than that of lawyers!

Where does education fit in?

One of the differences between the lawyer and the rubbish collector is that the lawyer has particular educational qualifications. So education plays a role here in differentiating between workers. The same can be seen with skill divisions in factories. Usually there is a hierarchy of skilled, semi-skilled and unskilled workers. One of the differences between these three groups is the amount of training they have. Skilled workers like boilermakers, welders and electricians, have usually been trained as apprentices, on the job and at technical colleges. Semi-skilled workers like machine operators are not as fully trained. They usually learn most of their skills on the job. Unskilled workers have no basic training and no specific skills.

Almost all jobs require some kind of training – whether this lasts a week or six years. And, in capitalist societies, there is a connection between the amount of training that a job has, and its status and pay.

We'll talk more about the link between qualifications and jobs later in this chapter.

At this point, we're trying to get a picture of capitalist work, and how education fits in. So let's continue our discussion of work under capitalism.

Division of labour

One of the main features of capitalist work is that jobs are divided up into a number of smaller tasks, each done by different workers. This process is known as the *technical division of labour*. So, for example, in a car factory a single worker doesn't make a whole car. Single workers make only one part of the car, over and over again. Different workers make different parts, and in that way a whole car is made. With this division of labour a worker only needs to know how to do one part of the whole job.

If we look at the production process as a whole, we can see three features: jobs are divided up into separate parts; people become specialized workers; and these workers are grouped together into a single unit. This unit works together in the production process. In fact, we can see this unit as a collective worker – a living mechanism of manufacture.

It's argued that this collective process of production is more profitable. Repeating a specific task speeds up production. And this increases profits for capitalists.

Where does education fit in?

Education is also linked with the technical division of labour. The argument is that the smaller the divisions of tasks, the less education or training workers need. Certainly, people don't need much education to perform some of the repetitive tasks within the technical division of labour. Other tasks are more skilled.

The argument is that people can be given only the specific training that they need to do a particular job. They don't need to be taught a whole lot of extra things as well. This would cut down on expensive education.

The other side of this is that if people are well educated, they needn't spend their time doing jobs that less educated people could do (and be paid less to do!).

Either way, there's no doubt that education influences the sort of work that people do in the division of labour.

The technical division of labour and the social division of labour are two quite different things. With the **social** division of labour, people do only certain kinds of tasks. For example, they may be a salesperson or a teacher. But within their own task areas, they do all the parts that make up a whole job.

With the **technical** division of labour, jobs are divided up or fragmented. A worker does a small part of the job, over and over again. Each worker is part of the collective labourer.

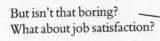

But isn't that boring?
What about job satisfaction?

Well, it obviously isn't very satisfying to do boring, repetitive work. Some writers use the word **alienation** to describe how this kind of work affects people. Alienated workers feel unfulfilled and cut off from themselves. They also feel cut off from the products they produce, which belong to someone else and not to them. Alienation is an important result of the way work is organized under capitalism.

But are there other ways of doing things? Would it be possible to organize production differently?

Certainly, it would be possible for production to be organized differently. People tend to think that the way things are presently organized is the only way. But history shows us that change is always possible. Change is part of life.

But let's move on with our discussion of the organization of work under capitalism. Let's look at the way mental work and manual work are separated.

Split between mental work and manual work

In the present-day organization of work we often see a split between mental work and manual work. Very often, tasks are divided up so that people either do the **thinking** part or the **doing** part. So, for example, someone may design a building, and someone else will build it. Factory workers who make motor cars usually don't design them. An engineer designs them, and workers then build them.

The architect and the bee

The split between mental work and manual work is quite important.

Think of this example. You can compare a bee with an architect. Both of them are builders. Architects design houses for people; bees build wax cells. So what makes human labour different from the work of the bees?

One difference is that bees can't think about what they do. They work by instinct. Human beings think about what they are doing. They can imagine all sorts of things before they actually make them; bees can't do this. So, basically, human labour has two parts: a thinking part and a doing part. We can also call these two parts **conception** and **execution.**

In the modern organization of work, conception and execution have become separated. People who execute tasks – for example, factory workers – have no opportunity to think about or conceive of these tasks.

If we use the example of the bee and the architect, we could argue that the separation of conception from execution is very important. If people can't think about what they're doing, their work is no different from the bees' work. They are deprived of the aspect of work which is special to human beings – that is, the thinking part.

186

Where does education fit in?

Education reinforces the mental/manual split. The more education people have, the more likely they are to do mental work. Education is often an essential rquirement for mental work. People with less education more often do manual work.

In schools manual or vocational subjects – like woodwork and typing – have lower status than academic subjects – like maths. Often, students who are not doing well at school are 'streamed' into vocational subjects. And if they do these subjects, it's harder for them to go to university and college. So they are more likely to be manual or semi-skilled workers.

The problem doesn't necessarily lie with typing or woodwork as such. Rather, the problem lies with the status they are given in society, and the way they fit in with the mental/manual split.

We'll talk more about vocational education in the next chapter.

Let's now look at our fourth feature of capitalist work: labour markets.

Segmented labour market

The labour market is a central feature of capitalist society. In theory, wage labourers are free to sell their labour power to any employer and to get the best wages and conditions they can. Labour power is bought and sold like anything else on a market. That's why we talk about the labour **market.**

In practice, however, the labour market is not as free and open and equal as the theory claims. In practice workers don't compete equally for the same jobs. We can say that the labour market is **segmented** or divided up. Some jobs are done mainly by women and others by men. In South Africa some jobs are done mainly by blacks and others by whites. The contract labour system, labour bureaux and pass laws all operate to restrict the freedom of black workers. There have been laws to prevent black people from doing certain jobs.

Basically we can see two labour markets in operation. They are often called the primary labour market and the secondary labour market. Jobs in the primary, or main labour market have certain advantages which jobs in the secondary labour market don't have. The following table compares the two labour markets.

187

Primary labour market	Secondary labour market
• Jobs are well paid.	• Jobs are less well paid.
• Jobs have high status.	• Jobs have lower status.
• People tend to stay in the jobs for a long time. Jobs are stable.	• People change jobs quite often. Jobs are less stable.
• There are extra benefits, like pensions and bonuses.	• There are fewer, or no extra benefits.
• There are possibilities for promotion and change within the job.	• There are few possibilities for promotion and change within the job.

Where does education fit in?

Obviously, education plays a part in preparing people for the labour market. The more education people have the more likely they are to get jobs in the primary labour market. If they have less education they more often get jobs in the secondary labour market. So if people don't have equal chances in education they are not likely to have equal chances in the labour market either.

In South Africa there are also specific examples of education being used to exclude people from jobs. For example, before the Wiehahn Commission, the Apprenticeship Act of 1922 prevented blacks from training as apprentices. Without apprenticeship training they couldn't work as tradespeople. Another example is that in the past, black miners have not been allowed to be issued with blasting certificates. This means in effect that they could not work officially as blasters. The following example of the Ford Motor Company shows how education has been used to block some workers, but not others.

Many of the workers also feel that they are not eligible for promotion to their level of worth as educational barriers operate against them. Promotion from grade 7 to 8 becomes extremely difficult for them as many do not possess a standard 8 certificate, a necessary qualification for mobility above the seventh grade. According to shop stewards, these educational barriers do not operate in respect of white workers. Interviews with white workers and shop stewards revealed that 45 percent of the sample did not possess a standard 8 certificate even though all were employed above the eighth grade. The reasons given by Ford officials for the more rapid progress of white workers into the higher grades was their exposure to a more sophisticated educational system and their longer experience of work in industry.   (*SA Labour Bulletin* 6 (2 and 3) 1980:25)

So far, we've looked at work under capitalism and some of the ways that education fits in with capitalist work.

Obviously, education is only one of the factors which influence the kind of work that people do. But it does have its part.

That ends our discussion of part one of this chapter: the link between education and work. We can now turn to part two: certificates and qualifications.

Part Two: Certificates and qualifications

It's easy to see that certificates are tied to jobs. But how does the link actually work? Obviously certificates alone don't guarantee jobs – as some of the statements above show. But it's also true that in our society we can't do certain jobs if we don't have qualifications. It's true that some jobs do need training – imagine an untrained bridge-builder! But does training necessarily imply certificates? What function do certificates and qualifications play in our society?

The meaning of 'certificates' and 'qualifications'

Here's what the *Concise Oxford Dictionary* says:

> **certificate** n. & v.t. **1.**n. document formally attesting a fact, esp. birth, marriage, death, medical condition, *abilities, fulfilment of requirements,* etc.;
> **qualification** n.**2.** quality or accomplishment fitting person or thing (for post, etc.); condition that must be fulfilled before right can be acquired or office held; document attesting such fulfilment.

What else do we know about certificates and qualifications?

- Certificates and qualifications usually indicate that people have undergone training so that they are able to do certain jobs – and they have some form of document to prove this.

- Usually certificates are indications of a fairly general training or ability. For example, a secondary teaching certificate enables people to teach in any secondary school – not just one particular school. An electrician's ticket indicates a general ability in the field of electrical work.

- But equally, an electrician's ticket doesn't qualify such a person to do plumbing. Certificates usually indicate general competence in a specific area.

- Certificates are usually issued by special institutions, like schools, universities and technikons. This gives the certificates authority. You could easily sit at home and draw up a certificate for your friend, but it would probably have no meaning at all for her or his employer. The more status the institution has the more status its certificates have. So if South African universities are not of equal quality it follows that their certificates don't have equal status.

Why have certificates?

We all know that people need certificates to do certain jobs. But why is this? There has been a lot of debate around the issue of certificates and qualifications. This debate raises interesting questions about how certificates really operate, and what they actually do in our society. One group of debaters argues that certificates are valuable and necessary. Another group argues that certificates aren't really helpful.

Basically, there are three questions that these people debate:

1 Are certificates necessary for certain jobs?

2 Are qualified people better workers?

3 Do qualified people deserve rewards like higher status and higher salary?

For each of these questions, we can look at the two opposing arguments.

1 Are certificates necessary for certain jobs?

Supporters of certificates argue as follows:

> In modern society, many of the jobs which people do are very complicated and difficult. Training is essential for these jobs, and having certificates is one way of making sure that people have the right training. Can you imagine an untrained accountant? How could a person with no training possibly fix a computer? Or remove someone's appendix? Or design a bridge? Obviously qualifications are essential.

Opponents of certificates reply as follows:

> Certainly there are jobs that need specific training. No one could deny that there are highly trained, specialist workers, like doctors, lawyers, economists, engineers, etc. But not all work needs such high training. We need to look more carefully at the qualifications people have, and the work that they actually do.

- Firstly, we can't assume that people actually use the knowledge that they learn at schools, colleges and universities. It is certainly true that a mechanic gains knowledge about how machines work, and this knowledge is necessary for the job. But what about more general education? Does a clerk actually use her knowledge of matric history – even though she needs to have a matric to get her job? People learn a lot of things which they don't actually use for their jobs.

191

- Secondly, people learn a lot on-the-job. Sometimes this on-the-job learning may be even more important than what they learn at special institutions like schools. Also, the information that people learn while they're studying often becomes out of date. In areas like engineering, medicine and computing, there are always new advances. These people would soon be out of date if they did not upgrade themselves, either on-the-job or by getting more qualifications. We shouldn't undervalue on-the-job education.

- Thirdly, a lot depends on the society you live in, and also the time period. For example, at one time a junior certificate was enough 'training' for a clerical position. Now you need a matric – and sometimes even a degree. This doesn't mean that the job itself has changed. The job is usually still the same – but the qualification requirements have shifted. We call this 'the spiral of certification'. The certificates that employers ask for go up and up like a spiral – but the actual job doesn't change.

You can see that the debate raises questions about the real reasons why we have certificates. The debate gives us food for thought.
Let's now look at the second question.

2 Are qualified people better workers?

Supporters of certificates argue as follows:

Qualified people are definitely more productive. Education provides people with knowledge and skills. It also teaches people to think and to reason. Educated people know more. They have a better understanding of their work. They are able to perform better on the job and to do more complex work. There's no doubt that educated people are more productive.

Opponents of certificates reply as follows:

- Firstly, just because people have certificates, this doesn't mean that they are really educated. We must be careful not to confuse 'education' with 'schooling'. Just because people have been to school or university doesn't mean that they've learned valuable knowledge or the ability to think critically. Some educationists argue that formal schools *stifle* critical thinking and reasoning powers! And we can all think of people in school who passed without knowing very much. Simply passing exams is no indication of being educated. So we can't assume that people with qualifications know more or have a better understanding of their work.

- Secondly, we can't assume that qualified people are more productive. A lot of the jobs that people do are boring, repetitive and unstimulating. It may be the case that better educated people are dissatisfied with these jobs, and actually perform less well! In fact we could argue that people with *less* education may actually be *more* productive in certain jobs.

  One American writer, Ivar Berg, argues that better educated workers may sometimes be less productive. In his study he found that, quite often, better educated people were more critical of their work situation and less satisfied with their jobs. They were more likely to stay away from work or change jobs more often than less educated workers. So we shouldn't be too quick to assume that people with certificates make better workers.

What do you, as reader, think of these arguments?

Let's now go on to the third question.

3 Do qualified people deserve rewards like higher status and higher salary?

Supporters of certificates argue as follows:

People with qualifications have sacrificed years of their lives to study. Often their study has cost them money. These people are usually intelligent, and they have worked hard. Therefore they deserve rewards. They deserve jobs with high status and high salaries.

193

Opponents of certificates reply as follows:

> We shouldn't see education as a sacrifice; rather, it is a privilege. People who are able to study are fortunate. Even when they have to pay fees to study their training costs more than they actually pay; the society pays part of the costs, through taxes. How can we say that these people deserve even more rewards?
>
> Often people's life and work experience is more valuable and more relevant than formal qualifications. We don't need certificates to be valuable members of society.
>
> In South Africa many people who have the ability don't have the opportunity to study for certificates. People who are privileged enough to go to universities and colleges aren't necessarily the most intelligent or most able people in the community. So we must avoid the trap of assuming that qualifications measure ability.

The opponents of certificates certainly have a lot to say!

Whichever arguments you support, you can see that we shouldn't be too quick to assume that certificates make better workers!

But, in either case, the truth is that in our society there is a link between certificates and jobs.

How does this link actually operate?

Certificates sort people out for jobs

Both supporters and opponents of certificates agree that in our society certificates are a way of sorting people out for jobs. They are a way of 'screening' people – of deciding who is eligible to apply for, and do, certain jobs.

Sometimes certificates are a quick way of showing employers that people have studied appropriate things for the job; for example, a first aid certificate for a first aid job. Sometimes it's more general than that. Employers may see certificates as indicators of general ability; for example, a matric certificate for a clerical job. And sometimes certificates may just indicate that people come from a privileged background – and this may be what employers want.

So it's not that people with certificates are necessarily more intelligent or better workers. Rather, it's that certificates are a way of making it easier for employers to choose workers. The general rule is: people with less education get lower level jobs; people with more education get higher level jobs. Of course there are exceptions to this, but it is a general trend.

But there's also another issue here.
In South Africa, certificates are a *political* issue as well.

Political issues

- In South Africa, the different population registration groups go to different schools, colleges and universities. They get different certificates. As we've seen, there is no doubt that the different education systems are not equal. This raises questions about whether the certificates are of equal value. And this is a political issue – it involves questions of power and questions of who has the right to choose.

- In South Africa, the different population registration groups don't have equal amounts of schooling either. As we say in Chapter Four, the drop-out rate for black children is much higher than the rate for white children. Far more whites than blacks go to universities. Far more men than women go to universities. Some black schools don't offer the necessary subjects for university entrance. In practice people don't have equal access to qualifications. The privilege of qualifications isn't equally distributed among all groups of people. And again, this is a political issue.

- In some cases job reservation has prevented black people from doing certain jobs, even though they may have the necessary qualifications. White people with lesser qualifications are allowed to do these jobs. Clearly this is a political issue too.

195

- There have been cases where the government has refused to recognize certificates. For example, after the Bantu Education Act of 1953, Mariannhill Teachers College continued to train black teachers. But the Bantu Education Department refused to recognize their qualifications. This was for political reasons, not for educational reasons.

- In South Africa there is a long tradition of boycotts, especially among black university students. Students have chosen to boycott their exams – and lose their chances of getting certificates – as a protest against the apartheid system. Again, this means that the issue of certificates is political.

Let's see how these issues are viewed from our three familiar standpoints: conservative, moderate and radical.

Conservative

Education and politics shouldn't mix. People who boycott are looking for trouble.

You say that very few blacks have a chance to get colleges and universities and that very few have certificates. That may be true. But if you consider the past situation, things are now certainly better than they were. More blacks are going to universities than before, and they are getting qualified. And there will be openings for these people in their own areas.

Just because people have certificates doesn't mean that they should come into the white society. They should serve their own societies.

And people who boycott deserve what they get.

Moderate

There certainly are problems with the way politics has entered education. There is no justice in the situation where race and gender influence people's educational chances, and their chances of becoming qualified.

We need to do all we can to give equal educational opportunities. People should have equal chances to get degrees and diplomas.

The economy needs trained people. It needs a well-trained and well-qualified workforce. We should be spending more money training people for jobs.

Allowing black people to become better qualified would be a good move away from the racism of apartheid. It would also be beneficial to the country as a whole.

If we had this sort of policy people wouldn't need to boycott.

Radical

Education and politics are linked – there's no getting away from that.

Until we have a more equal and more just political system there will continue to be inequalities and injustices in education.

Certificates are just one example of these inequalities and injustices. And boycotts are one example of how people may choose to respond.

As long as certificates are linked with privilege they will contribute to social inequality. Simply giving more certificates to more people won't solve anything. We need to think of ways of reducing inequality, not increasing it.

We need to recognize the different ways in which education maintains the inequalities of the wider society. We need to do some fundamental rethinking about all of these issues – education, certificates, jobs and general inequality.

One thing is certain. Doing away with certificates would mean a major change in our society.

What do you, as reader, think about these issues? Student opinion certainly varies, as the interviews below indicate.

"I want to be a teacher.

It's important that I get my qualifications so that I have some foothold to work from. I'm totally opposed to the government and the apartheid system. I know my certificate is just a piece of paper. But if I don't co-operate with the system, and get that paper, I'll have no way of doing the work I want to do."

197

"I boycotted Fort Hare exams, and that cost me my degree. This certainly affects my job chances. In fact some people will never hire me because of my record. I wanted to do science. Now I do clerical work.

But, for me, it's political. If you collaborate with the system, you just help to keep it going. There is just so much provocation you can take, then you have to act. If you want change, you can't put self-interest first."

"I wrote my university exams, even though others of my classmates decided to boycott. I believe that individuals pay the price if they boycott. They're the ones who suffer. The government doesn't care – it doesn't suffer.

Unless there's solidarity with all students, it seems there's no point in boycotting. Even then, you can all just lose out. Boycotting is no answer."

Dilemmas

What do *you* think about the issue of certification? Here's a specific problem to think about:

In June 1976, the Soweto Students representative Council (SSRC) decided to boycott Bantu Education matric exams. Some students decided to defy the boycott and to write anyway. In certain centres boycotting students then ripped up the papers which the other students had written.

What would you have done if you were a Soweto student at that time?

Another view

To end this chapter, here are some interesting comments by Julius Nyerere, President of Tanzania, who has tried to bring about changes in education in his country.

198

There are professional men who say, 'My market value is higher than the salary I am receiving in Tanzania.' But no human being has a market value – except a slave. There are educated people in positions of leadership in government, in parastatals, and still seeking jobs, who say, 'I am an educated person but I am not being treated according to my qualifications – I must have a better house, or a better salary, or a better status, than some other man.' But the value of a human being cannot depend on his salary, his house or his car; nor on the uniform of his chauffeur.

When such things are said, the individuals saying them believe that they are arguing for their 'rights', as educated people. They believe that they are asserting the value of their education – and of themselves.

In reality they are doing the opposite. For in effect they are saying, 'This education I have been given has turned me into a marketable commodity, like cotton or sisal or coffee.' And they are showing that instead of liberating their humanity by giving it a greater chance to express itself, the education they have received has degraded their humanity. For they are arguing that as superior commodities they must be exchanged with commodities of equal value in an open market. They are not claiming – or not usually claiming – that they are superior human beings, only that they are superior commodities. Thus their education has converted them into objects – into repositories of knowledge like rather special computers. It is as objects, or commodities, that they have been taught to regard themselves and others.

With such an attitude a person will inevitably spend his life sucking from the community to the maximum of which is capable, and contributing the minimum he is able to contribute and live as he desires to live. He sucks from the local community as he is fed, clothed, housed and trained. He sucks from the world community when he moves like a parcel of cotton to where the price is highest for his acquired skill.

Such a person is not a liberated human being. He is a marketable commodity.

We condemn such a person, or feel sorry for him as one of society's failures. But it would be much more appropriate to condemn the system which produces such people, and then to change that system.   (1974:49)

Of course, Nyerere has a particular social aim, and a particular view of the purposes of education.

In this chapter we've looked generally at issues of education, work and certificates. In the next chapter we'll look at education in the workplace in South Africa.

References and further readings

Berg, I. (1973) *Education and Jobs: The Great Training Robbery,* Penguin, Harmondsworth

Blaug, M. (1970) *Economics of Education,* Penguin, Harmondsworth

Braverman, H. (1974) *Labour and Monopoly Capital: The Degradation of Work in the Twentieth Century,* Monthly Review Press, New York

Callinicos, L. (1981) *Gold and Workers: A People's History of South Africa, vol. 1,* Ravan, Johannesburg

Dore, R.P. (1976) 'Human capital theory, the diversity of societies and problem of quality in education' *Higher Education* 5

Marais, A. (1984) 'Education, growth and income inequality' *Africa Insight* 14(3)

Nattrass, J. (1981) *The South African Economy: Its Growth and Change,* OUP, Cape Town

Nyerere, J.K. (1974) 'Education and liberation' *Development Dialogue* 2, 46–52

SALB (1980) Vol. 6 nos. 2 and 3

SALB (1983) *Briefings*

Chapter 8

Education on the job

So far in this book, we've looked mainly at formal education which happens in schools.

In this chapter we're going to take a different focus. We're going to look at an important new trend in education: education at the workplace.

On the job training

Since the early 1980s there has been an important development in education in South Africa. This is the growth of on-the-job training. Many privately owned companies and businesses have been running courses and training programmes of all sorts, offering educational opportunities to employees. There are programmes for managers and supervisors to help them to extend their educational levels and open up their careers. There are also courses for artisans, apprentices and operators to teach skills needed for the job. Some companies are even providing literacy courses and basic education for their workers. Huge numbers of people are involved: in 1983, more than one million people were being trained on the job. The companies get money back from the government to cover some of their expenses, but even so, private enterprise has been spending a lot of money on education.

Many people have not really questioned why so much on-the-job training is happening or whether or not it's valuable. For many people training programmes offer an opportunity to get education which they wouldn't otherwise have. Most people think that education is a good thing, and they don't ask too many questions about it. But, as we've seen in earlier chapters, education is a complex issue, and there can be a lot of disagreement about it. Education involves more than simply know-how. There are all sorts of political issues too. And there's also the hidden curriculum to think about. Education programmes teach all sorts of hidden attitudes and values, which we need to be aware of and to question. So we need to think carefully about this new direction of private enterprise, on-the-job training.

We could ask a number of questions:

- Why is there a growth of on-the-job education?

- Why is private enterprise prepared to spend money on education?

- What is the hidden curriculum of private enterprise education?

- Are there alternative ways of linking education and work? What about trade union education?

Let's start by asking why there has been a growth of on-the-job training, and see what answers we come up with.

Let's look first at the answers which private enterprise usually gives, and then see what critics say in reply.

Business person

The reason for on-the-job training is obvious. There's a shortage of skilled workers. That's why training is happening. You only have to look at newspaper headlines and you'll see that the country is short of suitably qualified people.

There are not enough skilled white workers to meet the needs of the economy. So private enterprise must provide training for white workers, and also upgrade black workers. But then, we meet up with the problems of Bantu Education. Many black workers have had poor schooling or no schooling at all. The government is either unwilling or unable to provide the necessary education. So the task has fallen onto the shoulders of private enterprise.

We have to put money into training so that we can get the workers that we need for economic growth.

Critic

No doubt there is some truth in these arguments. It's true that private enterprise *is* training workers to meet its needs. But there are also problems with this argument.

Firstly, there's all this talk about shortages of skilled workers. But at the same time people can't get jobs. There's a lot of unemployment, and it seems to be increasing. Why are there shortages of workers and unemployment at the same

202

time? It seems that we need to look more closely to see what is actually going on in the economy and at the workplace.

Secondly, the business person's argument makes it look as though private enterprise is being generous, and taking over the government's task of providing education. But again, we have to look more closely at what's actually happening. In the last few years, there's been a lot of worker militancy. Workers have been organizing into trade unions and making a lot more demands. Has this not influenced capitalists to provide education? Perhaps they are trying to create better employees?

The arguments of the business person and the critic give us three possible reasons for the increase of on-the-job training:
1 shortages of skilled workers
2 changes at the workplace
3 worker militancy.
Let's look at each of these in turn.

Shortages of skilled workers

This is the usual reason which is given for the growth of on-the-job training programmes. Business people have complained loudly about shortages of suitably qualified employees. Newspapers and government statements have echoed these complaints.

These people claim that there are shortages of qualified workers of all sorts and at all levels. There are shortages of professional people, like doctors and engineers; there are shortages of trained office personnel, from managers down to clerks; and there are shortages of technically trained people for the factory production process. But most importantly, there are shortages of artisans, technicians and engineers. Some of these are key people in the production process, and they need to be trained in greater numbers if the economy is to grow.

There is certainly some truth in the arguments about shortages of skilled workers, and no doubt this is one reason why private enterprise is spending money on training. But, as our critic pointed out, this argument doesn't tell us the whole story.

Some researchers have looked at figures of job vacancies, and they argue that there are *not* great shortages. According to these researchers, the shortages have been exaggerated. Charles Meth, for example, argues that the shortages are not so great as to plunge the country into crisis. In some cases, the shortages are very specific: for example, there certainly are shortages of engineers and nurses. But we cannot conclude from this that there are *general* shortages.

And then there is the problem of unemployment. Black unemployment has risen sharply over the years. According to the South African Institute of Race Relations, unemployment figures are:

11,8% in 1970
21,1% in 1981
24,0% in 1982

Many workers have been retrenched, and black school leavers are finding it difficult to get jobs.

It's all very easy to say that the unemployed people don't have enough education to get jobs. But again, this doesn't seem to be the case. A study done by SALDRU on African unemployment in 1977 showed that more than half of the unemployed African males had at least 7 – 9 years of schooling (Loots 1978:4).

All of this means that we need to look more carefully at the arguments about skills shortages. Certainly, there are shortages, but there are also other processes that we need to look at.

Let's turn to our second point, and look at some of the changes that have been happening at the workplace in recent years.

Changes at the workplace

In recent years there have been important changes in the economy and also changes at the workplace. During the 1960s there was an economic boom. This was a period of expansion for capitalism. But the 1970s saw an economic downturn. And now in the 1980s there has been a recession. Capitalists are facing difficulties in maintaining their rates of profit. Issues of productivity have become even more important for capitalists today than before.

As we say in Chapter Seven, the division of labour and job fragmentation have long been part of the capitalist labour process. But this has been increased by the greater use of new technology in the production process. As part of a worldwide trend, new machines are being introduced into production. These machines are changing the way work is done, and they are also changing relationships at the workplace.

In South Africa there are important changes happening in the racial division of labour. Before the new technology, there was a hierarchy of skilled, semi-skilled and unskilled workers. Skilled work was usually done by whites; unskilled work by blacks. The new technology has meant that machines have taken over a lot of skilled work. These workers are increasingly losing their skills and becoming des-killed. Many white workers in this position are being upgraded into technical or supervisory jobs. Machines are being operated by semi-skilled operators – mostly blacks. And as part of the same process, many unskilled workers have lost their jobs and become redundant.

The implications of these changes for skills training are obvious. There may well be a need for training at many levels, since people's jobs are changing. People may well need technical and supervisory training, and also operator training.

These changes in the production process give us an explanation of the contradiction: on the one hand there are skills shortages, and on the other hand there is unemployment.

But besides changes in the production process, there have also been changes in worker consciousness.

Worker militancy and education

Since the 1970s there has been increasing worker militancy. Trade unions have grown in size and effectiveness. They have negotiated for better wages and conditions and there have been waves of strikes and stoppages. Worker organizations have put pressure on capitalists. This labour pressure, combined with the recession, has threatened capitalism's concern with profits.

We could argue that all of this has meant a greater need for private enterprise to put effort into maintaining a stable, efficient, motivated workforce. One of the ways of doing this is to encourage the growth of a black middle class. And another way is to invest in training programmes, which help to build up the new middle class and to make the workforce more stable. It may appear that people are being trained simply because there are skills shortages, when in fact they are also being trained to make sure that they have appropriate work attitudes. Training programmes may actually be a form of work discipline.

When we look at education we need to remember that it plays an important part in class formation. It teaches people skills and know-how for different kinds of work. It also instils attitudes and values. But we shouldn't see this process as being too simple and automatic. We shouldn't forget that education itself is part of broader struggles. We can't simply look at changes in the economy or the needs of capitalism, and assume that education will automatically respond. Education doesn't only reflect what capitalism wants. It also reflects the struggles of worker and student movements.

When we look at the three sets of reasons for the growth of on-the-job training, I can see that the reasons aren't as straightforward as I once thought.

But what about the training that's going on at the workplace? Why is private enterprise prepared to spend its money on training programmes?

Why training?

Both the government and private enterprise have been providing more opportunties for blacks to get technical and vocational training. Technical courses and technical subjects are being introduced into schools. In 1980 Jabulani High School was built in Soweto. This was South Africa's first urban technical high school for blacks. There is now a National Technical Certificate alongside the ordinary matric certificate. Technical courses at schools provide training for semi-skilled and operator level jobs.

At a higher level there are also technikons for blacks. By 1981 there were four, and there are also specific provisions for black students to attend white colleges. Here, courses are training higher-level technicians and also middle management.

But even more important than these government provisions is the amount of private sector training which is going on within industries. As we've said, this is going on at all levels of work. It is estimated that there are over one million people being trained, or more than 15% of the workforce. This is a lot of training. Training courses are being paid for by private enterprise itself, though in most cases there are tax rebates from the government. Recent estimates are that the tax rebates for 1982 were worth R95 million. The government, however, does not give rebates for all training. For example, there are no rebates for courses in basic literacy and numeracy, unless this relates directly to specific skills. And there are no rebates in the mining industry. But even where the state isn't giving pay-backs, a lot of training is going on. This training is costing money.

The questions we come back to are:
– Why is private enterprise prepared to pay to train workers?
– And what sort of education are they giving?
Let's go back to our two earlier debaters, and see what they say.

Business person

As I've said already, businesses are prepared to train workers because we need a qualified workforce. Obviously, it would be better if the government paid. But as it is, the government is either unwilling or unable to pay. Either way, it falls on us to pay.

The point is, the education system doesn't provide adequately trained workers. Bantu Education, in particular, doesn't give people an adequate background for our needs. That's the main reason why we train.

Our training programmes also give opportunities for our employees to improve themselves. It's up to them to make the most of the training opportunities we offer. If they do well, they can be promoted to more interesting jobs with higher status and higher rates of pay.

We also spend money upgrading schools. For example, we put money into the Adopt-A-School Programme and other upgrading programmes. We have a duty to the future of this country. One way of providing for the future is to give better education for all people.

Critic

We all agree that there may be shortages of qualified workers, especially in certain jobs. And changes in the production process have also meant the need for certain training. Also, we certainly agree that Bantu Education is inadequate.

But I think we need to look at what is taught in the training programmes. We need especially to look at the hidden curriculum of training programmes – at the attitudes and values which they teach. I don't think capitalists are being as generous as they claim!

If we look at management and supervisor level work, the shortages which people talk about aren't always shortages of technical skills. People often have the right qualifications. But they may not know how to *behave* like managers and supervisors.

Let's think for a moment about the position of managers.

In capitalist production, there are definite relationships at the workplace. Managers are there to control production on behalf of owners. So they need to be able to manage workers, to keep running costs down to a minimum and to keep productivity at a maximum. The underlying motive is to make as much profit as possible.

I would argue that the main aim of management training courses is to teach about human relations, how to control people and how to increase productivity. These are the *social* skills of management, rather than simply technical skills. Perhaps it is that there is a greater need for these skills, to make labour more productive in changing economic times, when there is also an increasing challenge from trade unions.

Looking at operator training, I would argue that these training courses are more to do with encouraging 'the right attitudes' in workers than about learning new skills.

So, on-the-job training isn't just a matter of capitalists being generous with their money. Capitalists are giving the sort of education that suits their own interests.

These arguments are quite complicated. Is there any evidence to support what the critic says? Is a lot of the training promoting the values of capitalism?

To answer your questions, let's look in more detail at what goes on in some of the training programmes. We'll start by looking at management and supervision training, and then we'll look at the training of operators.

Management and supervisor training

The National Manpower Commission Report of 1980 had this to say:

208

> "The high level manpower of the country should not only have enough qualifications and knowledge, but should combine these with certain important personality traits, such as a sense of responsibility, enthusiasm, initiative, tenacity, and especially boldness." (1980:2,4)

There can be no doubt that managers need more than qualifications if they are going to support the interests of capitalism. They also need to have capitalist attitudes and values; for example, they need to believe that it is a good thing to work hard for maximum profits. And, indeed, some of the training programmes are openly geared towards teaching trainee-managers about productivity in the free enterprise system. One of the most popular training programmes is the *6M Simulation Training Course*. (The 6 Ms are men, money, machines, materials, management and markets.) According to one writer, 'it uses models and artificial money to simulate in a concrete way the establishment and operation of a business in a free enterprise system.' (De Lange Commission, Technical and Vocational Subcommittee, 1981:14) These people don't hide the fact that they're promoting capitalist values among trainees.

Many businesses recognize the difficulties that black supervisors face, and they are running programmes to help them to deal with interpersonal relationships. One motor company, for example, runs a six-month training programme for supervisors. As part of the course supervisors are taught things like 'how to improve employee performance', 'how to improve work habits' and 'how to take effective disciplinary action.' These people are being trained in the skills of controlling workers.

Industrial relations is another common subject in training programmes. This is hardly surprising in the light of trade union activity. In fact black managers and supervisors are often specifically trained so that they can be used to control black workers. Here's what a representative of Timber Manpower Services had to say:

> "What we need is the appointment of educated and experienced blacks in management positions. They should be in a position to communicate with black workers – not only to convey the policy of management to them, but also to convey the attitudes, opinions and feelings of black workers to management." (Proctor-Sims 1981:196)

This quotation shows clearly that the aim of management training involves more than teaching technical skills.

These examples give a clear picture of the hidden curriculum of management training. Black managers and supervisors are certainly being given broader opportunities. But at the same time many of them are being promoted specifically as a means of increasing the productivity of black workers, and controlling them. And it's no secret that they are being trained in the spirit and values of capitalism.

Operator training

Here again there's evidence that capitalist values are promoted, as well as skills. At this level of work qualities like steadiness, punctuality and diligence are applicable. Research has shown that when training components are built into the job this is likely to encourage such work values. Operator training courses may teach specific skills such as welding, fitting and machining, and electrical work. But they seldom teach any wider understanding of the work that's being done, where this fits into the industry, or where the industry fits in with the wider society. These are all dimensions of 'education' as opposed to simply 'training'.

Again, this education is better than nothing. But here we need to ask whether it's really enough. Is it a substitute for a general education in a good school?

Also, if education is happening on-the-job, what about people who don't have those sorts of jobs? This education isn't available to them. And what about women? The chances are that they have fewer opportunities for this education.

Let's go back to sum up on our question: Is there evidence to support the arguments that a lot of training is supporting the spirit and values of capitalism?

The benefits of training to capitalism

What emerges from this is that we *can* support the claims that a lot of training is promoting the spirit and values of capitalism. Some important aims are certainly to increase the productivity of labour, to train managers in free enterprise values and practices, to meet the needs for stable workers and to encourage general acceptance of work discipline.

But there's also another hidden message. When it is private enterprise which is supplying education there's a positive spin-off for capitalism. Capitalism is seen as a provider of good things: it has a chance to show its good face. There are promises of mobility and greater opportunity for workers. At all levels it seems that workers can get the training they need to improve themselves and do better. The underlying promise is: you can make it if you try hard enough. And, certainly, a few people do make it. They are promoted to higher positions, with better benefits. And this also suits capitalists whose interests are served if workers support capitalist values. But for most people mobility doesn't happen. What mobility there is happens mainly for artisans; so far progress of blacks to management has been very slow. In fact very often the training which is given to people is so narrow that they can't even use it to look for a better job somewhere else.

What about the workers?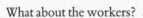

Dilemmas

We've said all along that education isn't neutral. And this applies to education at the workplace as well. Training programmes which are run by private enterprise have a hidden curriculum of capitalist attitudes and values. The question is: Can workers take the benefits of this education, without taking on the hidden curriculum, if they don't want it?

Often the training programmes seem to be offering benefits and advancements. Workers may be given educational opportunities which they wouldn't otherwise have. They may be increasing their knowledge, and learning new ideas and new techniques. But they are learning all of this within the context of capitalist values. Can they avoid these values if they want to?

211

 What follows are two interviews with people who were undergoing training programmes in 1984. These interviews should highlight the issues we've raised so far.

Interviews

George and Bongi work for the same company in Johannesburg. Both of them are attending training courses. George is a trainee production manager, doing a three-year diploma course run by a management institute. His company offered to send him on the course; it gives him paid study time and also pays the cost of his course. George is now in his third year part-time and plans to go on to study for a Master's Degree in Business Administration.

Bongi is a supervisor who has been attending a series of in-house training programmes. His courses are shorter; usually, his courses last three hours a day for one week. He has just completed his second course on safety measures in the factory.

We'll start with George's interview, and then give Bongi's.

Interviewer: Why do you think the company is prepared to pay so much money for your training?

George: The main reason is to get a skilled person to do the job. In the past they could employ fully qualified people for the job. But with economic expansion they couldn't get qualified people. They thought it better to train from within. They usually say that a person who is from within is fully acquainted with the atmosphere. To employ an outsider costs them more. They are lazy to pay more to a qualified outsider.

Interviewer: So you think there is a shortage of skilled workers?

George: Yes, I definitely believe so. That's why they're doing this training.

Interviewer: Will your qualification help you to get a job somewhere else if you want to?

George: Yes, it's general enough. There are a lot of companies that I could work for. I am presently being paid less than whites doing the same job. When I finish my course I must get the same pay as whites, or I buzz off.

212

Interviewer: What sorts of things does your course teach you?

George: The main objectives are really how to control the people. By creating teamwork, by understanding each other, we can produce more. We need better communication. Because of my business training, I would put the management point of view – for higher production. I can support higher production, provided we are paid more. If I get more production then I and the workers must get remuneration.

Interviewer: Do you think black managers are used to control workers better?

George: I think I can control workers better than a white. The main thing is to get down to my people's level. I have to be sympathetic to a problem on a factory level. I help them with ideas. They mustn't see me as something far higher.

Interviewer: Do you see yourself as part of management, or as a worker?

George: As a co-worker. I have been sent by someone else. I am a worker. I joined the union before, and I don't think I'd ever do away with the union.

I'm sure that readers can see certain contradictions in George's position. To a large extent he has accepted management's explanations and their aims; yet he still sees himself as a worker. He wants to be a union member; he wants better wages for workers; and he sees exploitation around him. Yet he is going for management. He believes in values like productivity, but this means productivity in a capitalist business. In fact, he wants to use his skills to get on top of the production process in a capitalist business. George is in a difficult position. He wants to be on both sides.

What about Bongi, answering similar questions?

Interviewer: Why do you think the company is prepared to pay so much money for your training?

Bongi: They are practising cheap labour. They don't want to hire qualified people to do those jobs. It costs them less to train me. I just go there to pass the time. They won't pay me for what I learn.

Interviewer: Do you think there is a shortage of skilled workers?

Bongi: I don't believe there's a shortage. They don't want to pay the qualified people.

Interviewer: Will your qualifications help you to get a job somewhere else if you want to?

Bongi: I can't say. I don't know if the other companies would accept my certificates. George can leave the company tomorrow. With my certificates, it probably wouldn't do to mix companies.

Interviewer: What sorts of things does your course teach you?

Bongi: The courses are trying to teach attitudes that are more favourable to management. They teach you how to handle workers, for example, you must know their moods; how you should approach them; know their surnames; their domestic problems, everything.

Interviewer: Do you see yourself as part of management, or as a worker?

Bongi: I regard myself as a worker, not management. As a supervisor I have to get the foreman's ideas to the workers. From supervisors downwards we work as a production team. Management pushes us to produce more for their gain. We get nothing; they get the profits.

Bongi's position as a supervisor is clearer than George's position as a trainee-manager. Bongi is less torn by contradiction. But then, by comparison, his training also gives him limited benefits. And here the question really applies: Is his training a substitute for general school education?

This leads to our final issue: Are there alternative ways of linking education and work? What about trade union education?

Trade union education

We saw that worker militancy was one reason for business-sponsored education programmes in the 1980s. The same militancy was responsible for the development of independent trade unions, in the 1970s, with their own education programmes.

Let's look briefly at the union movement and the education programmes which have been set up by the unions. You'll see that these education programmes are very different from those which are provided by management.

In 1973 thousands of workers in Durban went on strike. They demanded wage increases from management. Although they succeeded in winning some advances they realized they needed more permanent forms of organizaton to defend the gains they had made and to fight to extend these gains in future. As a result trade unions grew up, not only in Natal but all over South Africa.

The emerging trade unions are generally not in favour of joint management-labour education programmes. This is because they believe that gains for workers are costs to management. They believe that improvements in the workplace should be negotiated between representatives of workers and management. Workers had to struggle for many years to get their representatives (usually called shop stewards) recognized by management. It is very important to workers and their trade unions that there are effective shop stewards. Trade union education in the 1980s therefore primarily aims to establish worker leadership. Here is how one trade unionist describes it:

Trade unionist

We want to equip shop stewards and union organizers with the sort of skills that would make them effective worker leaders within their union and within the wider society. Both in the short and long term we are giving people skills to deal with grievances, negotiations – to deal, that is, with the internal workings of their trade union. At the same time we are conducting political education so they can develop a perspective on events around them from a working class position in society. We also see these people as spreading their knowledge through our factory-based organizational structures.

215

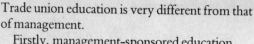

Trade union education is very different from that of management.

Firstly, management-sponsored education frequently trains individuals to do specialist – and often isolated – work. Trade union education aims to unite workers by showing the connections between what goes on, both inside and outside the factory.

Secondly, management education and trade union education have different aims. Trade union education aims to change the workplace and the relationships within it in favour of the workers, while management education focuses on the need to control workers.

Interview

Lizeka is a shop steward in a factory outside Johannesburg. She has attended a number of trade union courses.

Interviewer: As a shop steward, do you think trade union education is important?

Lizeka: Yes. Trade union education is important because you are not only taught how to solve problems in the factory, you are also taught about the relationship between capital and labour. In this education you are also being groomed to be a worker leader. Trade union education is very important because it teaches you about international trade unionism and the links between our local workers and overseas workers, and the way multinational companies exploit us. In fact it is important because it teaches us to question everything that management does. It teaches you to be militant.

Interviewer: How is trade union education spread from the shop stewards to the other workers in the factory?

Lizeka: Well, the shop steward who has been to a seminar has to make report-backs in the factory. For example, I must call a shop stewards' meeting about what I have learnt. Then each shop steward calls together the workers in their department and explains the main points. That doesn't only happen during lunch break; it also continues after working hours because that is a time when we can get people together.

If I address the workers and they don't seem to understand, then I make everyday examples about what I'm talking about. The

216

workers will not all understand in a day; some will, but some will take a longer time. Those who understand quickly will also explain – not only the shop steward but the workers themselves, the shopfloor.

Interviewer: How is trade union education conducted?

Lizeka: Well, seminars are different from management ones in the sense that you all participate and we have discussion. What I mean is, for example, if we are being taught about history, you are given a question like 'What was the first black trade union in South Africa?' That develops into a discussion on the reason why the union organized workers in the way it did and why it failed. What we also learn is that we don't have to repeat the same mistakes that were done by the first trade unions.

Interviewer: What do you think is the main aim of management education as opposed to trade union education?

Lizeka: Management's main aim of education is to teach us to be more productive and to be more responsible, but it does not teach us about safety at the workplace. For example, I'm operating a press machine, and the safety requirements are that that machine should be fenced and also that it should have a safety gate. So management doesn't put fences around press machines because he's more worried about production than the safety of my hands. One worker was injured for the same reason, because management didn't provide safety goggles, but the guy was grinding. They only provided the goggles *after* he was injured which was really useless because he had already lost one eye.

Interviewer: Do you think trade union education links up with wider issues?

Lizeka: I would say it links in this way: Firstly, I am a worker in a factory and I get a low wage; that low wage means I can't pay increased rents in the township. Well, the way of fighting this is first by raising the issue with management. That is where it starts.

Lizeka is in a very different position from both George and Bongi. Her trade union education will not help her get promotion. Nor will it help her get a certificate. But Lizeka's motives are also different. She is not concerned to strive for her own betterment only. She sees herself fighting for workers in general – through the trade union.

Conclusion

These examples of education at work show that
education isn't neutral. We saw clearly that
management education embodies certain
attitudes and values. Trade union education
embodies other attitudes and values. Both
groups are trying to use education to further their
own aims.

It's important to recognize that education is
part of broader political and economic struggles.
We can't view it otherwise.

References and further readings

Chisholm, L. (1983) 'Skills shortage: Black education in South Africa in the
1980s' *Comparative Education* 19(3)

Chisholm, L. and Christie, P. (1983) 'Restructuring in education' in SARS
South African Review, vol. 1, Ravan, Johannesburg

Financial Mail (1983) 'Manpower' Survey Supplement 16 September

HSRC (1981) *Investigation into Education* Vol. 12T: *Technical and Vocational
Education* (De Lange Report), HSRC, Pretoria

Innes, D. (1983) 'Monopoly capitalism in South Africa' in SARS *South African Review*, vol. 1, Ravan, Johannesburg

Loots, L.J. (1978) 'A profile of black unemployment in South Africa: Two
surveys' *SALDRU Working Papers* 19

Meth, C. (1979) 'Trade unions, skills shortages and private enterprise' *SALB*
5(3)

Meth, C. (1981) 'Shortages of skilled labour power and capital reconstruction
in South Africa' African Studies Seminar paper, University of the Witwatersrand, Mimeo.

Meth, C. (1983) 'Class formation: Skill shortage and black advancement' in
SARS *South African Review*, vol. 1, Ravan, Johannesburg

National Manpower Commission (1980) *Report on High Level Manpower*,
Pretoria

Proctor-Sims, R. (ed) (1981) *Technical and Vocational Education in South Africa*,
Proceedings of the 1981 Conference of the Technical and Vocational Education Foundation of South Africa, Johannesburg

SAIRR (Annual) *Survey of Race Relations in South Africa*, SAIRR, Johannesburg

Chapter 9

Resistance in education

June 1976 was a highpoint in the history of black resistance in South Africa. The opposition of these school students to Bantu Education and the apartheid system has become a landmark in South African history. It was also the beginning of a new era of resistance in education.

Yet 1976 does not stand alone as a single and isolated example of resistance in schools. There is in fact a long and continuing history of resistance by black people to the schooling system. 1976, 1980 and 1984 are part of a long process of boycotts, protest and opposition in schools. Sometimes this protest and opposition was mainly confined to schools; sometimes it was linked to events outside of schools. Sometimes it was well organized beforehand; sometimes it was spontaneous. Sometimes it was effective and brought changes; sometimes it did not. But whatever these differences there is no doubt that resistance has always been present in South African schools.

As we would expect, our three thinkers have different views on resistance in schools. Let's see what they would say.

Conservative

There are always trouble-makers in society. And there are trouble-makers in schools too.

If you look at June 1976, it's obvious that foreign agitators and tsotsis were responsible. Foreign agitators aroused the students with false promises, to get their support. Within minutes of the first stones thrown in Soweto, the students were joined by hundreds of Soweto's roughnecks. Among them were big-time bandits, tsotsis, drug-addicts, drunkards and won't-works. These people looted and rioted, and committed arson. The destruction was mindless and purposeless. The rioters even burned down the schools which the government had provided them. How could they have been serious about wanting education?

Such destructiveness endangers the whole society. It must be stopped, by whatever means. And the ring-leaders must be severely punished. People must learn that they can't oppose the system and get away with it.

Resistance in schools? It's caused by trouble-makers, who must be taught a lesson.

Moderate

Those people who protest about schooling have probably got good grounds for being unhappy. But I don't think that boycotts and strikes and violence are the way to get improvements.

Take June 1976. There's no doubt that the events of June 1976 were race riots, against the racially segregated and unequal schooling system. The cause of the conflict was undoubtedly the racial policies of the apartheid government.

Yet look what happened. Hundreds of people died. There was terrible looting and destruction. Even the schools were burned. There was a terrible cost in lives and in money. And what was achieved? Very little.

I can see why people are unhappy with the schooling they have. But I don't see that boycotts and riots are the answer. They are too extreme, and too destructive.

What we really need is to reform the system – to build on what's there and make it better. For a start, we need to get rid of the racist education system. We need to work for equal education for all.

Radical

It's not surprising that there's always been some sort of opposition going on in schools. As long as the society is unequal, opposition will always be there. In fact I think that resistance is *part* of schooling in capitalist and racist societies. Schools themselves are places of struggle.

Think of June 1976. The children showed clearly that they were rejecting the imposition of Afrikaans as medium of instruction. But they were also rejecting the whole racist, capitalist system of apartheid. Certainly, the Afrikaans issue sparked things off. But the real causes of the uprising were the racism and poverty that children were experiencing. June 1976 wasn't just about problems in schools. The issues involved were much broader than that. Look at the targets that the children went for: they were symbols of apartheid (like WRAB offices) or symbols of economic exploitation (like beer halls).

Resistance in schools reflects issues in the wider society. And it's these wider issues that must be changed. Reforms in education alone won't bring equality, as long as South Africa remains a racist, capitalist society. To get equality we need fundamental social change.

In this chapter we're going to trace the story of resistance and opposition in black schools, from the earliest days up to 1984. We'll be able to see the different forms that resistance has taken. And hopefully, we'll have a better understanding of what's going on in schools today.

And hopefully, also, you'll be able to judge the debates on resistance and opposition for yourselves.

We'll divide our study of resistance into seven periods or themes:

Earliest resistance
Resistance to mission schools after 1920
Opposition to the Bantu Education Act of 1953
Opposition from 1954 onwards
Black Consciousness and resistance
June 1976
1980 boycott
Resistance in 1984.

Earliest resistance

The slaves resist

As we saw in Chapter Two, the first school in South Africa was set up in Cape Town for slaves (mostly adults) in 1658. This school opened a month after the slaves arrived.

Why was the school set up? Some historians claim that the colonizers were concerned about the 'intellectual and moral welfare' of the slaves – and that is why they opened a school. Other historians argue that the colonizers were more concerned about the slaves as workers.

And schools were one way of teaching slaves to understand and accept their masters' orders.

Whatever the reasons, the slaves resisted these attempts to school them. The earliest form of their resistance was to run away. Once, the whole school stayed out for five days and hid in a cave near Hout Bay. The teacher was instructed to try and win their attention with a tot of rum and a few inches of tobacco each. But the slaves continued to run away until the school was closed down.

So we can see that opposition to schooling certainly has a long history – it started with the very first school! We can see clearly that these people resisted the imposition of schools. And they were probably resisting their whole position as slaves in the society.

Resistance to mission schools

There was also resistance to the early mission schools by African people. As we saw in Chapter Three, African chiefdoms did not always welcome the missionaries and their schools. Sometimes they avoided sending children to mission schools altogether. But sometimes they sent their children for long enough to get specific benefits – like clothes – and then removed them, or rotated them with other children. So it certainly wasn't a simple matter of Africans accepting the missionaries and their schools. It was only later that people began to value mission education as a way of advancement in the colonial society. In the beginning, they resisted it.

Here we see whole groups of people who were opposing the schooling system, or trying to take it on their own terms. So even the introduction of schooling was resisted!

And people continued to resist once they were in the schools – as we'll go on to see.

Resistance to mission schools after 1920

From 1920 up to the introduction of Bantu Education in 1954 there was periodic unrest in black schools across the country. Students protested, demonstrated, rioted, and boycotted chapel or classes.

Actually, there is not much information about events in the schools in this period. The newspapers reported only some of these 'strikes' (as they were called). Two official commissions of inquiry, set up to investigate grievances and disturbances at black schools, were never published.

But the information we do have shows a consistent pattern. Almost all of the unrest happened at rural secondary schools or teacher training institutions. And in most cases it was led by students who were boarders. Generally speaking, the strikes were directed against conditions in the mission schools, like poor food, compulsory manual labour and harsh punishment from teachers.

In the mission schools food was an important indicator of difference – and also a source of protest. In some schools the staff, and students who paid higher fees, received much better food than the students who paid less. Here is a description given by a student waiter at Lovedale in the 1930s:

> **"**The students were divided into four categories, and sat at separate tables. There were the R28 students, the R34 students, the R44 students and the R54 per year students. The first category of students received meat once a week with their samp, the R34 students had meat twice a week, and so on up the scale.**"**

The colour and class distinctions of the wider society were repeated in the schools. And food was one way in which these distinctions were made.

I'm not sure how to assess these protests – especially the food protests. How significant were they?

Well, that's a matter for debate. Some people argue that students were simply protesting about their conditions in schools. They say these protests were not linked to any broader issues, so they were not really political.

Other people argue that the students were protesting against general and deep-rooted discrimination – so their food protests were actually political protests. What do you think?

223

Certainly there were long periods of quiet in the schools, in between the protests. School authorities were easily able to punish students (as we all know!) and could also threaten to expel them. Also, we should remember that those blacks who were in secondary and higher education were a tiny minority (no more than 2% of the total black population). Many of them were hoping that education would open the way to high status jobs and a middle class position in society. Problems at school would threaten their chances. But on the other hand, these students had access to books and newspapers, and could have discussions and debates about current affairs. And this made them more aware of problems in the society around them.

Let's look at some instances of student unrest in the mission schools.

1920: Student strikes at Kilnerton and Lovedale

In February 1920, students at Kilnerton Training Centre went on a hunger strike 'for more food'. A few months later, theological students at Lovedale set fire to the buildings, in protest against the poor quality of food. The damage they caused was between R6 000 and R10 000 – a lot of money in those days. One hundred and ninety eight students were tried in court, and received sentences ranging from strokes with a light cane to three months' imprisonment, with a fine of R100.

1939 – 1945: Strikes during World War II

During this period, some of the resistance in schools coincided with events outside. At the beginning of World War II, there were at least six strikes at mission schools. Students were discussing and debating the problems of South Africa and the world. The staff took steps against this, calling it 'an unnatural interest in politics'. Es'kia Mphahlele, who was at Adams College, wrote in his autobiography:

> In a great number of mission schools, certain political journals were banned, and topics for school debate were severely censored. As the World War raged on, the tempers of the students raged to the extent that certain school buildings were burned down. (1962:146)

In the period 1939 to 1945, there were more than twenty strikes and serious riots in schools. Each strike led to expulsions.

1946: Strike at Lovedale

In August 1946 there was a serious strike at Lovedale which attracted a lot of attention. School premises were damaged, and prefects and white staff members were attacked. The Lovedale Governing Council set up a Commission of Inquiry. The Commission found that there had been unrest in the school since 1945. They also suggested that students were influenced by the 1946 mine workers' strike.

A hundred and fifty-two students were arrested and charged in the courts with public violence. Most of the students were fined. All of them were excluded from attending any school in the future. Later, another eighty students were excluded and Lovedale was closed for nine weeks.

Later strikes

After the Lovedale strike, there were at least five other strikes in 1946 in the Transvaal and the Cape. At the end of 1946, there was a sit-down strike at Bethesda Bantu Training College near Pietersburg. In 1949, after the National Party came to power, Fort Hare students supported a sit-down strike called by the nurses at Victoria Hospital. Strikes, stoppages and demonstrations continued.

Here is how a newspaper writer saw the situation at the time:

> At almost every African mission boarding school, conditions for students are deplorable, and this has been the root of all the minor revolts which have taken place from time to time at these institutions. Food and the Nazi-like control are usually the main causes for dissatisfaction. Last week the authorities were expecting some sort of explosion at Healdtown Missionary College. Police at 5 Eastern Cape towns were asked to stand by, in case something should happen at the College.
>
> Earlier, last week, 100 senior pupils were sent home after a passive resistance strike - escorted off the premises by 20 armed police.
>
> (*Torch*, 3 November 1953)

So the picture of mission education would really be incomplete without this story of ongoing resistance by students.

That's true. Sometimes opposition was linked to what was going on outside of schools. But mostly the opposition was not co-ordinated. And it was not linked with outside organizations.

But this is different with the next phase of resistance we'll look at – namely, the opposition to the Bantu Education Act, organized by the ANC, the NEUM (Unity Movement) and by various teachers' and students' organizations. In this case, we see an established political group – such as the ANC – organizing opposition in schools. And we see schools responding directly to broader social issues.

Opposition to the Bantu Education Act of 1953

The earliest resistance to Bantu Education came in fact from the teachers – who were immediately affected by the new education system. Bantu Education meant that they would have to work for double sessions each day; class sizes would be larger; salaries would not be improved; and they would be government employees.

In 1952 the Cape African Teachers' Association (CATA) condemned the Eiselen Report, and called meetings to discuss ways of resisting Bantu Education. They called on teachers and parents to do everything in their power to oppose the new system. The government responded by taking recognition away from CATA. Instead they gave recognition to a newly established teachers' organization, the Cape African Teachers' Union (CATU). Militant teachers were dismissed from schools.

The Transvaal African Teachers' Association (TATA) also condemned Bantu Education. TATA also called meetings of teachers and parents to organize resistance to Bantu Education. However, their activities were less widespread than CATA's, and not as many of them were dismissed.

As the historian Lodge argues, the activities of the teachers were 'an important part of the backdrop to the communal boycott of schools that took place in those areas'. (1983:120)

What was this boycott?

In May 1954, the ANC launched a 'Resist Apartheid Campaign'. Bantu Education was one of six issues in the campaign. The other issues were: the pass laws; the Group Areas Act; the Native Resettlement Act; the Suppression of Communism Act; and anti-trade union measures.

It's important to understand that Bantu Education was only one of the many new apartheid measures that were beginning to affect people's lives. The education boycott was not centre-stage. It was part of a larger campaign.

The ANC did not have the resources to fight all six issues of the Resist Apartheid Campaign. In fact, the National Executive of the ANC decided to hand over the question of Bantu Education to the Women's League and the Congress Youth League (CYL).

The schools boycott campaign was full of uncertainty and disagreement. Certain people favoured an indefinite boycott of schools, to begin as soon as possible. Other, more cautious people felt that fuller preparations should be made first. Eventually, the National Executive decided in December 1954 to launch an indefinite schools boycott as from 1 April 1955. But no full-scale programme of action was drawn up. Instead, it was left to local branches to organize people and make preparations. In fact, the day chosen to start the boycott was not even a school day – it was in the Easter holidays!

In March the ANC National Executive decided to postpone the boycott because there had not been enough time to organize properly. They also agreed that the boycott should not begin until arrangements were made for the children who would be out of school during the boycott. They set up a committee to plan alternative education. This committee later became the African Education Movement (AEM).

But the CYL was not prepared to call off the boycott. Even though there had not been proper preparations for a widespread campaign, they called a boycott for 12 April (the first day of term). The boycott was called in two areas: the Eastern Cape and the East Rand.

The boycott began on the East Rand on Monday, 12 April 1955. In Benoni, Germiston, Katlehong, Brakpan and Alexandra, children stayed away from school. Here is how Lodge describes the boycott:

> By Wednesday, 3 000 Brakpan children were out of school – the highest figure for any single location. In Germiston, parents marched with children in a procession. All Benoni and Germiston schools were empty, and in Katlehong Township only 70 of the 1 000-odd pupils at a community school attended. On Thursday a march by women and children in Benoni was broken up by police. By the following Monday, the boycott movement had penetrated Johannesburg. Six primary schools in Western Native Township and Newclare were abandoned by their 3 500 pupils after visits from the Youth League and the Women's League.
>
> The marches and processions continued more or less daily in the locations, and became increasingly violent. By the end of the week two unsuccessful attempts at arson had been made against school buildings in Benoni and Katlehong. On Friday the total number of children out of school exceeded 10 000, and the boycott had spread to Moroka/Jabavu schools in Soweto, and to Sophiatown.   (1983:124, adapted)

In the Eastern Cape, the boycott was a little slower to start. But altogether 2 500 children were involved, from Uitenhage, New Brighton, Korsten, Kirkwood, Missionvale, Kleinvee, Kleinschool and Walmer location.

The government soon took action against the boycott. The Minister of Native Affairs, Verwoerd, issued a statement. He said that all children who were still absent from school by 25 April would receive no further education. The ANC Executive was divided on what to do. Several ANC members called on parents to end the boycott. As a result, many children did return to school. But thousands stayed out and were expelled. The boycott was at its end.

Meanwhile, during the boycott, the AEM tried to organize alternative education programmes for children who were out of school. Although it was against the law to set up schools or hold lessons, some independent schools were set up, and were quite well attended. The main work of the AEM was to set up a network of cultural clubs. The aim was to use songs, stories and games to teach basic maths, history, geography and general knowledge.

Some of these cultural clubs were well attended. For example, the Brakpan cultural club still had 700 members a year after the boycott began. But usually they suffered from shortages of money, facilities and teachers. Many of the AEM committee members were banned; club leaders in townships were harassed; and clubs were subject to police raids.

The cultural clubs were a very important attempt to set up an alternative education programme. They weren't simply like schools. They were an attempt to offer education of a different kind – in their aims, their methods and their general approach.

But I can see that it was hard to keep an alternative going, especially when government schools began to open again.

Even so, the clubs were important in educational terms. Lodge argues:

> The AEM's approach involved a reversal of normal South African educational conventions. Even in terms of formal criteria, the clubs could be successful. Some of their members wrote and passed Std 6 exams. As late as 1956, clubs in Benoni and Brakpan were even winning over students from government schools. The AEM and the cultural clubs were a brave experiment, but their significance became increasingly symbolic as numbers dwindled and children went back to government schools. But they show an interesting attempt by Congress members to spell out an alternative world view in educational terms. (1983:129, adapted)

In 1960, the cultural clubs finally closed down.

So those were the events of the 1953 boycott. As we know the protest against Bantu Education didn't manage to prevent the system from going into operation.

Why did boycott against Bantu Education fail?

Different historians have given different answers to this question. Let's look at two of these answers:

"I say that the ANC was not well enough organized. The leadership was in confusion. They did not put enough effort into planning the programme for the schools boycott. And they didn't think enough about what would happen to children who were out of school.

If the boycott had been properly organized, it would have had more chance of success."

"Maybe part of the problem does lie with the ANC. But I think we also need to look at the government's repressive actions. The government was able to expel children from schools, and it was able to intimidate and harass the leaders of the boycott. This made it very difficult for the boycott to succeed.

In a situation where the government was able to take such strong action, I don't think the boycott could have been more successful."

These are just two views on the boycott. But I think there are important educational questions to ask as well:
1 What were the problems with closing schools?
2 Why didn't the cultural clubs last longer?
Let's look at each of these questions in turn.

What problems were there with closing schools?

One of the problems with the 1953 boycotts was that they involved *primary school* children. Parents were asked to keep their young children out of the Bantu Education primary schools. And there were problems with this.

Firstly, there were not enough schools anyway, so parents often struggled to get their 7 or 8 year olds into school. It was a difficult decision, in the face of that, to withdraw them. But secondly, what would happen to the children? Many parents relied on schools to keep their children busy and off the streets. For these parents, boycotting school left a practical problem: Who would look after the children? The ANC and its cultural clubs did not have the facilities for thousands of small children.

Why didn't the cultural clubs last longer?

As we said before, the cultural clubs were an important experiment in alternative education. They weren't just like other schools. In some ways this was a strength. Teachers could move away from restrictive syllabuses and classrooms. They could try to teach more relevant things.

But there were also problems. There was the problem of getting people to accept that this alternative education was worthwhile. Once the government schools were operating again there was the problem of competing with these schools, which could offer certificates and job prospects. As we've said throughout the book, education can't be viewed in isolation from the wider society. And this is always a problem for people who are trying to set up alternatives.

Let's now move on with our story of resistance in education. Let's look at resistance after 1954. We'll start by looking at the responses to separation in universities – there we'll see resistance of a different sort.

Opposition from 1954 onwards

Extension of University Education Act

In 1959 apartheid was applied to univesities. The 1959 Extension of University Education Act said that 'open universities', like Wits and UCT, would not be allowed to register any new black students, except with special permission. The Act also brought Fort Hare under the power of the Minister of Bantu Education. It could now accept only Xhosa-speaking students. Two new 'tribally-based' university colleges were established – the University College of the North at Turfloop for the Sotho-, Pedi-, Tswana- and Venda-speaking people; and the University College of Zululand at Ngoye for Zulu-speakers. 'Coloureds' were to go to the University College of the Western Cape at Bellville, and 'Indians' to the University College of

Durban/ Westville.

The resistance to these apartheid measures was mainly symbolic. There were no stay-away campaigns or militant actions. Instead, Wits and UCT declared that they were committed to being 'open universities', and they decided to hold an 'academic freedom' lecture each year. (These lectures are still given.) There were also mass meetings and one-day boycotts of classes. Members of the universities dressed in their academic gowns and marched through the streets in protest against the Act. There were also student and staff groups who organized against the Act. But none of this prevented the Act from being passed.

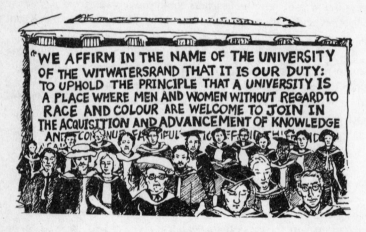

At Fort Hare staff and students passed resolutions condemning the extension of apartheid to universities. The government responded by dismissing certain staff members. Others resigned. One of these was the ANC member Prof. Z. K. Mathews, who was Vice Principal. In 1960 a number of students were refused readmission. Authorities forced students to sign a declaration accepting College regulations, or leave. In these ways opposition to the new system was brought under control by the government. But unrest at the university did not completely end.

So again there's a different form of resistance. I can see that the 1959 resistance was different from the 1954 boycotts. It was more symbolic, and not really a mass movement.

But again, the government was able to assert its control – by dismissing staff and expelling students. You can see the power that the government gained through bringing these universities under its authority. The government could then decide who would be able to teach, and who could get what education.

But this doesn't mean that the government could completely stamp out protests – as we'll go on to see.

Continuing protests at schools and universities

There was considerable unrest at many colleges and schools at the end of May 1961, when South Africa became a republic. According to various press reports, the students at Fort Hare stayed away from their lectures on 29 and 30 May as a protest against the republic. The College was closed until 18 July.

On Republic Day students at a number of schools refused to accept the medals and flags handed to them, and they also boycotted flag-raising ceremonies.

Throughout the 1960s there was ongoing unrest at schools across the country. There were strikes, protests and demonstrations, and there are many reports of students being expelled or punished because of 'insubordination' and 'misconduct'. In some cases students were arrested and brought to court. There were charges of public violence, malicious damage to property and contravention of the Riotous Assemblies Act.

Even although the 1960s were quiet years in terms of the general resistance movement, schools unrest continued.

These examples show the ongoing nature of upheavals in schools and universities. The question is: Were they mainly school-based, or were they linked to broader issues and organizations?

I'm sure we'll see the influence of the Black Consciousness movement in the 1970s. That's well known.

Black Consciousness and resistance

In the early 1960s many black university students wanted to affiliate to the white student body NUSAS, though there were influential groups, such as the CPSU, which were against talking with 'liberal' organizations. By 1968 many black students felt that NUSAS was not radical enough. The black student body, led by people such as Steve Biko, broke away from NUSAS and founded SASO.

SASO inspired the formation of the Black Consciousness (BC) movement. SASO believed that black students should organize on their own, independently of whites. For them, the word 'black' re-ferred to all the oppressed people of colour: Africans, 'Coloureds' and Indians. One of the BC slogans was: 'Black man, you are on your own.'

In the 1970s, BC was an important resistance movement. It began in universities, but it soon spread into a more general political move-ment. Many organizations were set up which reflected BC views. BC supporters included educational groups, cultural and community groups, journalists and theologians. BC was not a single and cohe-rent philosophy; it covered a number of different views and tenden-cies. But centrally it stood for a rejection of white domination in all its forms – political, economic, psychological and cultural. It strongly rejected apartheid, and it supported the liberation struggles elsewhere in Southern Africa.

In 1972, three important BC organizations were established:

- SASM (South African Students' Movement)
- BPC (Black People's Convention)
- BCP (Black Community Project).

Here is a statement on BC. It should give an idea of what BC stood for:

> **"**It is the inalienable birthright of any community to have a political voice to articulate and realize the aspirations of its members.
>
> In this, our country, Africans, Coloureds, and Indians, comprise the Black Community, which has been deprived of this inalienable right; and for too long there has been a political vacuum in the black community.
>
> We are therefore working towards the formation of a black people's political movement, whose primary aim is to unite and solidify black people with a view to liberating and emancipating them from both psychological and physical oppression.
>
> It is imperative and essential that all black people, individuals and organizations, should pool their resources together in order to achieve their aspirations. Their future, destiny and ultimate happiness lies in their own hands. **"**

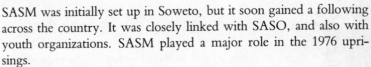

This statement gives an idea of BC's general position. You can see that BC places all black people together, regardless of social class and other differences. And, in fact, BC has often been criticized for this.

But during the 1970s BC was very influential, and groups like SASO and SASM featured prominently.

SASM was initially set up in Soweto, but it soon gained a following across the country. It was closely linked with SASO, and also with youth organizations. SASM played a major role in the 1976 uprisings.

SASO and BPC were involved on a day to day basis in literacy campaigns; health projects; the building of schools, clinics and community centres; home education; and co-operative bulk buying. They were also involved in drama and poetry in the townships.

During the 1970s, there was continuing resistance on campuses and in schools. And SASO and SASM were prominent in this resistance.

Black student protest: the 'May Revolt' of 1972

In April 1972, Onkgopotse Tiro, a past-president of the SRC at Turfloop, made a speech to the student assembly. In this speech he criticized discrimination in education, and the entire apartheid system.

In May, Tiro was expelled. A boycott of lectures took place, and Turfloop was closed. The boycott spread to other black campuses, and by June all black universities were boycotting. They were joined by M. L. Sultan Technical College, and a few colleges of education. The white universities launched a 'Free Education' campaign, which the police crushed with violence, using baton charges and dogs. Resistance on black campuses continued.

Strikes

Meanwhile, black workers took the lead. From January 1973 to June 1974 there were more than 300 strikes, involving some 80 000 black workers. In September there were major revolts on the mines, and clashes between mine workers and the police. At least 152 mine workers were killed, and more than 500 were injured. Immediately, the students protested.

SASO condemned the shootings. The University of Durban/Westville held protest prayer meetings. Turfloop students dismissed their SRC for not organizing protest meetings. And the white campuses held demonstrations and protests. Again there were clashes with the police. Some white students marched on Anglo American Corporation to demand an inquiry into the shootings.

This period of student activity seems to have tied in very much with wider political protest.

And – as you predicted – much of the student activity was inspired by BC and its organizations. Student protest responded to events outside the universities – like the miners' strikes – and also the victory of Frelimo in Mozambique, as we'll see.

Viva Frelimo rallies – September 1974

In 1974 the government in Portugal was overthrown. Shortly after that Frelimo won its struggle for the independence of Mozambique, which was a Portuguese colony. The independence of Mozambique spurred SASO and BPC to further action.

SASO and BPC called for nationwide Viva Frelimo rallies on 25

September 1974. The Minister of Police immediately banned all SASO/ BPC gatherings for a month. But in Durban a huge crowd gathered at Currie's Fountain to hold a meeting. The police moved in to disperse them. Many SASO and BPC leaders were detained, and remained in detention throughout 1976.

At Turfloop students responded to the Viva Frelimo call. They decided that the ban on meetings did not apply to them. Some 1 200 students gathered for a meeting, but they were dispersed by police with guns and dogs. The resistance continued for a short while. But as exams approached, students chose to write exams, rather than to continue boycotting.

For the next two years, until June 1976, there was no further news of student protests in the universities.

SASO and BPC trial – 1975

There were a number of political trials in 1975. The biggest and longest was the trial of SASO and BPC leaders. They were accused of promoting anti-white feelings, and encouraging racial hostility to prepare for violent revolution. The ideas of BC were on trial.

After two years of trial, SASO and BPC leaders were acquitted on the main charges. But they were found guilty on alternative charges and they received sentences of five and six years in jail. The trial and sentences put many of the BC leaders out of political action.

BC was a very controversial political movement. Many people accused it of lacking proper theory and organization. But it certainly had wide support. And it met with strong disapproval from the government – leaders were arrested, detained and banned in great numbers.

I'm interested to see that BC was actually started by students, and that students remained an important part of the movement.

And that in this period protests were not simply school-based. They were part of a broader political struggle. And it is in this context that we can move on to look at June 1976.

237

June 1976

The story of the beginnings of June 1976 is well known. In 1975 the Minister of Bantu Education instructed that half of the subjects in Std 5 and Form 1 must be taught in the medium of Afrikaans. There was widespread opposition to this regulation. Some people opposed it for educational reasons, saying that children would suffer. Others opposed it for political reasons. Protests spread from school to school in Soweto.

On 13 June SASM decided to hold a mass demonstration against the enforcement of Afrikaans. An action committee was formed, which later became the SSRC. On 16 June 20 000 students marched through Soweto in protest against Afrikaans. The police opened fire, and the first victim, Hector Petersen, died. The Soweto uprising had begun.

The students responded with violence. They attacked WRAB, burned its offices and destroyed its vehicles. They attacked and burned beer halls, liquor stores, post offices, a bank and a hotel. They burned buses and taxis. Within a day, unrest had spread throughout Soweto.

The government replied immediately. Prime Minister Vorster told Parliament that he had instructed the police to maintain law and order at all costs. And the costs were high.

In the following weeks the uprising spread fast. Townships on the Reef and around Pretoria were soon blazing. The protests also spread further afield: there was violence in Nelspruit, Jouberton (near Klerksdorp), Bothaville (OFS), Galeshewe (Kimberley), Langa and Nyanga (Cape Town), and also the universities of Turfloop and Ngoye.

During July the uprising spread across the country, and included the homelands as well. In August, the 'coloured' students in Cape Town joined the protests. A full-scale, nationwide uprising was in process.

According to the sociologist Molteno:

> Tens of thousands of men, women and children, students, parents and workers, in some 200 black communities throughout the country, including the bantustans, actively participated in the uprising.   (1979a:54)

They clashed with the police. They set fire to Bantu Affairs buildings, schools, beer halls, liquor stores, white-owned businesses and vehicles. They went on marches and stay-at-home campaigns. They managed to close down the Soweto Urban Bantu Councils. And they blocked a rise in rents.

And what about the police? They used dogs, guns, teargas, armoured cars (hippos) and helicopters. They raided houses and searched people at roadblocks. They prohibited gatherings. They detained without trial. And they shot.

Huge numbers of people were rounded up. Among them was Biko, the BC leader, whose death in detention in 1977 shocked the world.

Throughout 1976 and 1977 there were repeated skirmishes between students and the police. In October 1977 virtually all BC organizations were banned, including the SSRC. According to the writer Kane-Berman:

> These bannings constituted the severest act of political suppression by the state since the outlawing of the ANC and the PAC in 1960.   (1979:9)

It was only in 1978 that the uprising finally settled.

In 1980, the Cillie Commission, which the government had appointed to investigate the uprisings, tabled its report. The Cillie Commission concluded that:

> Bantu Education was not a cause of the riots. It was, to a certain degree, a cause of dissatisfaction; this dissatisfaction was to some extent stirred up and exploited by those bent on creating disturbances.
>
> (SAIRR Survey 1982:501)

The Commission acknowledged that there was considerable dissatisfaction with Bantu Education. It also mentioned other sources of discontent. These included influx control laws, the Group Areas Act,

239

the homeland policy and compulsory homeland citizenship. The Commission found that SASM had played a supportive role and that the SSRC had organized much of the resistance. It also found that organizations such as the ANC, the SACP, PAC and SASO had played an active role.

There's no space here to tell the whole story of the 1976 uprising. That would need a book of its own.

Perhaps we should discuss the causes and the results of the uprising a bit more fully?

Yes, and also look at the students' attempts to broaden the base of their struggle by linking up with workers.

Causes of the 1976 uprising

As we saw at the start of this chapter, people give very different reasons for why the schools exploded in 1976. Some people blame outside agitators and outside influences. Other people see the uprising as a race riot, which was sparked off by the introduction of Afrikaans medium. And others see it as a protest against the whole South African system.

So deciding on the causes is no easy matter! But if we look at the background events before 1976, we can get some general ideas about the circumstances in which it occurred.

- Firstly, there was a crisis in schooling. The general conditions in schools are well known. There was a shortage of classrooms and teachers. There was overcrowding and high student-teacher ratios. Teachers were poorly qualified. Buildings and equipment were of poor quality. There was a high failure rate.

  In the 1970s, the situation worsened. There was a large increase in the number of secondary school students. One reason for this was that the last year of primary school was moved into secondary school. This put more pressure on the already overcrowded schools.

  And into this already difficult situation came the introduction of Afrikaans medium.

- Secondly, the economy of the country was in recession. Many black workers were laid off, and unemployment rose. Black matriculants faced poor employment opportunties. There was high inflation, and food prices soared. The poverty datum line for Soweto was estimated at R129,05 per month; but the average black family was estimated to be earning R75 per month. So people were experiencing economic pressure at the time of June 1976.

- Thirdly, there were problems of apartheid. Townships such as Soweto were overcrowded and there were inadequate facilities, like transport and housing. Problems like pass laws, influx control and compulsory homeland citizenship – all of these were grievances which people felt. These grievances were also part of the background to June 1976.

- And then, there was also what Molteno calls 'an atmosphere of revolt' in the 1970s. There were the liberation struggles in Mozambique, Angola, Zimbabwe and Namibia. There were the black workers' strikes in the 1970s. And there were the ideas of BC and its organizations.

  All of this contributed to the background of the uprising.

There's no doubt that 1976 should be seen as part of this wider context. But it's up to you to try to assess what you think the actual causes were.

Let's now look at how the students attempted to win the support of workers during the uprising.

Students and workers

The June uprising started as a student protest. But it was not only students who were involved. Students also made attempts to broaden their struggle to include workers as well. And some of their demands were not simply about education.

Initially, students were more concerned with preventing workers from going to work rather than with recruiting them as supporters. The students' tactics varied from persuasion, to stoning buses which carried workers to the city, to jeering at workers who were seen going to work.

But at the beginning of August 1976 the students called on workers to stay home from work. They wanted parents and workers to march with students to John Vorster Square in Johannesburg. It seems that at least 60% of Soweto workers responded to the call and stayed away from work.

Altogether there were four stay-away (*azikwelwa*) calls. In August and September 1976, parents and workers responded, and 70% to 80% did not go to work. But the last time – in November – workers did not respond. At Christmas time students called for a boycott on liquor and Christmas shopping – and it seems that this was more successful.

Some writers view the stay-aways positively. They conclude that the workers played an important part in the 1976 uprising. Other writers dispute this. They point to the failure of the November *azikwelwa* call, and they argue that the students did not successfully forge links with the working class. They argue that people who responded to the earlier *azikwelwa* calls responded as parents and township dwellers. They were concerned about their children, and about the repression in Soweto. These people were not responding as members of the working class.

And the story of student-worker links must also include the fact that migrant workers from Mzimhlope Hostel went on the rampage in August 1976. Many people thought the police backed the migrant workers who attacked students, their parents and their property.

In looking at student-worker links, it is also true that student demands were not only about education. One of their most successful campaigns was to prevent rent increases in Soweto. They also caused the collapse of the Soweto Urban Bantu Council. And they supported the establishment of the Committee of Ten, which Kane-Berman calls 'the most widely representative body to emerge in Soweto in years'.

 The relationship between students and workers was not always an easy one. June 1976 was mainly a student struggle. But it's interesting to see that students were attempting to create links outside their own ranks.

Assessing achievements

Kane-Berman writes of the uprising:

> June 1976, like Sharpeville 16 years before, was another turning point at which South Africa did not turn. (1979:232)

How do we assess the achievements of 1976? Is Kane-Berman correct?

Certainly, the costs were enormous. More than one thousand people died; and many, many more were injured. Many others fled the country. A generation of lives was disrupted.

On the one hand, we can look for concrete achievements to make this cost worthwhile. In education, Afrikaans medium was withdrawn. The Department of Bantu Education was renamed the Department of Education and Training. More money was put into schooling, and more attention was paid to schooling conditions. And four years later, the De Lange Committee was set up to investigate the provision of education of equal quality for all in South Africa. But the 1976 uprising was not able to bring an immediate end to Bantu Education. Schools remained segregated and unequal.

But it isn't only in such concrete terms that events like June 1976 can be assessed. Here is a statement made by an ex-student, now a teacher, six years later:

> **"***Question:* What was achieved by the events of 1976?
>
> *Answer:* Firstly, we got an unexpected response. We wanted an educational reaction and we got war. A very one-sided war. We learned a lot from this.
>
> We saw that the white society was living in a world of dreams. When people are killed, one expects some reaction. There should have been some response from white education. Instead, they were as negative as the government. Then the industrial bosses continued to fire workers as if they were responsible for the disturbances. White schools were totally unaffected by the boycotts, as if South Africa consisted of two worlds. As if Soweto and Lower Houghton were two distant islands.**"**

(quoted in *NEWSA*:67)

The events of 1976 brought greater awareness to those who were involved. Here is a statement made by the Cillie Commission of Inquiry into the uprising:

> **"**When, in the course of the riots, Bantu Education had virtually superseded Afrikaans as the rioters' dissatisfaction there were many who described the object of this system as a deliberate attempt to train the black pupil in such a way that he be subservient to the white man, that he would remain the oppressor's slave.**"**   (1980:556-7)

Even the Cillie Commission recognized that people's political awareness grew during the uprising. And this is not something that can be measured in concrete terms.

One thing is certain: the students' revolt of 1976 is a landmark in the history of black protest – no matter what it achieved.

    Let's now move on to look at the 1980 boycotts.

1980 boycott

April 1980 marked the beginning of the famous schools boycott that started in Cape Town and rapidly spread throughout the country. Tens of thousands of black students left their desks to protest against the education system. In certain regions they completely closed down the formal working of first 'Coloured' and Indian schools, and then DET schools. The boycott was soon supported by 140 000 students in the Cape, the Transvaal and also Natal. Furthermore hundreds of teachers came out in organized public support of the boycott, and they pledged their solidarity with the students.

    Again, the state responded with warnings and with police action. Political meetings were banned, student leaders were intimidated and students were threatened with expulsion. People were injured and killed.

    What were the causes of the boycott?

    As with June 1976, there were school-based issues which led to dissatisfaction. Schools were poorly equipped and in a bad state of repair. There were shortages of qualified teachers and dismissals of political teachers. Students also protested against corporal punishment and against the presence of security police at schools. And they demanded independent SRCs.

Also similar to June 1976, the boycott happened in the context of economic problems. There was steadily increasing inflation and unemployment. Black unemployment rose from 11,8% in 1970 to 21,1% in 1981. Again people were experiencing economic pressure.

But the 1980 students had the example of 1976 before them. They could learn lessons from the experiences of 1976. They saw the need for organization and co-ordination. They also made attempts to link their demands with the wider society. Here are two statements made by students in 1980. They show the link between education and the wider society.

> **"**We must see how short-term demands are linked up with the political and economic system of this country. We must see how the fail-pass rates in schools are linked up with the labour supply for the capitalist system.**"**

> **"**Our parents, the workers, are strong. They have power. We, the students, cannot shake the government in the same way. We have got to link up our struggle with the struggle of the black workers. Our parents have got to understand that we will not be 'educated' and 'trained' to become slaves in apartheid-capitalist society. Together with our parents we must try to work out a new future. A future where there will be no racism or exploitation, no apartheid, no inequality of class or sex.**"**

The 1980 boycott was inspired by a different political understanding from June 1976. Whereas June 1976 showed the influence of BC, the 1980 student manifestos and slogans talked more about capitalist exploitation under apartheid. They also talked about how schools prepared students for a subordinate role in apartheid-capitalist society.

It seems that in 1980, as in 1976, students were not only challenging the education system. They were challenging the political system as well.

Exactly. But an interesting feature of the 1980 boycotts was the students' attempt to set up alternative education programmes. Let's see how these worked.

Organization of boycott activities

During the boycott committees were established in most centres to co-ordinate the boycott as efficiently and democratically as possible. School buildings were used as places where students could assemble, as well as centres from which alternative education programmes could be run.

Mass meetings were a regular feature of the boycotts. At many schools they were held every day during the boycott. For example, in the Cape Town region, the boycott was co-ordinated by the Committee of 81, which had representatives of SRCs from schools in the area. After meetings of the Committee, representatives would report back to their schools on the meeting. Leaders would present issues to the students for discussion and decision. They arranged for people to come and address students on the bus and meat boycotts which were happening at the same time. Some attempts were made to link the students' protest with the workers' struggle.

You can see that leaders were making efforts to be democratic, and to involve students actively in the issues of the boycott. This didn't always work, but it was an important feature of the organization of the Committee of 81.

Alternative education

During the boycotts student leaders organized alternative education programmes at schools. There were talks, discussions and debates to raise people's awareness on many topics. These included, for instance, the history of black people in South Africa, the June 1976 uprising, the nature of the education system, politics in South Africa and sports policy. Relevant films and music were also popular parts of these alternative programmes.

246

These programmes differed from school to school. Some were better organized than others. Some were better attended than others. But throughout the boycott period, students attempted to provide alternative education at school.

This is an interesting comparison with the cultural clubs of the 1950s. In both cases people were trying to provide education of a different sort. In both cases they were trying to make education more relevant – and also to give it a different political purpose.

We saw that the cultural clubs had difficulties in keeping going. How successful were the alternative programmes in 1980?

Success of alternative programmes

The alternative programmes at different schools were very different in quality. At some schools students learned a great deal and actively took part in the alternative education they were being offered.

Molteno describes this process as follows:

> At certain schools, the students were for the most part of the boycott in classrooms, earnestly participating in awareness programmes. They remained interested and responded enthusiastically to the opportunity of being able to contribute to a process of collective learning and of being able to criticize openly teachers who in the normal way were figures of unchallengeable authority. (1983:12, adapted)

But many of the programmes were less good, and some programmes had virtually no activities going. Sometimes they ran out of ideas, and they also ran out of steam. Molteno describes how some of these programmes achieved very little:

> For long stretches of the boycott, little or nothing went on at many of the schools. The students would mostly stand around chatting; some would play a ball game; others would drift off home or with groups of friends; the rest would leave school around midday. (1983:13)

For these students, the 'boycott' became the 'borecott'. And many turned the 'borecott' into a stay-away.

This highlights the fact that not all resistance is political. Not all resistance is inspired by ideas of social change. There is a difference between the resistance of the 'boycotters' and the resistance of the 'borecotters'.

It's important to keep a critical perspective when we look at times of resistance.

The end of the boycott

Evidence shows that there was substantial support for the boycott for all the time it lasted. But it was very hard to keep the boycott going. As Molteno writes:

> Much of the early sense of excitement, fun and adventure was consumed by boredom and depression. The initial orderliness and discipline broke down in many quarters. The tremendous solidarity and cohesion of the early phases of the boycott developed divisions as time passed.
>
> (1983:15, adapted)

By the beginning of 1981, most of the schools were back, and the boycott was over.

But that doesn't mean that the boycott was a failure. To judge that, we need to look at some of the achievements of the boycott.

Assessing achievements

How do we assess the achievements of 1980?

Certainly, there was not as much violence as June 1976; not as many people were killed or injured. So the costs were not as high. Nevertheless, the boycotts were disruptive of many people's lives.

As with 1976, we can look for concrete achievements. Some of the immediate, school-based grievances of students were attended to. More textbooks were provided, and school buildings were repaired. But, as with 1976, schools remained segregated and unequal.

However, the unrest of 1976 and 1980 did result in action by the government. The De Lange Committee was set up, partly in response to schools unrest. The government accepted certain of the De Lange recommendations. But it rejected the major recommendation that there should be a single education department for all in South Africa. Nevertheless, resistance in schools has put education onto the political agenda.

But, as with June 1976, we can't only look at concrete achievements. As one student said in 1980:

>"It was not anything that was granted by the authorities which was felt to be important, but rather the spirit and what had happened amongst the people."
>
>(Quoted in Molteno 1983:16)

And a pamphlet, issued just before the end of the boycott, said:

>"Apart from promises of material reform and improvement, the major gains of this campaign have been political and organizational. The degree of unity attained is almost unprecedented anywhere in the country at any time in its history. A base has been created upon which lasting buildings of the future can be erected."
>
>(Quoted in Molteno 1983:16)

Perhaps we can best view the boycotts as a particular event in an ongoing story of resistance. The boycotts are an important part of the history of resistance in South African education. And that story is by no means finished, as we'll see when we look at the situation in 1984.

It's too soon to say in 1984 what the full story of the schools resistance is. But we can tell part of the story.

Resistance in 1984

At the time of writing this book, schools were again erupting in protest against unequal education and against the apartheid state in general. And, at the end of 1984, it does not look as if the protest is at its end.

What are the reasons for the mobilisation against the education system?

As you'll expect by now, different people give different reasons for what is presently going on in schools. The students blame the DET, the local councillors, self-interested capitalists, and the apartheid state for their grievances. And the government and the DET blame trouble-makers and extremists who are not genuinely interested in improving existing school arrangements.

249

The 1984 resistance can be looked at in a broader context – as we did with 1976 and 1980.

- As in 1976 and 1980, there are school-based issues which are causing dissatisfaction. COSAS, AZASO, AZASM, SOYA and SAC point to segregated and unequal education; lack of schools and facilities; poorly qualified teachers; shortages of textbooks; leakages of exam papers; age limits in black schools, and so on.

    But as well as these long-standing grievances, the 1984 student complaints have centred around the extremely low black matric pass rates and the demand for democratically elected SRCs.

- Secondly, people are experiencing economic difficulties as the country is facing recession. There is high inflation and prices are rising. Unemployment is very high. School leavers face great difficulties in getting jobs – whether they have a matric or not. And in this situation of economic hardship, increases in rents and transport prices have worsened people's problems.

- Thirdly, many people have been angered by the constitutional arrangements which have excluded Africans from the Tricameral Parliament. At the time of the elections in August 1984 thousands of students boycotted schools.

    On the local level, there have been protests against maladministration and corruption in local government. A number of councillors have resigned or fled, and some have been killed.

The 1984 boycotts took place against a background of general dissatisfaction. Problems in schools were only part of people's discontent – but they were a very real part.

Let's now look at how events developed in the 1984 school protests.

The course of events

In early 1984 schools unrest broke out in Atteridgeville and Saulsville near Pretoria, and in Cradock and Port Elizabeth in the Eastern Cape. Within a month the unrest claimed its first victim, Emma Sathekge. Students marched, stoned, and burned buildings, buses and cars. Police fought students with birdshot, bullets, sneeze-machines, tear-gas and casspir and hippo vehicles. Students were expelled and schools were closed. But the schools protest increased in momentum

and spread to other areas as well. By the middle of the year, thousands of students were boycotting schools across the country.

In the meanwhile in February 1984 COSAS, AZASO and NU-SAS launched the Education Charter Campaign. The basic objectives of the Charter Campaign are contained in the box below.

The Education Charter Campaign aims:

1 To establish an Education Charter that would streamline student demands and present a view of a viable alternative to our present system of education.

2 To reach out to and consult all students in all corners of our country together with our communities and to receive contributions from them so that the document arises out of the principle of democracy.

3 To develop the organizational network of both AZASO and COSAS and all other participatory organizations.

4 To establish branches of AZASO and COSAS in those areas where they do not exist presently.

5 To demonstrate to South Africa and all the world that the students and community have rejected the present system of education.

6 To create a document around which students can organize and rally in striving for a democratic and relevant system of education for all.

(Source: *Africa Perspective* 24 1984:74-6)

The DET offered to introduce its own form of SRCs, but the students rejected this on the grounds that DET SRCs would not be properly democratic.

In August 1984, rents and service costs were increased in townships around Pretoria, the East and West Rand, the Eastern Cape, and also in the Vaal Triangle. The Vaal Triangle erupted. Rent protests and education protests joined together in a wave of anti-state action. There were protest meetings and marches; rent and school boycotts; increased police activity; and increased violence. A stay-away campaign of Vaal residents was supported by more than 20 000 people.

On 23 October the state retaliated with Operation Palmiet (Bullrush). The army – the SADF – was brought into the townships with the police. In a joint effort, 7 000 police and soldiers searched 19 500 houses, and arrested 354 people. Such a raid had never happened before.

Meanwhile, a joint campaign was arranged by 37 organizations for a two-day stay-away on 5 and 6 November. These organizations included independent trade unions – CUSA, FOSATU, and others; student organizations – COSAS, AZASO, AZASM, YCS and others; and also community groups and civic groups. Over half a million people participated in the stay-away.

Protests have continued in other centres across the country. Unions, the UDF and the National Forum have been active; and so have student groups. As 1984 draws to an end, FOSATU has called for a black Christmas. Schools have closed for holidays, but there is every indication that schools protests will continue.

If we look at some of the main events of the 1984 resistance, we can see a number of important themes.

Assessing the trends

- Firstly, as well as spontaneous student boycotts, we see the presence of organizations like COSAS and AZASM. These organizations have been trying to mobilize and co-ordinate student activity throughout the country.

- Secondly, there are clear links between school-based issues and broader struggles. Students have been part of the Vaal rents boycott campaign. Also, students and independent trade unions have organized around the same issues, e.g. the November stay-away. So the protests and unrest are not only based in schools.

- Thirdly, there is the Education Charter Campaign, which is attempting to build democratic involvement around educational issues and to work towards an alternative educational future for South Africa.

As we said earlier, this book has been written before the 1984 schools boycotts have reached their end. We can't predict the outcome or how long the present unrest will last. But we can be sure that resistance in education is not over.

Conclusion

That ends our story of resistance in South African education, from the earliest schools to 1984. It's a story with many parts. And it's also a story that has many different interpretations.

For reference here are brief surveys of teacher and student organizations, past and present, involved in the story we have been telling.

Black teacher organizations

South Africa has a rich history of black teacher organizations. From the outset many teacher organizations saw their role as political as well as educational. In the Cape **CATA** (Cape African Teachers Association) was the earliest teacher organization to link educational demands and activity with broader political demands and activity. It was formed in 1921 in Ciskei, with D.D.T. Jabavu as chairperson for sixteen years. During the 1940s, CATA resolved that:

> It is in the best interests that our struggles be co-ordinated with those of the masses, and to this end we consider that this can be best effected by the affiliation of CATA with the AAC (All Africa Convention).

The AAC was launched in 1936, with a Marxist leadership different from that of the SACP (Communist Party).

CATA thus proceeded to act both inside and outside of the educational field. On the one hand, it helped to organize resistance to the retribalization scheme in the Transkei and the Ciskei. On the other hand, it mobilized and organized public opinion against the Eiselen Commmission regulations in 1952.

CATA had a great deal of mass support. But its increasingly militant position and its affiliation to the AAC resulted in the government withdrawing recognition of CATA. Recognition was given to a newly-established body, **CATU** (Cape African Teachers Union). CATU was vigorously denounced by CATA as 'boss boys' and 'herrenvolkers'.

TATA (The Transvaal African Teachers Association) also organized opposition to Bantu Education when it was introduced. TATA was influenced by both the ANC and the AAC, but it did not affiliate to either. Yet it experienced the same fate as CATA – withdrawal of recognition.

By giving recognition to moderate teacher organizations, the government hoped to reduce the influence of CATA and TATA. The moderate, government-supported teacher organizations usually do not challenge the hierarchy as a whole. Most of the executive positions are held by principals. These organizations are not supported by the more radical students. Thus, in 1976, the offices of **ATASA** (African Teachers Association of South Africa) were burned down.

TLSA (The Teachers League of South Africa) was connected with the NEUM (Non-European Unity movement). Throughout the 1950s, 1960s and 1970s, it maintained a consistent critique of the educational system in its journal, *Educational Journal*.

At present, there are government-recognized teacher organizations representing teachers in different black education departments. These include **UTASA** United Teachers Association of South Africa), **TASA** (Teachers Association of South Africa), **CTPA** (Cape Teachers Professional Association) and ATASA. There are also unofficial teacher organizations which adopt a stronger stand and attempt to organize in very different ways. Examples are the **TAC** (Teachers Action Committee), **TLSA,** and **NEUSA** (National Education Union of South Africa). These organizations see the problems in education as part of broader social and political problems.

Student organizations

AZASM (Azanian Students' Movement) was formed in 1983, under the inspiration of the youth wing of AZAPO. It believes that the Azanian People's Manifesto 'is the only document in our history that has deliberately pointed out that we are working towards a socialist Azania'. AZASM is a nationwide organization.

AZASO (Azanian Students Organization) was formed in 1979 as a national organization of black university students. In 1980 AZASO split with AZAPO (Azanian People's Organization) and Black Consciousness. Since then it has worked closely with NUSAS and COSAS. AZASO later joined the UDF (United Democratic Front). In 1982 AZASO's major campaign was to draw up an Education Charter, containing student rights and demands. The Charter campaign aimed to co-ordinate demands for changes in the education system.

COSAS (Congress of South African Students) was formed in 1979 'to meet the needs and aspirations of the post-1976 situation'. COSAS organized students nationally at pre- university level. One of its aims was: 'To strive for an education for all that is dynamic, free, and compulsory for the betterment of society.' COSAS was banned in August 1985.

NUSAS (National Union of South African Students) was formed in 1924 to unite all white university students. In 1936 Afrikaans-speaking white students left NUSAS. In 1945 Fort Hare applied for membership and was accepted. But in 1968 black students broke with NUSAS and formed SASO. Today NUSAS has links with one black university student organization – AZASO.

SOYA (Students of Young Azania) was formed after a split in AZASO at Cape Town University in 1983. One of the causes was AZASO's decision to join the UDF. According to their pamphlet, SOYA believes that the struggle is against racial-capitalism and not only against apartheid. SOYA operates only in the Western Cape.

References and further readings

Africa Perspective (1984) 24

Cillie Commission (1980) *Report on Riots, 1976,* Pretoria

Kane-Berman, J. (1979) *South Africa: The Method in the Madness,* Pluto Press, London

Lodge, T. (1983) *Black Politics in South Africa since 1945,* Ravan, Johannesburg

Maurice, E. (1981) 'What did you learn in school today? 80 years of educational protest' *Sash,* Journal of the Black Sash, Johannesburg

Molteno, F. (1979a) 'The uprising of 16th June: A review of the literature on events in South Africa 1976' *Social Dynamics* 5(1)

Molteno, F. (1979b) 'South Africa 1976: A view from within the liberation movement' *Social Dynamics* 5(2)

Molteno, F. (1983) 'Reflections on resistance: Aspects of the 1980 students boycott', Conference papers, Kenton-at-the-stadt Education Conference, Mmabatho

Molteno, F. (1984) 'The evolution of educational policy' in P. Kallaway (ed) *Apartheid and Education,* Ravan, Johannesburg

Mphahlele, E. (1962) *Down Second Avenue,* Seven Seas, Berlin

NEWSA (undated) 'June 16: Recollections of resistance' NEUSA, Johannesburg

Rose, B. and Tunmer, R. (1975) *Documents in South African Education,* Ad. Donker, Johannesburg

SAIRR (Annual) *Survey of Race Relations in South Africa,* SAIRR, Johannesburg

SAIRR (1978) *South Africa in Travail: The Disturbances of 1976-77,* SAIRR, Johannesburg

Torch (1953)

Chapter 10

Alternatives

Well, we've looked at a number of issues and debates around apartheid education.

So now, where do we go to from here? What are the solutions? What are the alternatives?

I wish I could answer your questions! But, in fact, there are no ready-made answers. There are no ready-made solutions.

The best we can do in this chapter, is to find ways of thinking about alternatives.

In this chapter, we'll start by looking at some of the themes that have emerged in earlier chapters of this book. Then we'll look more specifically at South Africa.

To begin with, let's ask the question: What guidelines emerge from earlier chapters for thinking about education?

Education and the wider society

One of the earliest points we made in Chapter One is that education can't be seen as separate from the wider society. It is part and parcel of the wider social system. So for example, as the wider society has changed, education has changed as well. When we looked at the history of South African education we saw that education was part of broader processes of social change. Today education is part of apartheid, capitalist society. We can't see it as separate from other apartheid capitalist features.

So we shouldn't make the mistake of looking just at education. We need to view education in a broader context.

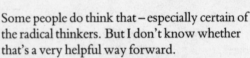

That seems to mean that we'll only be able to change education after we've changed the wider society.

Some people do think that – especially certain of the radical thinkers. But I don't know whether that's a very helpful way forward.

- Firstly, change is a process that is always happening and never finished. How often in life can we say 'This is finished. Now let's start the next thing.' Change doesn't happen so neatly! We need to be building now for what we want later.

- Secondly, we've also seen that education is part of the processes of change. Remember that we said that education is a site of change and struggle. We can't simply leave education off the political agenda. The story of resistance shows us clearly that education is part of broader social struggle.

- And thirdly, what about all the students who pass through schools? We can't simply set aside their education needs to some future time. We can't simply sacrifice present generations for the future. We have to think about the here and now as well.

But, on the other hand, we mustn't be too optimistic about education and social change. The debates of this book have shown that change is no simple matter. We need to be aware of the limitations of the situation we're in. We need to balance what we'd ideally like with what we can actually strive for in the concrete situation.

So you're saying that we should give thought to education as part of other processes of social change, in a particular context?

Exactly. Which brings us on to look at our next point: What the aims of education and schooling are.

Aims of education in schools

We've seen that schools perform many functions in society. And only one of these functions is to pass on valued knowledge to young people! For example:

- Schools socialize people. They pass on attitudes and values. Through the hidden curriculum they teach all sorts of things about what people should do and how they should behave.

- Schools also prepare people for work. They teach knowledge and skills, and they give certificates. In these ways schools link in with the work that people go on to do.

- And schools keep people off the streets. They are a kind of child care, or pre-employment service, as well. We saw that this was one reason for the failure of the 1954 schools boycotts.

Throughout the book we've seen that people have different aims for education. And we've seen that education isn't simply neutral. We've also seen that education is bound up with issues of power, and issues of social class, and race and gender. The education system embodies many different aims and purposes.

259

One thing is clear: there can be many different purposes behind the education system.

So if we want to think about alternatives, we need to think about or own aims also. What are we trying to achieve through alternative education programmes, bearing in mind the context we're working in?

And I suppose we can also watch out for the hidden curriculum. We can try to get textbooks, school practices and teaching methods that fit in with our broader aims.

It's important that our schooling embodies the principles we value. It's one thing to talk about principles like 'justice' and 'fairness' and 'equality'. But we've got to do more than this. We've got to look carefully at what this means in practice in schools.

So, for example, if we're working for democracy we must be sure that our schooling system embodies democratic practices. We can't say that our aim is democracy and then act in an authoritarian way.

Exactly! It's very important that we keep this wide view of education. Education is a process with many parts, and we've got to look at them all if we're thinking about alternatives.

We need to see schools as part of the broader struggle. We need to strive for changes in schooling practices. Changes in the subject content, changes in the relationships between teachers and students, changes in the exam system, changes towards more democratic practices in schools – all of these are important when we are working towards an alternative.

But, we also shouldn't think that schools are the only places where we can get education.

Education outside schools

Schools are very much part of our society. But that shouldn't lead us to think that schools are absolutely necessary for education. In past societies there were no schools as we know them today. And future schools may also be quite different from today's schools.

We shouldn't fall into the trap of thinking that we have to keep the same schooling system in the future. In fact we should be thinking about making changes to it – such as, for example, bringing schools and work closer together, and making education more relevant to life outside schools.

We also shouldn't fall into the trap of thinking that we can only learn through schools. There are all sort of educational programmes that can be run outside formal schools.

When we think of alternatives, we also need to give thought to non-formal education.

Would cultural clubs count as non-formal education?

Certainly, they would. And they also alert us to some of the problems of non-formal education.

We saw the difficulties which the cultural clubs had in being accepted by people and being regarded as worthwhile education. It can be very hard for non-formal education to succeed alongside formal schools.

And there's also the issue of certification that needs to be confronted. If people want and need certificates, then that poses something of a problem for non-formal education.

Also, we've seen that education reflects and shapes social classes. If some people have non-formal education and other people have formal education then this could also be part of social inequality.

Even so, non-formal education is very important, especially when we're thinking about alternatives.

261

I can see that these are problems that come from
the link between education and the wider
society. Education doesn't just have a free hand.

Yes, indeed, that's true. But we must be careful
not to make society into a thing that's
completely separate from us, and that we can't
change.
Let's discuss this point a little more fully.

Social change

We've seen throughout the book that different people have different
views about society and social change. But when we think about
social change it's important to remember that our own actions go to
make up society and social change. Society isn't fixed and static.
There are always processes of change, and people are part of these
processes of change. This isn't to say that people can change society
as they like; there are certain concrete conditions that we find ourselves in. We live in an existing society – whether we like that society
or not. And the important thing is to recognize that people can and
do change society. People are part of ongoing processes of change.

Think, for example, about the history of schooling and resistance
in schooling. The schooling system grew and developed and changed
over time, as the society grew and developed and changed. The
schooling system wasn't always imposed from above; it was also
shaped by people from below. There are many examples to think
about: think of black resistance, CNE schools and workplace education.

Schooling has been shaped and influenced by those who are at the
receiving end of the system, and especially by their protests and
struggles.

So that's another reason why we can't just sit
back and wait for change to happen. Our actions
are part of society and social change.
But there's another issue about schooling and
change – and that's the issue of education and
social awareness.

Education and social awareness

When we look at how the schooling system operates, we see a contradiction. On the one hand, in apartheid South Africa we see a schooling system that divides people and is unequal. And very often the curriculum, the textbooks and the teaching methods may actually prevent people from thinking critically.

But on the other hand, education can and should help people to think critically. It should help them to develop a better understanding of the world around them. Education is one way in which people may come to analyse, and assess, and act on the situation they are in. Education is part of the development of individuals and also of the society.

And I can see that for this reason, also, it's important that we think about education as part of social change – and it's important to think about alternatives as well.

Certainly. And this is also where questions about education and the wider society come in again.

Our ideas about educational alternatives are very much part of our ideas about the wider society. We can't just think about alternatives in education without thinking about alternatives in the wider society.

And again, this is where education becomes part of broader struggles. So, in a sense, an alternative education system will be shaped in our general struggle for an alternative social system. But that doesn't mean waiting for social change. It means linking our ideas of educational change with our ideas of social change.

Alternative programmes?

The issues that we've discussed so far give some basic guidelines for thinking about alternatives in education. There are many educational strategies that we could think about. But it's important that we don't look at these strategies as solutions in themselves. It is only once we know what our broader aims are, that we can develop educational programmes.

What follows are some of the 'alternatives' that are often mentioned:

And we could continue with many more. But the message is clear: we can't treat these as educational solutions – until we know what our broader aims are. Each of these 'alternatives' could be used in different ways. For example:

- Some literacy programmes are aimed at social change; others are not.

- Some labour education programmes are directed towards management or capitalist ends; others are directed towards trade union ends.

- Some distance education programmes are aimed only at giving people certificates; other distance education programmes don't give certificates at all.

And so we could go on.

The point is that education strategies are linked to broader aims. We can't simply look at the strategies and see them as alternatives in themselves.

Let's now turn to the question of alternatives in South African education.

To start, here is an example of an alternative education programme which ran very briefly in South Africa: People's College.

People's College

People's College was a 24-page weekly educational supplement which appeared in the newspaper *Weekend World* from March to October 1977. In October 1977 *People's College* and the *Weekend World* were both banned by the government.

Aims

People's College was an experiment in alternative education in South Africa. By using a low-cost newspaper it hoped to give large numbers of people access to information and educational material which they could not get through the formal schooling system. In particular, it was aimed at people who were subject to the deficiencies of Bantu Education.

People's College also intended to encourage a new attitude to learning. It aimed to stimulate critical independent thought, and community and social awareness.

In order to achieve its aims, *People's College* provided two resources:

1 There was an educational supplement to the newspaper, which offered a wide range of content, covering different subjects at different levels. Students could study an entire course at the cost of only R3,80 – the cost of the newspaper.
2 A system of learning groups was set up around the *People's College* materials. Specially trained regional organizers were appointed to train group leaders who would then organize learning groups to study the material. *People's College* was designed to be used by groups of people, without trained teachers.

Content

Some of the material was 'informal' – it covered subjects of

265

general interest and use that werenot based on syllabuses and exams. Topics covered were Worker Education, Food Co-operatives, Basic Economics, Pregnancy and Childbirth, and so on.

Some of the material was 'non-formal'. These were courses that were designed to meet the needs and interests of adults and students who had left school early, and they included exams and certificates. Courses were run in Money Management, a Social History of Black South Africa, Elementary Typing and Elementary Accountancy.

Some of the material was 'formal' – it was aimed at JC and matric students. It contained material on the more difficult sections of the core syllabuses.

Responses

In the first month of *People's College, Weekend World* sales increased by 20 000. This sales boost was maintained at 10 000 for the rest of the year. During the 33 weeks that *People's College* ran, the publishers received an average of 327 letters a week. There is no doubt that people were using *People's College*.

People's College banned

In October 1977 *Weekend World* and a number of organizations were banned. It is not known whether the supplement was the cause of this banning, but *People's College* could no longer be published.

It became an offence to possess and distribute back-issues of the paper. The regional organization system also had to end, otherwise it could have been seen as an attempt to promote a banned publication.

People's College as an alternative

There is no doubt that *People's College* aimed at providing a very different system of education in South Africa. Its content was different; it had informal and non-formal education, as well as formal. Its teaching methods were different; it tried to set up independent learning groups instead of classrooms with teachers. And its overall educational aims were different; it aimed to promote critical, independent thought, and community and social awareness. Whether or not *People's College* could succeed in its alternative system will never be known.

(Summary of Lawson 1979)

The story of *People's College* has a lot to tell us about educational alternatives in South Africa. And part of that story is how vulnerable an alternative programme is when it is not promoting the interests of the government.

Now let's consider more fully the issue of alternatives in education in South Africa.

Educational alternatives in South Africa

When people talk about alternatives they often have very different ideas in mind. The alternatives which people put forward for education are linked to the aims they have for education. And their alternatives are also based on their views about society and social change.

Let's return briefly to our three thinkers.

Conservative

Alternatives? A lot of people talk about improving things when they really mean destroying things.

In South Africa there are many different and diverse cultures and ways of life. These need to be preserved. One of the functions of schools is to preserve group identity.

Certainly, systems must change. Education in South Africa will change in time. It has changed already. There are now many more black people in school, and there is a homeland system which is growing.

Growth is possible within this present system. I think alternatives must preserve this framework.

Moderate

Alternatives? Certainly! The education system in South Africa must change. The present system is out of date. We need an education system which looks to the future needs of the country – especially the needs of the economy. Unless we can provide better education for more people – especially black people – the economy will suffer.

And of course there are a lot of problems with the present system. A lot of black people are refusing to accept it. We can't let schools unrest continue indefinitely.

We've got to change the present system as peacefully as possible. We need to put more money into education and start providing equal opportunities. We must make some moves to improve the system before it's too late.

Radical

Alternatives? The only alternative is fundamental change. We need change in the education system and change in the society at large.

The present education system is completely unequal. There are inequalities firstly of social class and also of race and gender. The present system actually promotes inequality. There can never be social equality while we have this system.

And the students know this. They're rejecting the education system and what it stands for. And their ongoing protests won't end unless things change fundamentally.

Trying to adjust the present education system isn't the answer. Change needs to be more fundamental than that. The alternative we need is a different society. Alternative education will be part of this new society.

These three views show that different groups of people would propose very different alternatives for education.

This is illustrated very clearly by one 'alternative' that has been proposed for South African education – the De Lange Report.

The De Lange alternative

In 1980 the government appointed the HSRC (a government research body) to conduct an investigation into education in South Africa, and to make recommendations for an education policy. These recommendations should 'provide for the manpower requirements of the RSA' and 'make available education of the same quality for all population groups' (HSRC 1981:1).

There were a number of reasons why the government appointed a commission of inquiry into education. The De Lange Commission followed a number of other commissions (like Riekert, Wiehahn and Rabie) which were trying to find ways to modernize apartheid. Certainly, the government was responding to the unrest in schools – particularly June 1976 and the 1980 school boycotts. Another reason was the continual complaints made by business people about shortages of skilled workers (as we saw earlier in Chapter Eight). Business people were complaining that the education system did not meet the needs of the growing economy.

The De Lange Report put forward proposals for educational change in South Africa. It proposed a more comprehensive system of mass schooling, with one education department for all groups. And it proposed the principle of 'equal quality' in education for all groups.

The De Lange system of education proposed a move away from traditional, formal schooling patterns towards a new schooling structure. Instead of twelve grades of formal school, there would be a formal (academic) education structure running parallel to a non-formal (vocational) education structure. The formal structure would have three phases: pre-basic, basic and post-basic (similar to nursery school, primary school and secondary school). Basic schooling would take six years, and would be free and compulsory for children of all groups. Pupils would be streamed and channelled on the basis of academic achievement, and then move into post-basic education. There would be three post-basic possibilities for pupils. NEUSA describes these as follows:

1 They could be channelled into an academic school;
2 They could be channelled into a commercial or technical school;
3 They could leave the formal education system and enter into non-formal education. This could involve anything from in-service training to learning specific technical skills in a private institution. (undated: 8)

Post-basic education would be paid for by parents, business people and the government. The academic 'track' would not be free – it would be paid for by parents. Vocational education would be funded and provided mainly by the business sector.

Through this system children of all groups would receive a free, compulsory basic education. But only certain children would be streamed into academic education – at their parents' expense. Other children would receive technical or non-formal education for three more years, making nine years of education altogether.

In many ways the De Lange Report does present an educational alternative. It sets out different educational principles, and a different educational structure from the present one. It proposes a single system, with education of 'equal quality' for all people. It includes formal and non-formal education in the same system. And it addresses itself to the labour needs of the country.

But what sort of alternative is the De Lange system? Like all alternatives, the De Lange proposals are based on certain assumptions about education and about social change. The responses of different groups of people illustrate these assumptions clearly.

Let's look briefly at these responses.

Responses to De Lange

- At a Volkskongres, Afrikaners were divided. The conservative group saw the De Lange proposals as a threat to Afrikanerdom. A more moderate group saw the proposals as a possible strategy for reform. The conservative group won the day. The influential Afrikaner teacher organization, the TO, also opposed the De Lange proposals.

  Shortly after the Report was issued, the government rejected the proposal of a single education department for all. In 1983 they issued a White Paper accepting other De Lange proposals, but stressing that CNE principles would be the basis for all education in South Africa.

- Liberals and capitalists welcomed the De Lange Report. They supported the De Lange proposals, and urged the government to implement them as soon as possible. According to Chisholm and Christie, they hailed the De Lange Report as a 'revolutionary breakthrough in education', and they saw the White Paper as a setback for reform because it did not completely support the De Lange Report (1983:256).

- Radicals strongly criticized the De Lange Report. They argued that it was simply a modernization of apartheid. Under the De Lange system of education, class, race and gender differences would remain. Working class children (mainly black) would most likely be channelled into technical and vocational education. Middle class children (whose parents could afford to pay) would be more likely to have an academic education. Radicals argued that the De Lange system would not bring fundamental change to the educational and social inequalities in South Africa.

These responses illustrate the worldview that the De Lange Report is based on. You can certainly see which worldviews it doesn't reflect!

But what about the students, who are the main participants in education?

Student demands

In South Africa, we've seen that there is a long history of education protest. Particularly since 1976, students have shown their dissatisfaction with the education system. They have rejected the existing system, and they have demanded changes.

What the students have demanded has been different – for different groups at different times. But there are some demands which have consistently been made:

- non-racialism
- democratic practices
- equal opportunities for all.

Of course, all of these demands can be interpreted differently – and they are. But there's no doubt that the students are demanding an education system which is very different from the system we know today.

The issue of alternatives in education is a contested one. Different people have very different views. Whose views will shape the future? Probably all of them will, in one way or another.

There are no blueprints for alternatives. As we've said before, there are always processes of change in society and in education. Education is a site of struggle and change.

Ultimately, future alternatives for education in South Africa will be shaped by its people in the processes of struggle and historical change.

The right to learn

References and further readings

Chisholm, L. and Christie, P. (1983) 'Restructuring in education' in SARS *South African Review*, vol. 1, Ravan, Johannesburg
Davies, J. (1984) 'Capital, state and education reform in South Africa' in P. Kallaway (ed) *Education and Apartheid*, Ravan, Johannesburg
Gardiner, M. (1984) 'Redefining education: The White Paper on the provision of education' *Africa Perspective* 24
HSRC (1981) *Investigation into Education* (De Lange Report), HSRC, Pretoria
Kallaway, P. (ed) (1984) *Education and Apartheid*, Ravan, Johannesburg
Lawson, L. (1979) 'People's College: a South African experiment in NFE' in NUSAS *Education and Development*, Conference Papers, University of Cape Town
NEUSA (undated) *De Lange . . . Marching to the Same Order*, NEUSA, Johannesburg
Perspectives in Education (1982) Special Issue: The HSRC Report, University of the Witwatersrand, Johannesburg
Republic of South Africa (1983) White Paper on the Provision of Education in the Republic of South Africa, Pretoria